Nineteenth Century Modern

Nineteenth Century

Modern

THE FUNCTIONAL TRADITION
IN VICTORIAN DESIGN

Herwin Schaefer

PRAEGER PUBLISHERS
New York · Washington

To my children

Louisa, Christopher, and Andrew

BOOKS THAT MATTER

Published in the United States of America in 1970
by Praeger Publishers, Inc.
111 Fourth Avenue, New York, N.Y. 10003

© 1970 by Praeger Publishers, Inc.

All rights reserved

Library of Congress Catalog Card Number: 70–118021

Printed in the United States of America

CONTENTS

ACKNOWLEDGMENTS

The writing of this book was made possible by the grant of a Humanities Research Professorship by the University of California, and a grant from the Graham Foundation, and I am deeply grateful to both for their generosity.

I also wish to thank the many individuals and institutions who assisted me in assembling the material for this book. There are the museums where I received courteous and efficient and, above all, patient help: from the large and famous—such as the Smithsonian Institution, the Deutsches Museum in Munich, the beautiful Danish Kunstindustrimuseum in Copenhagen, the Science Museum and the Victoria & Albert Museum in London—to many smaller but equally fascinating collections in many places; I thank all of the staff, both curatorial and photographic, who assisted me. Librarians in many of these same institutions, such as Svend Eriksen in Copenhagen, and especially in the library of the University of California, have given much time and effort in helping to find material for the book; to all of them, too, I am indebted.

Many friends participated in fruitful discussions and made critical and helpful comments: Eugene Dodd read the entire manuscript at a critical stage and did much to improve it and set it on the right track; Janet Lee has faithfully and exactingly checked all details, and Maurice Barel has enhanced the quality of many of the photographs by his fine craftsmanship. My wife, Hildegarde, has been the ever needed, ever present spirit, whose comments, criticisms, insights, and calm judgment have guided the book through all its various stages, and who has contributed more to its final form than anyone else.

LIST OF ILLUSTRATIONS

RECOGNITION AND VINDICATION

We should have every thing in a house touched by the divining rod of the poet. An inkstand, instead of being a literal glass bottle . . . might be fashioned to represent a fountain, with a Muse inspiring its flow; our goblets might bubble over amongst hop leaves, and stems of blossoms; our decanters be composed of transparent vines, clustering in wild confusion, or drooping over trellis-work . . . ; our bellropes, . . . might be converted into hanging garlands; our water-jugs be made to flatter the palate with their look of coolness, snow creaming over the edges, and harts drinking at brooks, in the shadows down the sides: lively colours, tastefully toned and harmonized, might be scattered over our rooms, under a thousand pretences of necessity.

The redundant must be pared down, the superfluous dropped, the necessary itself reduced to its simplest expression, and then we shall find, whatever the organization may be, that beauty was waiting for us.

John Tallis, *History and Description of the Crystal Palace and the Exhibition of the World's Industry in 1851*, (London and New York: n.d.), I, iv.

Horatio Greenough, *The Travels, Observations, and Experience of a Yankee Stonecutter* (1852; Gainesville, Fla.: 1958), p. 172.

Introduction

It has been the generally accepted view that functional design—abstract, often geometric and devoid of decoration, but emphasizing utility—is peculiar to the twentieth century, and that nineteenth-century design was the very antithesis of this, with decoration lavished on all objects and function entirely neglected and obscured. One thinks of the nineteenth century as a confusing and deplorable interregnum after a past in which a succession of harmoniously ornamented styles were created and used by a leisured aristocratic society, and of the twentieth century as one in which a democratic industrial society developed a rational design of pure form based on function, quality of material, and workmanship. The nineteenth century is felt to have had no valid style of its own but to have resorted mainly to applying decoration derived from the styles of the past, debasing its forms, and using them to emphasize ornateness, sentimentality, and story-telling rather than function and purpose of the object. Further, it is part of the accepted view of design history that a small number of pioneers, beginning with the medievalizing William Morris and continuing with artistically innovative artists, architects, and designers around the turn of the century, led us out of this quagmire of Victorian design by creating a body of new designs that form the basis of twentieth-century design.

Our picture of nineteenth-century design and—if we are modernists—our censorious view of it are based on the inherited reactions of the generations since 1900, as well as on a vulgar vogue for Victorian trivia during the last few decades, which has confirmed the picture by reminding us of it. Our ideas of the process of change and reform are largely due to the initial and most influential writing on this aspect of the period, namely, Nikolaus Pevsner's *Pioneers of the Modern Movement, from William Morris to Walter Gropius*, which, in broad outline, sees eclectic Victorian design being reformed by the efforts of a few pioneers. Originally published in England in 1936, at the height of the modern period, it was republished in 1949 by the Museum of Modern Art in New York, under the slightly different title of *Pioneers of Modern Design*, and in this later, revised form, it achieved enormous popularity. In actuality, a careful reading of Pevsner's book shows that he was well aware that machinery and utilitarian functional forms played a major role in the thinking of at least some of his pioneers; but by emphasizing the artistic creativity of individuals and further relating it to contemporary painting, and by giving no examples of machine design or anonymous vernacular design, he leaves the reader with a fragmentary and distorted picture of the history of design in the nineteenth century and the beginning of the twentieth century. Though a good deal of literature exists today that would modify this picture, it was only very recently said that "the important point about [Pevsner's] book is that although it is mainly about architecture, it is also, for the modernists, the bible of industrial design."[1]

This canonical view has been modified, enriched, attacked, and corrected in the last decades. Sigfried Giedion's *Mechanization Takes Command* (1948) is a first and encyclopedic investigation into the effects of industrialization on the design of everyday objects. It is a book enormously rich in material to enlarge our vision of nineteenth-century industrial vernacular design. In this book, Giedion used the phrases "constituent facts" and "ruling taste," which have become a part of our design vocabulary. In the same year, John A. Kouwenhoven published *Made in America*, which explores the American contribution to the vernacular, contrasting it with what he calls the "cultivated tradition." In fact, Kouwenhoven suggests that the qualities of the vernacular, its plainness

1

and practicality, were particularly sympathetic to the American character and environment. It is easy to arrive at this conclusion in view of the frequent testimony of contemporaries in the nineteenth century and also later; nevertheless, equally fine vernacular forms are also found all over Europe, if perhaps not in equal measure in the industrial sector. An extensive survey of the vernacular form in Germany was published earlier, in 1939, by Walter Dexel: *Deutsches Handwerksgut, eine Kultur- und Formgeschichte des Hausgeräts*. The interest of Dexel's book lies partly in the fact that it stems from the experience of the modern style in Germany, represents a search for its antecedents, and seeks a justification for its formal preferences in history. Dexel postulates a dual design track: one, the highly ornate and decorated, for the aristocracy; the other, the vernacular, for the ordinary man. Though one may question Dexel's proposition that the ordinary man always preferred the simple functional form, the book does provide a corpus of such forms in the Germanic orbit, from the Middle Ages through the nineteenth century.

The sharpest challenge to Pevsner's pioneer view of design history comes from a series of articles by Herbert Lindinger in the German magazine *Form*, in 1964 and 1965. Far from being merely an investigation into an area neglected by Pevsner, the results of which would implicitly alter the pioneer view, Lindinger explicitly castigates its limitations and false emphasis, and, with reference to Dexel and others, suggests the key role of technical and vernacular design in the nineteenth century. Though the series of articles seems tentative and does not fully develop the theme, it is a suggestive and valuable contribution.

And there was always Lewis Mumford, that wonderfully wise and knowledgeable man who wrote *Technics and Civilization* (1934), in which the contribution of technology and function to the evolution of modern design is clearly stated with great insight. It is hard to imagine that Mumford would ever have fallen under the spell of the pioneer thesis; whatever has been written since to enlarge and rectify this thesis he knew, and had anticipated in his book.

My own interest and efforts stem from all these stimuli, not least from Pevsner's book itself, but I should also mention a crucial question put to me by a student some ten or twelve years ago: Lecturing in a course on the history of design in the nineteenth and twentieth centuries that I have been giving for about fifteen years, I was in the midst of the usual rapturous account of the various fascinating facets of Art Nouveau, when the student asked, "but what did the bicycle and the camera and the telephone look like then?" We discussed how these things differed, how they were rational and functional in form, in fact, anticipatory modern and quite the opposite of the caprices of Art Noveau, and that they should have at least "equal time" in a course such as mine. It brought home to me, as nothing else, that this aspect had been neglected and needed further investigation and representation in design history.

The crucial discovery is that design of functional form antedates the twentieth-century functional style with which we most often associate it. In the nineteenth century, functional form existed in the technical realm—in industrial and scientific equipment, which developed in intellectual, calculated, and precise forms for new purposes and functions during the industrial and technical revolutions of the eighteenth and nineteenth centuries. It existed in the field of transportation, in carriages, ships, trains, in sports equipment, and in musical instruments. And it existed in the vernacular: the design of age-old everyday useful objects whose forms were the result, over centuries, of intuitive adaptation to function, originally on the basis of traditional hand-craft production and, in the nineteenth century, more and more of industrial production. While "artistic" ornateness was the mark of the ruling taste, the vernacular flourished on a more modest level in all areas of the home furnishings field. It produced the unassuming and undecorated functional form in furniture, glass, pottery, and other household equipment as a matter of course. The common concern of technical and vernacular design was function. In both realms, throughout the nineteenth century, designs were produced that are "modern" in the sense that they strike us as apt and contemporaneous today, even though made long ago. In this sense, "modern" is not necessarily synonymous with machine design; it rather denotes an approach to design, the direct, practical, and best solution of a problem, regardless of technique. Nor does "modern" in this sense refer to artistic or stylistic peculiarities of a period —though that period be the modern period—but to the timeless qualities derived from the logic of function. Emerson once made the observation that "we read the verses of one of the great English poets, of Chaucer, of Marvell, of Dryden, with the most modern joy—with a pleasure, I mean, which is in great part caused by the abstraction of all *time* from their verses." [2] In a similar way, we experience a pleasurable recognition of the modern qualities in designs antedating the twentieth century.

The same recognition and appreciation occurred at the turn of the century and the following decades when the modern style was being formulated. The clear, rational forms found in the functional tradition became the models for modern design. It was after 1900 that one spoke of modern as synonymous with functional, meaning by that a quality as well as a style. In the first decades of our century, the advocates of modern design were confident that the adoption of the functional tradi-

tion would lead to a style beyond style, a world of permanently valid forms.

In the following decades, though function theoretically remained its determining rationale, modern design went beyond the simple grounds of the functional tradition to become a style influenced by currents outside of this tradition. Further, the very fact of the existence of functional design in the nineteenth century and its importance as the inspiration and basis for the growth of the modern style were lost sight of. This happened partly through the passage of time and partly through the historical writing referred to above, which emphasized the works of the so-called pioneers of modern design. In fact, these pioneers contributed less through their own usually artistically oriented designs than through their intellectual recognition and advocacy of the functional tradition.

The modern functional style reached its high-water mark in the 1920's and 1930's. As a style, it was undisputed until the middle of the century. The last two decades have seen a steady erosion of this position, a moving away from the orthodoxy of modern functional design. There has been more and more involvement in new experiments that, surprisingly often, include Victorian reminiscences and Art Nouveau, and, most recently, adaptations of the so-called Art Deco, the Cubist decorative art of the mid-twenties. We now look back on the period of the modern functional style as something almost, if not entirely, in the past. What had seemed like the millennium while it lasted has turned out to be a phase; what had been accepted as "timeless" forms "beyond style" turn out to have been manifestations of a style after all, with a life-span that has come to an end. "Modern" in common parlance is now something else. There is now a generation gap in the use of the word "modern"; to those who lived through at least part of the period of functional modern design, modern will retain the connotation of functional; while to the young, it will mean merely up-to-date, what "is" today, no matter how far that may be removed from function. A young student recently brought me up-to-date by writing in an examination: "The functionalist style was somewhat cold by modern standards." Functionalism is frequently explicitly rejected; it has become a bad word. The new phase, the postmodern phase of design emphasizes and seeks qualities opposed to what was thought of as modern design. As yet, it is impossible to define a new style or foresee the future. It is clear, however, that the austere, rational form derived from function is passé and that a search is on for color, gaiety, and sentimentality, often taken from forms of the past with results that are disparate, *outré*, and trivial. Fantasy is more real than function. Our new situation is permissive and has been called an umbrella style. In many respects, it bears an uncanny resemblance to the nineteenth century, when functional design existed submerged under the cover of a fashionable mélange of largely eclectic forms, then also appreciated as colorful, sentimental, gay, and romantic. Today, the perennial functional tradition also continues, but, once again, outside the scope of fashion and style. Once again, it continues underground, mostly in technical and nonconsumer directed areas.

The very fact that we can look back on the period of the modern functional style as something in the past gives us detachment, freedom, and vision to see without the blinders that a living style imposes. While a style lives, one does not see it as a style but identifies with it. We are able to see now that what we called modern functional design and considered a new and lasting order, because it seemed based on reason, was but a moment in which function was the proclaimed rationale for a style based, in practice, on a predilection for geometric forms—the Platonic forms of cone, circle, square—avidly avowed as a dogma by its creators, and made into a formula by its practitioners. It is, of course, no accident that the ascendancy of this modern functional style coincided exactly with that of Cubism, which espoused the same formal values. Modern functional design, as a style, was, in fact, part and parcel of the Cubist period; Picasso and Gropius, Braque and Breuer, Mondrian and Mies are all of one family. Though designers quoted function, they were compelled by the predilection of the time for geometric forms to adhere to a narrow pattern. Adherents of the style were blind, often deliberately blind, to the fact that formal values that were accepted, in fact demanded, did not always derive purely from functional considerations, though function was cited as source and reason. There was the harmony of geometry, the austere beauty of technology, and, for those who believed, this was enough. This is not to say that the modern functional style was "cold" and therefore emotionally barren; it was emotionally satisfying to its devotees, because the austere formal values it offered were precisely those desired. Also, one cannot say that no truly functional design was created during this period; often the best functional solutions were found in the abstract geometric forms relevant to the time. One must merely point out the irony in a period that proclaimed function as the determinant of form and yet was guided by formal values outside the consideration of function. Actually, the functional tradition existed side by side with the functional style, as well as having been absorbed into it. The functional *tradition* existed as a matter of course in areas remote from style and fashion, its products being timelessly modern; the functional *style* was a conscious and deliberate effort, a matter of aesthetic concern, accepted by informed and fashionable taste, but modern in the stylistic sense and not necessarily in the sense of being timeless.

I make a distinction, then, between functional design as a quality or an approach to design that we may call modern (in Emerson's sense) because of its timelessness and, therefore, its contemporary appeal, and the modern functional style that, though initially inspired by and ostensibly based on this same quality or functional approach, was, nevertheless, determined in its formal values by an artistic current of the time, and therefore time-bound.

The modern functional style dominated the first half of our century; but it was the more timeless functional design that existed throughout the nineteenth century that gave it its impetus and its initial inspiration. It is the aim of this book to emphasize and illustrate this functional tradition during the nineteenth century by assembling instances of functional design in the technical, scientific, and industrial fields, as well as in the broad area of the vernacular. In this way, its continuous existence may be seen as an essential part of the history of design in the nineteenth and twentieth centuries, indeed as *the* history of design, if it is

concerned with functional design. Its existence in the nineteenth century was the one indispensable basis, the all-important precondition for the genesis of modern functional design in the twentieth century; it was the grass roots of modern functional design. The efforts of reformers and pioneers, be they piously medievalizing or aesthetically artistic, pale to insignificance beside the strength and consistency of this tradition which furnished the solid core of modern design.

What I am presenting is, of course, not the whole of this tradition; that would be an impossible task for one man's lifetime. Not a systematic inventory, the book is essentially a fortuitous selection of objects, the result of chance—the chance of their own survival and of my chancing upon them in my searches. I have pursued areas that interested me, subject areas and geographic areas, to illustrate my thesis, and doubtless many objects that should have been included have been missed. But this is a field for discoveries by many people, and I hope that the material presented here will inspire others to look further—as I was inspired to do by earlier writers—and fill in the many gaps that remain.

NOTES TO THE INTRODUCTION

1. Corin Hughes-Stanton, "Nikolaus Pevsner: A Major Influence on Modern Design," *Design,* No. 222 (June, 1967), p. 56.
2. Ralph Waldo Emerson, "The American Scholar," an oration delivered before the Phi Beta Kappa Society at Cambridge, Mass., August 31, 1837, in *The Complete Works* (Boston, New York: Houghton, Mifflin Co., 1904), I, 91–92.

1 *Instruments and Machines*

If one examines machines, instruments, and tools of the eighteenth and early nineteenth centuries, it becomes clear that the industrial revolution brought a complete change in the approach to their design; there is a marked and conscious break with the past. This took place first in England, in the atmosphere of rationalism prevalent in the eighteenth century, and was influenced by the British philosophers' speculative writing on aesthetics. One of the problems they dealt with over and over again was that of the relation of utility and fitness to beauty. The entire nation was consumed with curiosity and interest in mechanical invention and the progress of industry; thus, it is not at all surprising that those concerned with aesthetic questions should seek to reconcile beauty with mechanical efficiency. E. R. De Zurko, in his *Origins of Functionalist Theory*, has collected and analyzed the relevant passages in philosophical writings. He finds that "the interest in the beauty of mechanical efficiency . . . appears at the beginning of the industrial revolution in England." [1]

In 1725, Francis Hutcheson, in *An Inquiry into the Original of Our Ideas of Beauty and Virtue*, wrote of beauty in machines as the result of wisdom, as denoting "the pursuing of the best Ends by the best means" and the choosing of "this frugal Oeconomy of their forces" that permits "many useful or beautiful Effects [to flow] from one general Cause." [2]

David Hume was concerned with the usefulness of the social virtues and saw utility as their chief foundation. He used "inanimate forms" as analogies and illustrations of his thesis, and when he refers to them, his phrases reveal prevalent attitudes. "What praise, even of an inanimate form, if the regularity and elegance of its parts destroy not its fitness for any useful purpose!" [3] In *A Treatise of Human Nature*, he wrote:

The observation of convenience gives pleasure, since convenience is a beauty . . . it must delight us merely by communication. . . . This observation extends to tables, chairs, scritoires, chimneys, coaches, saddles, ploughs, and indeed to every work of art; it being an universal rule, that their beauty is chiefly deriv'd from their utility, and from their fitness for that purpose, to which they are destin'd. [4]

Adam Smith, the political economist, stated:

that Utility is one of the principal sources of beauty has been observed by every body, who has considered with any attention what constitutes the nature of beauty . . . that the fitness of any system or machine to produce the end for which it was intended, bestows a certain propriety and beauty upon the whole, and renders the very thought and contemplation of it agreeable.

He also made clear that it is principally a pleasure by association. "The utility of any object . . . pleases the master by perpetually suggesting to him the pleasure or conveniency which it is fitted to promote." [5]

Henry Home, Lord Kames, in his *Elements of Criticism*, wrote of the difference between intrinsic and relative beauty and stated that it lies in the use of understanding and reflection. Again, it is association that evokes the feeling of beauty. "Beauty is not an inherent property or quality of objects at all, but the result of the accidental relations in which they may stand to our experience of pleasures or emotions. . . . Thus, a subject void of intrinsic beauty appears beautiful from its utility." In this way, new forms, such as mechanical structures and machines, of proportions not yet assimilated into the polite aesthetic consciousness, can be accepted as beautiful by the rational considerations of utility. In speaking specifically of instruments and machines, Kames wrote that "no single property recommends a machine more than its

1a. *Microscope, by John Marshall, London, 1704.*
Typical of the eighteenth century in its use of wood,
cardboard, leather with gold tooling, its finials,
baluster forms, moldings, and cabinet-work.
(Deutsches Museum, Munich)

1b. *Detail of Fig. 1a.*

simplicity, not solely for better answering its purpose, but by appearing in itself more beautiful," [6] an observation that became an axiom of all mechanics and engineers in the impending boom of machine invention and construction.

Another associationist, Archibald Alison, wrote that "in the mechanical arts, the object of which is utility, this utility is itself the principle by which we determine the perfection of every production." Further, in speaking of the quality of fitness as a source of relative beauty, he wrote:

that this quality in forms is productive of the emotions of beauty, every one must probably have perceived. In the forms of furniture, of machines, and of instruments in the different arts, the greater part of their beauty arises from this consideration; nor is there any form which does not become beautiful where it is found to be perfectly adapted to its end. [7]

The new men—instrument-makers, mechanics, and engineers—took for granted that utility and fitness are desirable. The demands of economy of form led them inevitably to the starkly simple and geometric designs of their instruments and machines, structures of the utmost economy of form, entirely undecorated, of an abstract modern beauty of form. To be sure, this did not happen overnight. Prior to the middle of the eighteenth century, technical apparatus—instruments, tools, machines—had been almost universally shaped and decorated in the forms of the prevailing style. But from at least 1750 on, there are examples of a new kind of design, free from all traditional forms and designed boldly in clear, rational forms, as though the instrument- and tool-makers and the engineers were confident that the beauty of these forms would be recognized by everyone, as they themselves recognized it. While the eighteenth century lasted, or until the end of the *ancien régime*, there were occasionally highly decorated instruments and machines that were made for aristocratic amateurs. More often during this century, there were remnants of traditional forms in designs that were otherwise very soberly utilitarian. The tendency was clearly to design and construct instruments and machines solely with the function and purpose of the apparatus in mind.

One of the more complex scientific instruments, the microscope, was developed in Holland in the seventeenth century, but soon the finest examples were made in England. In the eighteenth century, microscopes were known on the continent as "Dollonds," after the most prominent London maker,[8] and they were copied everywhere, much as were British machines of every sort a little later.

If we look at microscopes of the seventeenth and eighteenth centuries, it is interesting to see that from the start their appearance represents a compromise (*Figs. 1a, 1b*). Though the body of the microscope is usually covered with shagreen or with colored leather stamped in gold with floral or other patterns, in the manner of bookbinding, and though other details are ornamental, such as the turned finials of the pillar, it is unmistakable that decoration can only be applied in limited areas; the rest must be strictly and purely functional, thereby contrasting strongly with the decorated portions. The pillar, on which the microscope slides up and down for adjustment; the rod that attaches it to the sliding block, which is in turn held by a jamb screw; the threading, the eyepiece, the stage, whether of metal or glass; all of these are rigid and exact and give any otherwise graceful and charming decoration the appearance of having strayed into an area where it does not belong. This is evident in John Marshall's microscope of 1704, and in any of the many other types designed and made in the eighteenth century.

During the eighteenth century, brass tubes were increasingly used in microscopes in place of cardboard-and-leather tubes; eventually, the entire ap-

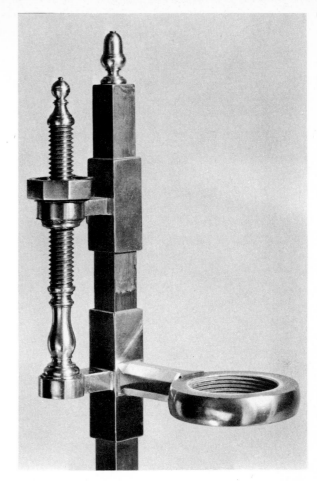

paratus—except, of course, the optics—was made of brass. From being the object of the goldsmith and bookbinder's art, it became the object of the instrument-maker proper, such as John Dollond in England. Though scrolls, moldings, engraving, and turning were used in the first half of the century (perhaps because eighteenth-century instrument-makers were often clock-makers and therefore ornamented instruments as they did their clock cases),[9] they were eventually eliminated altogether, and by the beginning of the nineteenth century the microscope was composed of the most austerely simple forms, circular and rectangular; only then did it present an appearance that was wholly consistent and, by virtue of that consistency, strikes us as entirely modern. Through the genius of Joseph von Frauenhofer, leadership in the field of microscopy passed to Germany in the first few decades of the century, to remain there practically until the present day. Typically, a fine telescope or microscope was known as "a Frauenhofer" in the course of the nineteenth century.[10]

The futile attempts to mix art and design, or rather to improve design by art, are particularly instructive in instruments of the seventeenth, eighteenth, and early nineteenth centuries. Most of those made in the seventeenth and eighteenth centuries were probably intended for the pleasure of aristocratic amateurs and their guests. Science was fashionable at the court of Charles II, especially after the founding of the Royal Society in 1665, and noblemen, on the Continent as well as in England, took an interest in scientific pursuits. Particularly in the eighteenth century, when the purely functional form began to emerge, the measure of decoration and elaboration of an instrument was directly in proportion to the aristocratic status of its owner.

By 1761, when instrument-makers had gone a long way toward eliminating all superfluous decoration, George Adams made a silver microscope for King George III, which, for the sake of its patron, was meant to be artistic as well as scientific and was therefore composed of stylish decorative forms of the period (*Fig. 2*). The instrument is built on and around a silver-cased Corinthian pillar on a pedestal, flanked by two further pedestals with putti and urns. The pillar carries a platform with two microscopes, a compound one and a single one. The higher compound one is upheld by two partially draped silver figures, while the body tube is decorated with acanthus leaves, ribbons, garlands, and spiral grooves. Every possible attempt is made to overcome the contrast of the rationally functional form and the imaginatively artistic form by covering up and smothering the necessary underlying functional form with the paraphernalia of stylish ornamentation. But to no avail: the necessary logic of the instrument breaks through and destroys the cohesion of the decorative scheme. The result is unsatisfactory on both counts. Reginald S. Clay and Thomas H. Court quite rightly say:

this microscope exhibits the sacrifice of usefulness to ornament [and, one might add, equally that of ornament to usefulness]. Though perhaps the most artistically and elaborately decorated instrument ever constructed, Adams must surely have been fully aware of its faults as a scientific instrument. For instance, the combination of the single and compound microscopes in one instrument makes it necessary either to bend across the instrument to reach the eyepiece of the compound body, or to illuminate the object from the side; while the compound body is inconveniently close to the head when using the simple microscope. It is too high for table use and it cannot be inclined . . . its scientific inferiority is such that one is forced to the conclusion that it was never really intended for serious practical work.[11]

In contrast, Frauenhofer's large achromatic microscope, of about 1817 (*Fig. 3*), is solely dedicated to its function and purpose. Gone are the finials, moldings, and turning; screws with butterfly heads are replaced by severe discs. The instrument achieves a refinement of form, a purity and exactitude that are the result of a new dedication to science and a new vision of form resulting from a new technology in the service of science. Here, at the beginning of the nineteenth century is the pure form language of the twentieth century, abstract geometric form of absolute mastery and sureness of use. Frauenhofer laid the foundation for the fame of the German optical industry during the rest of the nineteenth century. Steinheil, Abbé, Zeiss, and Voigtländer were his immediate followers and bear names still alive and famous in the field of optical instruments. Other instruments for precise observation, for measuring space, time, line, mass, weight, and numbers, can be found in abundance, each specific form derived from its individual task and function but having in common with other forms the quality of dedication to purpose—a quality of intellect given material form by the genius of the designer (*Figs. 4–24*).

Machine tools, particularly the lathe, also have a dual history in the eighteenth century. Many aristocrats amused themselves with lathes, which were elaborately decorated (*Fig. 25*), whereas actual work-a-day tools, even in the eighteenth century, were of a stark utilitarian simplicity (*Fig. 26*). In the nineteenth century, the functional form became universal for tools and machines. If an aristocrat was engaged in science or mechanical experimentation, his tools and instruments were no different from those of anyone else, just as his clothing, though of finer quality, was no longer distinguishable in style from that of the working population.

2. *Silver double microscope, by George Adams.*
London, second half of the eighteenth century.
(British Crown Copyright. Science Museum, London)

3. *Microscope by Joseph von Frauenhofer, Munich,*
ca. 1817. Its exclusive use of brass and its austere
geometric forms are the results of the new, rational ap-
proach to design by the instrument-makers and
scientists after 1800.
(Deutsches Museum, Munich)

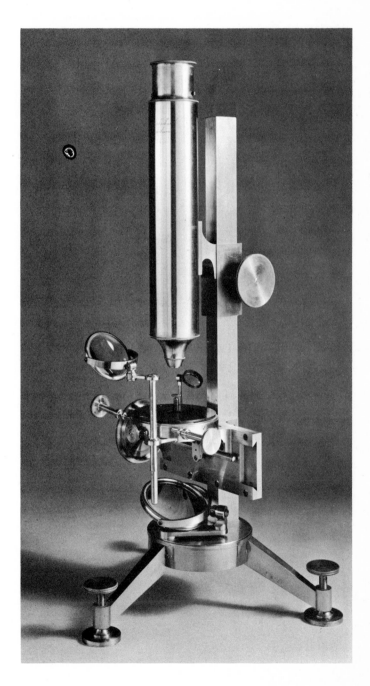

12

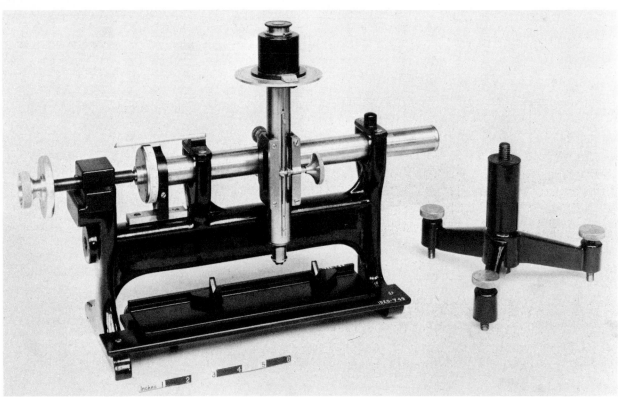

6. *Sun microscope, by George Adams, London,*
ca. 1790.
(Deutsches Museum, Munich)

7. *Inclinometer, its reading lens with micrometer*
adjustment, by J. Liebherr, ca. 1810.
(Deutsches Museum, Munich)

14

8. *Theodolite, by J. G. Studer, Freiberg in Saxony,
beginning of the nineteenth century.*
(Deutsches Museum, Munich)

9. *Galvanometer. Inscribed: Galvanomètre Deprez,
Ateliers Ruhmkorff, J. Carpentier, Paris, 1881.*
(Deutsches Museum, Munich)

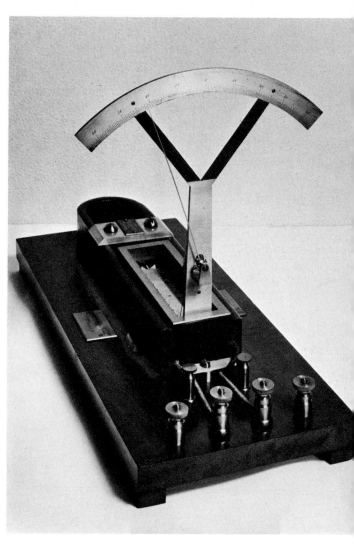

10. *Quadrant with two fixed and one movable diopter in a ball joint. End of the eighteenth century.*
(Deutsches Museum, Munich)

11. *Sextant of brass, by C. F. Oechsle.*
Pforzheim, first half of the nineteenth century.
(Deutsches Museum, Munich)

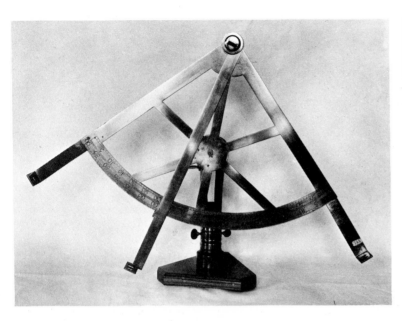

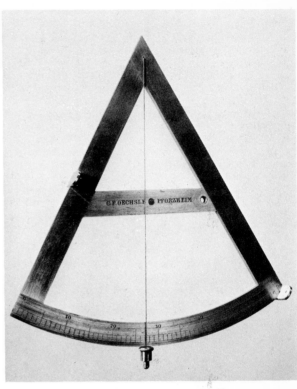

12. *Two-and-a-half-inch prismatic compass,*
by E. I. Dent, London, ca. 1845.
(British Crown Copyright. Science Museum, London)

13. *Diopter compass, ca. 1800. Inscribed:*
E. Petitpierre, Berlin.
(Deutsches Museum, Munich)

16

14. *Pedometer, by Johann Martin. Augsburg,* ca. *1700.*
(Deutsches Museum, Munich)

15. *Pedometer, beginning of the nineteenth century.*
Inscribed: Bikel, Augsburg.
(Deutsches Museum, Munich)

16. *Adding machine. Inscribed: Dr. Roth, Inven.*
Paris, 1842.
(Deutsches Museum, Munich)

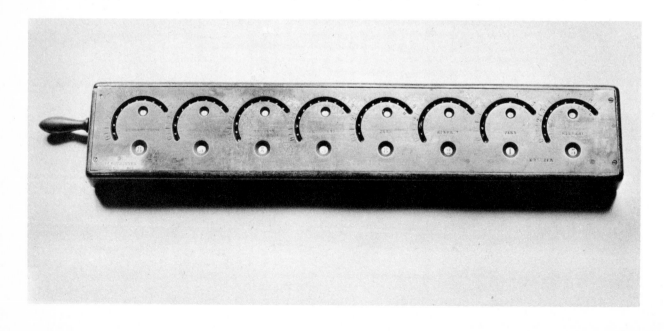

17. *Opera glasses in ivory, with ivory handle.*
Inscribed: Friedrich Voigtlaenders Patent 1823 in Wien.
(Deutsches Museum, Munich)

18. *Camera, by Steinheil, after Voigtländer, ca. 1842.*
(Deutsches Museum, Munich)

19. *Portrait camera, by F. Hanfstaengl. Munich, 1850.*
(Deutsches Museum, Munich)

20. *Telegraph (facsimile), by Samuel Morse, 1837.*
(Deutsches Museum, Munich)

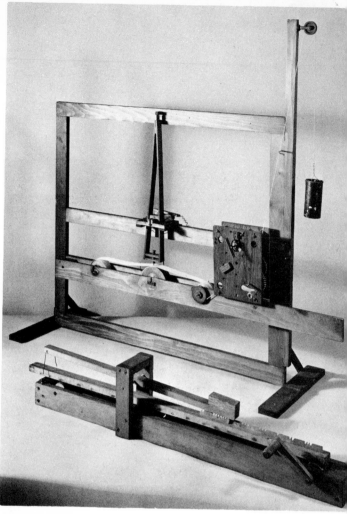

21. *Compound steelyard, made by George Adams for*
George III, toward the end of the eighteenth century.
(Science Museum, London, by courtesy of King's
College, London)

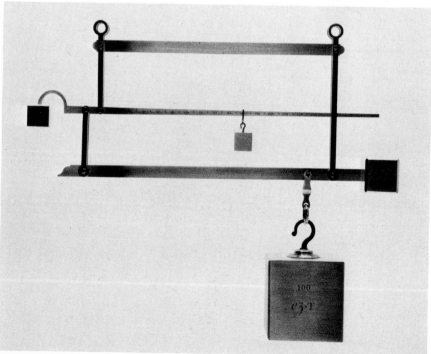

22. Standard fifty-six-pound balance of hardened steel, with copper pans and brass chains, made by Messrs. De Grave & Son, in 1825, for the Exchequer in Westminster, where it was used until 1870.
(British Crown Copyright. Science Museum, London)

23. British standard weights (facsimiles in nickel of the originals in platinum). Imperial kilogramme standard, 1878; imperial avoirdupois standard pound, 1824; imperial primary pound standard, 1855.
(British Crown Copyright. Science Museum, London)

24. British standard measures. Imperial standard gallon, quart, and pint, in conical form, 1824.
(British Crown Copyright. Science Museum, London)

25. *Ornamental lathe or rose engine, German, ca. 1750.*
(British Crown Copyright. Science Museum, London)

26. *Ornamental lathe, French, ca. 1740.*
(British Crown Copyright. Science Museum, London)

27. *First steam engine (facsimile), with rotary drive,
by James Watt, 1788.*
(Deutsches Museum, Munich)

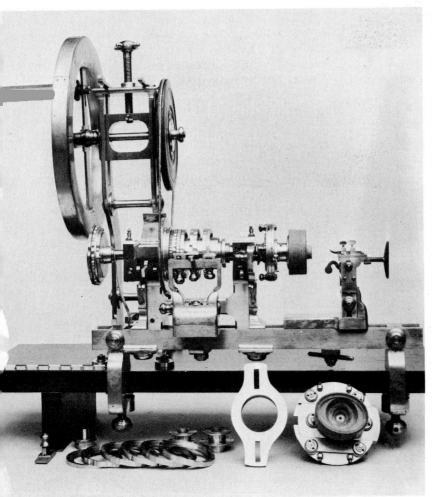

The first engines and larger machines of the Industrial Revolution were made almost entirely of wood, particularly their framing, and one sees the inventors so intent on realizing their mechanical ideas that no conscious thought was given to the appearance of the machine. And yet, the first engines of Watt have something grandiose about them, with their enormous wooden beams, studded with large bolts, and their purposeful metal gears and wheels lending a note of grace in their contrasting thinness and precise articulation (*Fig. 27*).

A milestone in the development of machine tools for mass production is a group of machines designed by Sir Marc Isambard Brunel for manufacturing ships' blocks at the Royal Dockyard at Portsmouth at the very beginning of the nineteenth century [12] (*Figs. 28, 29*). The blocks had previously been made on contract by various workshops using machine saws and lathes driven by a horse mill, but depending to a large extent on hand labor. The annual consumption by the Royal Navy at the beginning of the nineteenth century has been estimated at 100,000 blocks. Brunel's designs for machinery to manufacture blocks were submitted to Sir Samuel Bentham, Inspector General of Naval Works, who was quick to realize their merit and recommended to the Admiralty that the machinery be constructed and installed at the Portsmouth Dockyard. The proposal was accepted, and the work of building the machinery was given to the firm of Henry Maudslay (1771–1831), the first great machine-tool manufacturer. The machines were constructed entirely of metal, thus insuring greater rigidity and accuracy, a practice that henceforth became standard for the manufacture of machine tools. The entire plant was finished by 1807, and the machines operated by ten unskilled men did the work of 110 skilled block-makers. The machines were so well designed and constructed that some of them continued in use into the mid-twentieth century. But they were also the sensation of the day when they were built, and visitors flocked to the Navy Yards to see the mechanical wonder. Because of its interest as a new system of manufacturing machinery, every detail is fully described and illustrated in the contemporary *Cyclopaedia* of Abraham Rees, published in 1819. The final comment of the 18-page-long description is that Maudslay "made these machines with the most scrupulous attention to accuracy and durability, at the same time preserving an elegant proportion in their form, which is very agreeable to the eye." [13]

Brunel, like Watt, made use of Tuscan columns in his machines and later occasionally used Gothic forms, conforming to the then current taste. This may be regarded, on the one hand, as a remnant of the older tendency to beautify, inherited from the eighteenth century, and, on the other hand, as evidence of the dichotomy inherent in the nineteenth century, with its use of austere functional forms alongside of romantic forms. As late as 1851, at the Crystal Palace, machines with architectural forms in their framing were shown. They make those of pure functional form stand out all the more. In the case of Brunel's machines, the important point is that Tuscan columns are *remnants* and do not dominate the design or make it into a decorative plaything.

In Henry Maudslay, the manufacturer of the Portsmouth block-making machinery, we meet the first of a succession of distinguished engineers who, until about 1840, invented and designed modern machine tools as we know them today. The building of the block-making machinery was Maudslay's first large undertaking, and it was conceded by all that his contribution to the quality of the machines was as decisive as the designs of Brunel. Nasmyth, who learned in Maudslay's shop and became one of the great engineers of the next

28. *Mortising machine, ca. 1804. One of the historical series of machine tools known as the "Portsmouth Block-Making Machinery," designed by Sir Marc Isambard Brunel, manufactured by Henry Maudslay.* (British Crown Copyright. Science Museum, London)

29. *Detail of coaking machine, ca. 1804, of the "Portsmouth Block-Making Machinery."* (British Crown Copyright. Science Museum, London)

30. *Screw-cutting lathe, by Henry Maudslay, ca. 1800.*
(British Crown Copyright. Science Museum, London)

31. *Micrometer, by Henry Maudslay, 1805.*
(British Crown Copyright. Science Museum, London)

32. *Eccentric chuck, by Henry Maudslay, 1810.*
(British Crown Copyright. Science Museum, London)

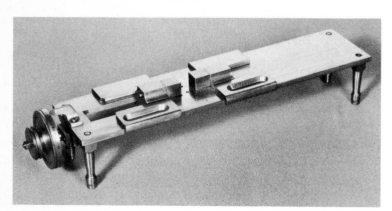

generation, said that "every member of it was full of Maudslay's presence and the mechanical perfection of its details, its practicality and adaptability show his handiwork at every turn." [14] One can see how, during the period between 1800 and 1840, the remnants of the old forms were dropped more and more and the new functional forms were adopted. One senses that the mechanics, engineers, and scientists who designed, built, and used these new machines and instruments were a new breed of men, whose conception of machines was worlds removed from the elegant aristocratic playthings of the eighteenth century. Their minds and hands would have revolted against the use of idle and superfluous decoration on their truly magnificient tools, machines, and instruments. They were exhilarated and enthused about the beauty of their own creations, about whose formal qualities and the newness of these qualities they were quite clear in their minds (*Figs. 30–48*).

In *Technics and Civilization*, Mumford illustrates Maudslay's screw-cutting lathe and comments that "perhaps the most original artists of the period were the toolmakers." He speaks of the English toolmakers of the late eighteenth and the early nineteenth century as "a new race of artists." [15]

Testifying before a parliamentary committee in 1836, Thomas L. Donaldson, an architect, said, "I find that old machines, when they were originally invented, had not any beauty of form: they were of large proportions, but as they were more studied, they became simplified, and have now acquired greater grace of form from that very simplicity. The steam engine itself is an example of that remark" (*Fig. 33*). And upon being asked by the examiner: "Has not a general use of iron in making machinery added very much to the beauty of the steam engine?" he answered, "Yes, it has relieved it from heavy cumbrous propor-

tions." And when the examiner asked: "There is probably no example of a perfect machine which is not at the same time beautiful?" his answer was, "I know none." [16]

Almost 100 years later, at the start of the "modern movement," the beauty of machines was discovered again. Very similar language was used, but it took the form of platonic rapture, whereas at the beginning of the nineteenth century, the actual inventing, designing, and making of machines and instruments and tools of the utmost refinement of form was the life and blood of the men concerned. Their conviction, involvement, and satisfaction spoke out of every detail of every machine, and, indeed, from their words. Many times they referred to the "beauty" of machines; they spoke of simplicity and economy of form, and they asserted that every excrescence is a deterrent to function, especially rejecting, as inappropriate, "traditional" forms. We have become very careful in assessing nineteenth-century calls for functional form, because, too often, performance does not match up with the verbal postulations of the same men, particularly in the second half of the century. But, like the microscopes of Frauenhofer, the machine tools of these pioneers are uncompromising in their devotion to simplicity, exactitude, and directness of approach. In many instances, the result cannot but evoke aesthetic pleasure.

Not only were the English proud and exhilarated by their own achievement, but the world came to admire and imitate. England's rapid industrial growth, its inventiveness, productivity, and wealth were the wonder and envy of the world. Emerson, who visited England several times during these decades and wrote his impressions in *English Traits*, observed that "the bias of the nation is a passion for utility. They love the lever, the screw and pulley. . . . They have impressed their direct-

26

33. *James Watt's "cabinet" steam engine, after 1800.*
(British Crown Copyright. Science Museum, London)

34. *Planing machine, by Richard Roberts, 1817.*
(British Crown Copyright. Science Museum, London)

ness and practical habit on modern civilization." [17] The anglophile Swiss manufacturer Johann Conrad Fischer, who came repeatedly to see and learn in English factories, kept a diary of his travels, in which he remarked again and again on the solidity and beauty of English machines.[18] He was perhaps more sensitive than some others to the aesthetic qualities of the machines, but he is representative of many.

Maudslay invented or improved many of the tools and machines that made possible all later developments, but his fame rests chiefly on the introduction of the slide-rest and the screw-cutting machine. The slide-rest is the foundation of all further machine tools. Only with the precision it made possible by supporting and directing the cutting tool on a lathe mechanically instead of depending on the human hand, could further machines be produced that would satisfy the demands for accuracy and dependability in technical production. In his screw-cutting lathe, Maudslay combined the slide-rest with a lead screw, operated by change gears, so that various pitches could be cut (*Fig. 30*). He was passionately concerned with accuracy. As ordinary calipers were too unreliable for his workshop, he developed a bench micrometer of an amazing accuracy for the time. He kept this in his own workshop, and it was always referred to as "The Lord Chancellor." It was designed merely and directly for performance. As in all the best work of this time, there is no false rhetoric; the tool consists of the necessary parts stated in the necessary geometric forms [19] (*Fig. 31*).

Though Maudslay kept up the custom of using architectural framing in many of his larger machines, the fineness of their proportions and the perfection of their workmanship gave them a character all their own. Samuel Smiles records Nasmyth's statement concerning Maudslay, that "you could see the man's character in whatever work he turned out; and as the connoisseur in art will exclaim at sight of a picture, 'That is Turner,' . . . detecting the hand of the master in it, so the experienced mechanician, at sight of one of his machines or engines, will be equally ready to exclaim: 'That is Maudslay.' " [20] (*Figs. 30, 32*).

Being vigilant and critical of his own work, it may be imagined that Maudslay would be a careful master over the workmen in his shop. The most notable members of the next generation of engineers who contributed further inventions were trained by him. "It may be said that what Oxford and Cambridge are in letters, workshops such as Maudslay's . . . are in mechanics. Nor can Oxford and Cambridge men be prouder of the connection with their respective colleges than mechanics such as Whitworth, Nasmyth, Roberts, Muir, and Lewis, are of their connection with the school of Maudslay." [21]

James Nasmyth (1808–90), one of the greatest of the next generation of engineers and known principally for the invention of the steam hammer (*Figs. 35, 36*), came to Maudslay as an apprentice in 1829. Not only has Smiles written extensively about him in his *Industrial Biography*, but Nasmyth himself wrote his recollections in the form of an autobiography later in life. These writings reveal his attitudes and ideas about machines in an appealing, personal way. He was twenty-one when he came to London with the object of entering Maudslay's workshop as an apprentice. Describing his first visit there, he speaks of his excitement and astonishment at the sight of "the beautiful machine tools, the silent, smooth whirl of the machinery . . . I observed the beautiful steam-engine which gave motion to the tools and machinery of the workshops." The young man won Maudslay's confidence. Maudslay "then proceeded to show me the collection of exquisite tools

of all sorts with which his private workshop was stored. They mostly bore the impress of his own clearheadedness and common-sense; they were very simple, and quite free from mere traditional forms and arrangements. At the same time they were perfect for the special purposes for which they had been designed."

Nasmyth's own philosophy of design for machinery is expressed a number of times very trenchantly and reveals with great clarity his kinship with what is thought of as modern design. His own "definition of engineering" is *the application of common-sense to the use of materials.*" (Italics his.) Of the training he gave young mechanics, he said: "This sort of [practical] training educated the perceptive faculties of the lads, and trained their ideas to perfect truth of form, at the same time that it gave them an intimate acquaintance with the nature of the materials employed in mechanical structures."[22]

In another context, Nasmyth wrote in 1841:

Viewing abstractedly the forms of the various details of which every machine is composed, we shall find that they consist of certain combinations of six primitive or elementary geometrical figures, namely, *the line, the plane, the circle, the cylinder, the cone,* and *the sphere;* and that, however complex the arrangement, and vast the number of parts of which a machine consists, we shall find that all may be as it were decomposed and classed under these *six* forms; and that, in short, every machine, whatever be its purpose, simply consists of a combination of these forms, more or less complex, for the attainment of certain objects and performance of required duties. [Italics his.][23]

One is, of course, immediately reminded of Plato's definition of beauty in *Philebus*, in which he states that he means "straight lines and circles, and shapes, plane or solid, made from them by lathe, ruler and square." But more important is the contemporary parallel of the severe geometric architecture of Boullée and Ledoux in France, Soane and Gandy in England, and Gilly in Germany, with its emphasis on the sphere, the cylinder, and the cube.[24] And, looking ahead, there is Cézanne's interest in "the cylinder, the sphere, the cone," and, of course, the work of the cubists and all that follows from it, in painting, sculpture, architecture, and design.

A still more thoughtful and far-reaching definition is given by Nasmyth in his *Autobiography*:

In mechanical structures and contrivances I have always endeavored to attain the desired purpose by the employment of the *fewest parts*, casting aside every detail not absolutely necessary, and guarding carefully against the intrusion of mere *traditional* forms and arrangements. The latter are apt to insinuate themselves, and to interfere with that simplicity and directness of action which is in all cases so desirable a quality in mechanical structures. *Plain common-sense* should be apparent in the general design, as in the form and arrangement of the details, and a general character of *severe utility* pervade the whole, accompanied with as much attention to gracefulness of form as is consistent with the nature and purpose of the structure. [Italics his.][25]

Though some of these statements may have the character of hindsight, since they were written later in his life, we do have a testimony that falls in this period and that was recorded contemporaneously, during his appearance in March, 1836, before a parliamentary committee constituted to "inquire into the best means of extending a knowledge of the arts and of the principles of design among the people (especially the manufacturing population) of the country." When asked, "How would you carry into effect the combination of beauty of design with machinery?" Nasmyth answered, "I would show the means of combining the most beautiful forms and the most scientific application of the materials employed in the forma-

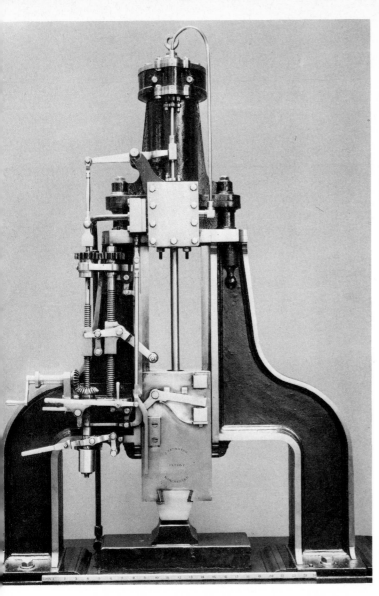

tion of machinery with the greatest economy. In the majority of instances, the most economical disposition of materials coincides with such a form as presents the most elegant appearance to the eye." Above all, he stressed "the entire reconcilability of elegance of form with bare utility." [26]

One last member of the early generation of English tool-builders was Joseph Whitworth (1803–87), trained, as was Nasmyth, in the workshops of Maudslay. His overriding concern was with accuracy and quality of workmanship, and for these purposes he developed better methods of achieving a true plane and improved methods of measure-

ment (*Fig. 37*). In 1856, he exhibited a machine capable of measuring one millionth of an inch. In his screw-cutting machine, Maudslay had provided the means for accuracy and uniformity in the production of an essential detail in machine construction. Whitworth carried this out further and fully realized the standardization of screw-thread practice in England.

More important for this study is the fact that Whitworth did away with every vestige of the architectural style of framing in his machines, introducing the box design or hollow frame for machinery and greatly increasing the weight of the metal used in order to insure stability. While elegance of machines had once been thought possible only through the use of such artistic conventions as architectural elements and splayed or curved legs, later engineers saw functional elegance in reducing weight to a minimum and proportioning of each member to its precise limit and function. In his pursuit of precision and accuracy, Whitworth added box-section supports of massiveness and weight to achieve his ends, thus changing appearance and proportions of the machines.

In contrast to the earlier versatile engineering workshops, Whitworth's Manchester works specialized in the manufacture of machine tools, and he was thus able to standardize his production and achieve high quality and reliable delivery at reasonable cost. By 1850, his machine tools were the standard of the world. The machines exhibited by

36. *Bench drilling machine, by James Nasmyth, ca. 1840.*
(British Crown Copyright. Science Museum, London)

37. *Workshop measuring machine, by Joseph Whitworth, ca. 1850.*
(British Crown Copyright. Science Museum, London)

38. *(left to right)* a: *Replica of the original micrometer invented and patented by Jean Laurent Palmer, France, 1849.*
b: *Pocket sheet-metal gauging micrometer, 1867, the first micrometer made by the Brown and Sharpe Manufacturing Co., Providence, R.I.* c: *The first micrometer with one-inch opening made by the Brown and Sharpe Manufacturing Co., 1877.* d: *Direct-reading micrometer, invented by J. Ciceri Smith of Edinburgh, 1893.*
(British Crown Copyright. Science Museum, London)

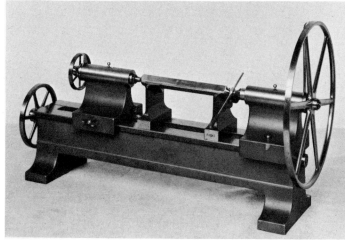

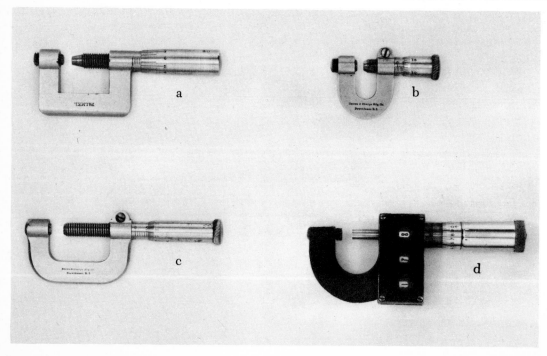

a

b

c

d

Whitworth's firm at the Crystal Palace in 1851 were commented on as being "of great beauty and power." [27] The fame and reputation of his firm meant that his machines, their forms, and their aesthetics became exemplary. "The proportions of the modern machine tool, massive, austere, strictly functional, owe more to Joseph Whitworth than to any other man." [28]

With the middle of the century, the pioneering workshops, in which the new engineers had built their machines with an intuitive knowledge and practical skill, and with a passion for precision of execution and an aesthetic delight in the elegance of their designs, were a thing of the past. Henceforth, engineering was more and more closely coupled with theoretical scientific investigation and procedure, a necessary combination as processes and machines, as well as the enterprises that produced and used them, became larger and more complex. In its pioneering phase, England had depended on the skill and intuition of its engineers and had neglected formal scientific and technical education, in contrast to the Continent, particularly France and Germany, where this was fostered not only by tradition but also in an endeavor to catch up with England. However, it is the early period that established the forms and the aesthetics of machines for the modern world (*Figs. 30–41*).

Although England had led in the first half of the century and had been the unchallenged workshop of the world, by mid-century, America had grasped the initiative in machine-tool design (*Fig. 42*). It was in America, in 1845, that the turret lathe was developed by Stephen Fitch, to meet the demands of a government contract to produce 30,000 pistols. The revolving cylindrical turret carrying eight tools permitted eight successive operations without stopping the machine to change tools. [29] This was the most important development in the lathe since Maudslay's inventions. It is significant that in 1853

a group of British engineers, which included Whitworth, toured America as a parliamentary committee; as a result of their visit and subsequent recommendations, England imported 157 American machine tools for the purpose of setting up and equipping a new government rifle-making plant at Enfield. [30]

The new prominence of the United States in the field was principally due to what was then called "the American system," namely the interchangeability of parts. First proposed in Europe for the manufacture of arms and reported on from France by Thomas Jefferson in 1785 as of importance to the United States, [31] it was successfully applied by Eli Whitney, in collaboration with government armories and a few other private armories, in the manufacture of guns in the United States. [32] The interchangeability of parts was essential to the further growth of industry, and its early introduction in America was to a large part responsible for the astonishing development of American industry in the second half of the century. Its application to the tools of industry as well as to the products of industry made possible the mass production of inexpensive, practical consumer goods for the American market as well as for export.

Even in 1851, at the Great Exhibition in the Crystal Palace in London, practicality and reasonable price marked the products shown by America, from the McCormick reaper to boots, pails, axes, and other tools. In 1876, the Centennial Exhibition in Philadelphia afforded an opportunity for the fruits of this development to be shown to the world on a grand scale. Just as in the other international exhibitions of the century, there was, of course, much that was "refined" and "artistic," but refined with borrowed finery and artistic in forms of the past. Though there was much gushing over that, a genuine enthusiasm was expressed for some of the machinery displayed, particularly the great

39. *Compression pump, by Natterer, 1844.*
(Deutsches Museum, Munich)

40. *Drilling machine for watch plates,*
patented by Richard Roberts, 1848.
(British Crown Copyright. Science Museum, London)

41. *Screw-rolling machine, 1860 (patented in 1851).*
(Photo Science Museum, London)

42. *Universal Milling Machine, invented by Joseph R.*
Brown in 1861. The number-one machine
manufactured by Brown and Sharpe of Providence, R.I.,
was granted patents in 1862 and 1865.
(British Crown Copyright. Science Museum, London)

Corliss engine; in fact, a kind of apotheosis of machinery was celebrated in the display of this huge steam engine (*Figs. 43, 44*). It aroused astonishment and admiration, not only by its size and its smooth and silent technical performance, but also by its shapes and forms and their relationships at rest and in motion, which was an exciting aesthetic experience for many. So impressed was one observer by the convincing expressive qualities and the various forms of motion in Machinery Hall, that he declared "surely here, and not in literature, science, or art, is the true evidence of man's creative power; here is Prometheus unbound." He also makes the astute observation that "probably those who understand nothing of what they see are more imaginatively affected than those who know all about valves and pistons." [33]

Other machines, such as those exhibited by William Sellers at the Centennial, showed beauty and grace on a smaller scale and in a less complicated, more direct way (*Fig. 45*). The forms have an astonishing refinement and, with all mechanical logic, a sculptural quality that satisfies the senses beyond and in spite of the mechanics.

"The sensation of the exhibition" was the Stow drill with a flexible shaft that could bring power into otherwise inaccessible places (*Fig. 46*). A European observer compared it to a dental drill, which had long been known there, but here it was three-horsepower strong! With genuine admiration, he said of American machinery in his report, "everywhere we are met with the results of serious thinking and we are astonished to see how many of our old tools could be improved . . . In numerous examples we see that in its achievements American industry breaks with every tradition and seeks new ways which seem to us fantastic" [34] (*Figs. 47, 48*).

Only two years later, at the Paris Exposition of 1878, American machines were especially admired, without envy, by the outdistanced English:

It may almost certainly be predicated of any modern mechanical congress that the Americans will carry off the palm for novel and ingenious application of force to practical purposes, the substitution of mechanism for hand labour in new and curious contrivances. . . . The New Englander invents normally; his brain has a bias that way. He mechanizes as an old Greek sculptured, as the Venetian painted . . . a school has grown up whose dominant quality, curiously intense, widespread and daring, is mechanical imagination . . . "Yankee" is almost a synonym of inventor. [35]

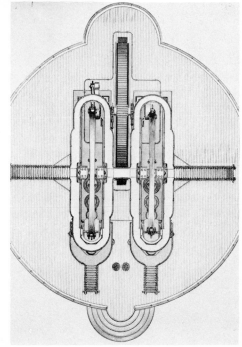

43. *President Grant and the Emperor of Brazil
starting the Great Corliss Engine in Machinery Hall
at the Centennial Exposition in Philadelphia, 1876.*
(From: Frank Leslie, Historical Register of the Centennial
Exposition *[New York, 1876], p. 79.)*

44. *Plan of the Corliss Engine.*
(From: Joseph M. Wilson, The Masterpieces of the
Centennial International Exhibition, *Vol. III: History,
Mechanics, Science [Philadelphia, n.d.], p. 5.)*

45. *Portable riveting machine, William Sellers and Co., Philadelphia, 1876.*
(*From: Joseph M. Wilson,* The Masterpieces of the Centennial International Exhibition, *Vol. III:* History, Mechanics, Science *[Philadelphia, n.d.], p. 96.*)

46. *Stow flexible shaft—in locomotive work, by Messrs. Stow and Burnham, Philadelphia, 1876.*
(*From: Joseph M. Wilson,* The Masterpieces of the Centennial International Exhibition, *Vol. III:* History, Mechanics, Science *[Philadelphia, n.d.], p. 264.*)

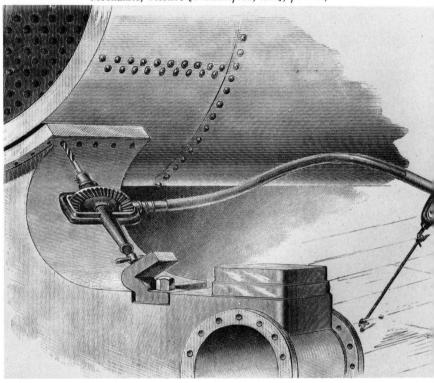

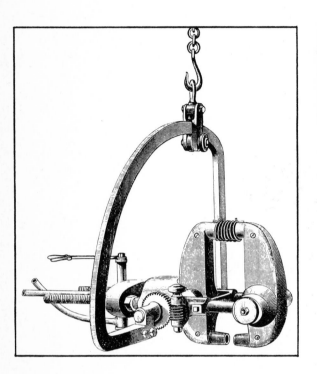

47. *Boring tool, American, 1872, patented by Q. S. Backus. A tool with a universal joint between bit and handle, so that boring can be done "around the corner" up to an angle of 135°.*
(*From: Georg Seelhorst,* Die Philadelphia-Ausstellung und was sie lehrt *[Nördlingen, 1878], Fig. 10*)

48. *Plane of cast iron, American, 1876. Adjustable for use on plane, concave, and convex surfaces.*
(*From: Georg Seelhorst,* Die Philadelphia-Ausstellung und was sie lehrt *[Nördlingen, 1878], Fig. 11*)

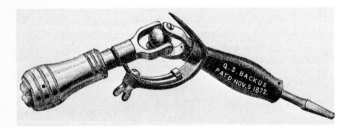

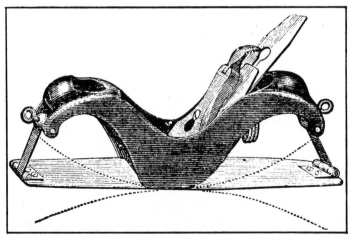

1. Edward Robert De Zurko, *Origins of Functionalist Theory* (New York: Columbia University Press, 1957), p. 80.

2. Francis Hutcheson, *An Inquiry into the Original of Our Ideas of Beauty and Virtue* (2d ed.; London: J. Darby, 1726), pp. 66–69.

3. David Hume, "Why Utility Pleases," Sec. V, pp. 202 ff., in *An Enquiry Concerning the Principles of Morals* (1751), Vol. II of his *Essays, Moral, Political and Literary* (London: Longmans, Green, 1882). See also Walter John Hipple, Jr., *The Beautiful, the Sublime, and the Picturesque in Eighteenth Century British Aesthetic Theory* (Carbondale, Ill.: Southern Illinois University Press, 1957), p. 41.

4. David Hume, *A Treatise of Human Nature*, Vol. II, *Of the Passions* (1739; London: Longmans, Green, 1882), p. 151.

5. Adam Smith, "Of the Beauty Which the Appearance of Utility Bestows Upon all the Productions of Art, and of the Extensive Influence of this Species of Beauty," chap. i, Part IV, *Of the Effect of Utility Upon the Sentiment of Approbation, of Essays, Philosophical and Literary . . . Including the Theory of Moral Sentiments* (1759; London: Ward, Lock, 1880), p. 158.

6. Henry Home (Lord Kames), *Elements of Criticism* (1761; New York: H. S. Barnes, 1866), pp. 120, 110, 114.

7. Archibald Alison, "Of the Sublimity and Beauty of the Material World," in *Essays on the Nature and Principles of Taste* (1790; New York: Harper & Bros., 1846), pp. 280, 284.

The associationist view was not unchallenged. See Lord Jeffrey's review of Alison's book in *The Edinburgh Review*, XVIII (May, 1811), 1-46; Victor Cousin, *Du Vrai, Du Beau et Du Bien* (lectures delivered in 1817) (Paris: 1853), pp. 166–67; John Stuart Blackie, *On Beauty* (Edinburgh: 1858), p. 47.

8. Moritz von Rohr, *Joseph Frauenhofers Leben, Leistungen und Wirksamkeit* (Leipzig: Akademische Verlagsgesellschaft, 1929), pp. 172, 204.

9. L. T. C. Rolt, *Tools for the Job* (London: B. T. Batsford, 1965), p. 119.

10. Frauenhofer also developed a new type of mounting for telescopes which was more rational, more stable, and more useful than those used before. The Frauenhofer type of mounting is known to this day as "German-type." Henry C. King, *The History of the Telescope* (London: Charles Griffin, 1955), pp. 183–84.

11. Reginald S. Clay and Thomas H. Court, *The History of the Microscope* (London: Charles Griffin, 1932), pp. 179–80.

12. Most of the following information is taken from K. R. Gilbert, *The Portsmouth Block-Making Machinery, A Pioneering Enterprise in Mass Production* (London: Her Majesty's Stationery Office, 1965). Mr. Gilbert also very kindly gave me additional information and answered queries by letter (May 12, 1967).

13. Abraham Rees, *The Cyclopaedia or Universal Dictionary of Arts, Sciences, and Literature* (London: 1819), Vols. XXI and XXII, Vol. II of plates. The volumes are unpaged. At the end of Volume XXI is the article "Machinery," which is continued at the beginning of Volume XXII, and this part, consisting of eighteen pages, is concerned solely with the Portsmouth block-making machinery.

14. Quoted by Joseph Wickham Roe, *English and American Tool Builders* (New Haven, Conn.: Yale University Press, 1916), p. 35.

15. Lewis Mumford, *Technics and Civilization* (New York: Harcourt, Brace, 1934), plate IX, p. 209.

16. Great Britain, House of Commons, *Parliamentary Papers*, Vol. IX, "Report from the Select Committee on Arts and their Connexion with Manufactures," Part II (1836), p. 32.

17. Ralph Waldo Emerson, *English Traits* (1856), in *The Complete Works* (Boston: Houghton, Mifflin, 1904), V, 83, 85.

18. Johann Conrad Fischer, *Tagebücher* (Schaffhausen: G. Fischer, 1951), pp. 265, 306–7, 434.

19. Roe, *op. cit.*, p. 45.

20. Samuel Smiles, *Industrial Biography: Iron Workers and Tool Makers* (London: John Murray, new ed., 1876; Preface dated 1863), p. 227.

21. *Ibid.*, pp. 232–33.

22. James Nasmyth, *An Autobiography* (New York: Harper & Bros., 1883), pp. 131, 132, 279, 310 respectively.

23. James Nasmyth, "Remarks on the Introduction

of the Slide Principle in Tools and Machines Employed in the Production of Machinery," appears as Appendix B in Robertson Buchanan, *Practical Essays on Mill Work and Other Machinery* (3d ed.; London: John Weale, 1841), p. 394.

24. See Emil Kaufmann, "Three Revolutionary Architects, Boullée, Ledoux, and Lequeu," *Transactions of the American Philosophical Society*, Vol. XLII, Part III (1952), 431–564; and *idem, Architecture in the Age of Reason* (Cambridge, Mass.: Harvard University Press, 1955).

25. Nasmyth, *Autobiography*, p. 443.

26. Great Britain, House of Commons, *Parliamentary Papers, loc. cit.*, pp. 28–29.

27. Charles Tomlinson, *Cyclopaedia of Useful Arts, Mechanical and Chemical, Manufactures, Mining, and Engineering* (London and New York: 1862), p. cxliii.

28. Rolt, *op. cit.*, p. 119. Whitworth is discussed at length, pp. 118–21.

29. *Ibid.*, pp. 164 ff.; Roe, *op. cit.*, p. 143.

30. Rolt, *op. cit.*, pp. 137–38; Roe, *op. cit.*, pp. 138–41.

31. Rolt, *op. cit.*, pp. 139–40.

32. Though Eli Whitney has usually been credited with the first realization of the interchangeability of parts in gun-making, recent research has shown that this view is exaggerated when his efforts are compared with those of some of his predecessors and contemporaries. See R. S. Woodbury, "The Legend of Eli Whitney," *Technology and Culture*, I, No. 3 (1960), and Edwin A. Battison, "Eli Whitney and the Milling Machine," *The Smithsonian Journal of History*, I, No. 2 (1966), 9–34.

33. "Characteristics of the International Fair," *Atlantic Monthly* (September, 1876), pp. 358–59.

34. Georg Seelhorst, *Die Philadelphia-Ausstellung und was sie lehrt* (Nördlingen: C. H. Beck, 1878), pp. 96, 102, 122.

35. *The Times* (London), August 22, 1878, p. 6.

2 Transportation

While the virtues of machine and instrument design were recognized by few other than their makers and may be said to represent an aristocracy of design, the whole field of transportation has a wider, more popular appeal and, at the same time, stands as a fine example for every critic and advocate of modern, functional design.

Carts and carriages and coaches link the nineteenth century, the century of change and progress, with the older ways of life of earlier centuries. However, the vehicles we admire and that have become classics are actually a development of the early nineteenth century. Before technical improvements could be made in the vehicles themselves, improvements that gave them the elegance we associate with them, it was necessary for better roads to be designed and built.

Road improvement began everywhere in Europe during the eighteenth century, mostly under state authority. But it was in England that the decisive development took place. There, the Industrial Revolution made cheap and rapid transport of goods and people imperative. Typically, the British relied on private enterprise and created the system of turnpikes in which trusts were allowed to levy tolls on roads for which they had the responsibility of upkeep. In the second half of the eighteenth century and in the first decades of the nineteenth, British roads were remarkably improved, mainly through the work of the engineers Thomas Telford and John McAdam, who reduced the curvature of the road and provided proper drainage to insure a hard, smooth surface in all weather conditions. Traffic increased rapidly, and regular coach service became a reality. The better quality of the roads meant that fewer coaches overturned; thus, the increased safety led to increased speed, which called for modification in the design of the carriages. Eighteenth century carriages and coaches were high off the road, heavy, and cumbersome. The need to increase both speed and safety led to a lowering of carriage bodies, made possible in 1804 by the invention of the elliptic steel spring, in which the carriage body hung suspended. The demands of speed also meant a constant trimming down of all parts to their slimmest possible dimensions commensurate with safety.[1]

The Prince Regent and his friends fostered this development; they made carriage-driving fashionable and the carriage became a highly prized possession as well as a means of conveyance. Though they belong to another era and a vanished way of life, the names of these vehicles still ring in our ears: cabriolets, landaus, victorias, phaetons, and broughams; occasionally the names of these carriages are brought to life and applied to the fashionable automobiles that long ago replaced them.

One might assume that in these vehicles of highest fashion there would have been a conflict between the demands of the ruling taste for ornateness and the strict logic of function appropriate to a means of transportation. If there was, function won out over the ruling taste, in fact *became* the ruling taste in this instance. Utmost simplicity was the mark of elegance and refinement in a carriage.

The cultivation of the carriage nevertheless provoked some thought on the part of Englishmen, as is interestingly shown in the review of a book on French industry in an *Edinburgh Review* of 1819. The article discusses the differences of the industries and tastes of France and England and finds England pre-eminent in carriage design. Curiously, the author is a trifle defensive about this, because he had just previously cited as England's chief glory her capacity to make the common, useful thing available to the many, and since a carriage could hardly be called a common article, he felt England's superiority in its manufacture needed some explaining.

There is but one branch of *luxury* in which we exceed [the French], but in this case we are unrivalled, and that is, in all that relates to horses and carriages. But these, more than any other article of splendour, are connected with things of the most essential importance to society; with an animal the most precious of all, in the most eminent of all arts, Agriculture; with the goodness of our roads, which allows our vehicles to be constructed with a lightness and delicacy, impracticable in any other country; and, finally, with speedy communication. In a word, it is of all luxuries the least sensual, the least selfish, and the most useful to mankind; and, in this respect, we look upon our immense superiority to be characteristic.[2]

Thirty years later, by the time of the Crystal Palace exhibition, American carriages, carts, and trotting wagons were as handsome and as beautifully made as those of the English, and evidently American roads were also as good, for commentators remark on both. Illustrations of vehicles, both British and American, show their lightness, their elegance, their comfortable construction (*Fig 49*). One American carriage was shown of which it was said that it was "so light, it may be moved with the finger; you may imagine it to be made of paper, and the wheels have not the breadth of a quarter of an inch." [3] In the illustrations, all the vehicles look extremely light in weight, the curves of their springs and bodies have beautiful fluency, and the entire elegant effect appears to have been achieved only with the irreducibly necessary parts.

If the carriages presented lines of steel and thin rails of wood, and flat and curved surfaces of lacquered wood, the American trotting wagons and the famous racing sulkies eliminated even the body of the vehicle and consisted only of a seat attached to the one-piece curved shaft: a minimum of weight for a maximum of speed. They are but gossamer lines spinning in motion, and Currier and Ives and others delighted in depicting them as part of the American scene (*Figs. 50, 51*). Horatio

Greenough couples the trotting wagon with the yacht *America* and declares that the men who have thus "reduced locomotion to its simplest elements . . . are nearer to Athens at this moment" than those who would imitate Greek forms.[4]

Carriages, along with ships and locomotives, become one of the touchstones of nineteenth century functional design to which the pioneer discoverers around the turn of the century refer again and again as exemplary. None does so with greater emotion than Henry van de Velde. In his essay "Amo," in which he cites the whole gamut of vernacular functional design, from the axe to the automobile, he climaxes his Whitmanesque phrases with a rhapsodic description of the procession of carriages on a day in May in Hyde Park. Never in the past has a spectacle more beautiful, more perfect, more noble and solemn been offered; not the Elysian mysteries, nor the processions that mounted the Parthenon, neither medieval tournaments nor the legendary feasts of Venetian gondolas could compare with the gripping harmony, the unique rhythm of this festival of modern beauty.[5]

One might say that carriages were displaced twice: the first time, by the railroads; the second time, more decisively, by the automobile. To both, carriages initially lent their forms and even their names.

The development of the railroads in a few decades in the first half of the nineteenth century is one of the marvels of the age. In the 1830's and 1840's, the completion of the railway network in England and elsewhere spelled the end of the coaches that had been, at least in England, a dependable and relatively speedy means of public transportation between cities as well as a colorful part of a way of life. The earliest locomotives were small and looked like steam engines set on wheels, which indeed they were. But by the 1840's, locomotive design had become essentially what it was

49. *Light park phaeton, by Messrs. H. & A. Holmes, of Derby, England; shown at the Crystal Palace Exhibition, 1851.*
(From: Art Journal Illustrated Catalogue, *p. 22.)*

50. *American trotting wagon, by Currier and Ives, 1853.*

51. *An American racing sulky, 1856. Lithograph by J. H. Bufford, after Charles S. Humphreys.*
(Courtesy Kenneth M. Newman, The Old Print Shop, New York)

52. *Patent express engine "Liverpool," London and North Western Railway Co. Made by Messrs. Bury, Curtis, and Kennedy of Liverpool, 1851. Patented by T. R. Crampton, London.*
(From: Official Descriptive and Illustrated Catalogue of the Great Exhibition 1851 [London, 1851], Vol. I, plate 50).

53. *Eight-wheeled passenger car on the Baltimore & Ohio Railroad, by John R. Niernsee, after 1840.*
(Deutsches Museum, Munich)

to remain until the end of the century, though locomotives were to increase enormously in size and many detailed improvements were to be made. The characteristic form, and one entirely indigenous to the nineteenth century was the horizontally placed cylindrical form of the boiler on four, six, or eight axles, with wheels often varying in size, ending at the back in the rectangular platform (*Fig. 52*). By the time of the Great Exhibition at the Crystal Palace in 1851, locomotives were shown that were speedy and powerful not only in terms of horsepower but also in terms of design. It was only toward the end of the century that new forms of power, electricity and the diesel engine, brought changes in the form of the locomotive.

Though locomotives were an independent, indigenous development of the nineteenth century, the form of the coaches was at first taken from older models. In Europe, passenger coaches were usually modeled after the old stagecoaches; indeed, they resembled stagecoaches set on a wheeled frame. This resulted in the European system of compartments, accessible separately from the outside, with varying degrees of comfort and privacy, according to class. In contrast, the American railway carriage, after a brief experiment with stagecoach bodies mounted on wheel trucks, soon developed into the double-truck eight-wheel car with a center aisle. It was first designed by Ross Winans for use on the Baltimore & Ohio about 1840, and soon a clear, rectangular, box-like form with the fine rhythmic pattern of windows and frames became standard (*Fig. 53*). This was essentially derived in its form and function from the cabin of canal and river boats (*Fig. 65*), accessible in front and back with a passageway down the center, and as a result became an open carriage that did not separate the classes. Not until 1870 were the American and European systems combined in Europe, when a passageway was put along one side of the

car, allowing access to the compartments (though the classes remained separate).[6]

The 1850's and 1860's brought a multiplicity of improvements in railroad cars in America; they were the constant concern of the restless American inventor. Adjustable, reclining, and convertible seats, lighting, ventilating, and heating systems, and various safety features were proposed, patented, and manufactured. The most celebrated name in railroad-car development and improvement, notably of sleeping and dining cars, is, of course, George Mortimer Pullman (*Fig. 54*). Though he is popularly considered to be the inventor of the sleeping car, it was really the product of a longer development and embodied the inventions of a number of men.[7] The mechanics of the sleeping car form a part of that ingenious functional aptitude of the American inventor catering to the public's desire for comfort. Pullman's patent drawings show that the unadorned functional aspects of his invention and many of the exteriors, from the first Pullman car, "The Pioneer," of 1865, to numerous later ones, retain an almost nautical simplicity that contrasts strongly with the rich interiors of the Pullman cars that were appropriately called "Palace Cars."[8]

Throughout the nineteenth century, trains retained their appearance of a string of coupled units, locomotive, and rolling-stock. An exception is the vision of an American, S. R. Calthrop, who took out a patent in 1865 on a train that was conceived not as a locomotive pulling a succession of carriages but rather as one articulated moving entity, with the forms we associate with later streamlining (*Fig. 55*). He specifically states that the object of his invention is to diminish atmospheric resistance by "regarding the whole train as an aerial ship and modeling its whole surface in accordance with the principles so successfully applied to shipbuilding, modified, however, by the [consideration] . . . that

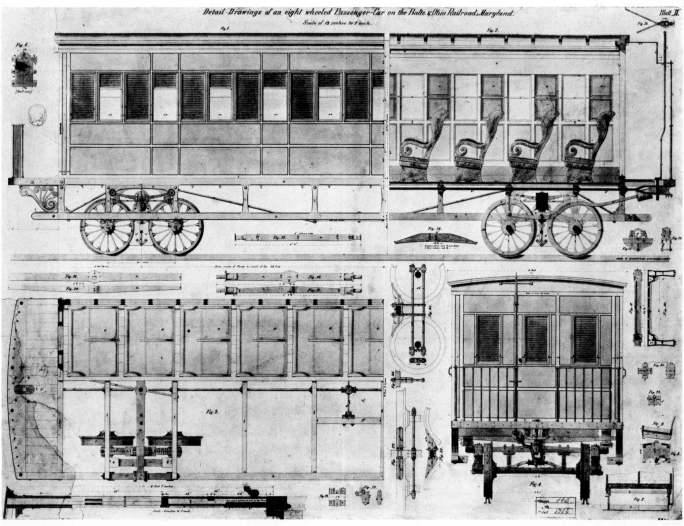

Detail-Drawings of an eight wheeled Passenger-Car on the Balte & Ohio Railroad, Maryland.

Scale of 12 inches to 1 inch.

56. *Aerial steam carriage "Ariel," a lithograph by W. L. Walton, British, mid-nineteenth century. (The Metropolitan Museum of Art. Gift of Paul Bird, Jr., 1962).*

54. *Patent drawings for sleeping cars, by George M. Pullman. Patented September 19, 1865. U.S. Patent No. 49,992.*

55. *Patent drawings, by S. R. Calthrop, for a streamlined train. Patented August 8, 1865. U.S. Patent No. 49,227.*

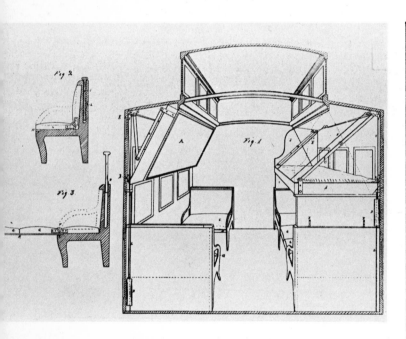

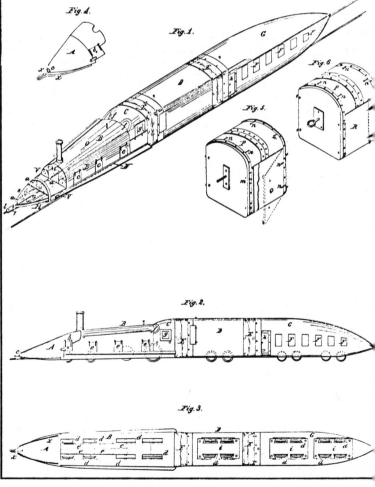

the railway train is wholly immersed in the fluid through which it is passing." To this end, he eliminates as far as possible all projections, he connects cars by means of flexible hoods, and he tapers both front and rear of the train, "the prow" and "the stern of the aerial ship." The rear is tapered in order to "overcome the chief part of the resistance arising from the drag of the air behind the rear car in trains as ordinarily constructed, in a word, presenting a smooth and curving outline to the pressure of the atmospheric fluid, whereby the train may obtain a greater speed with the same consumption of fuel than has heretofore been practicable." Not until the 1930's, when experiments with streamlining were being made everywhere, was this idea taken up again, and only the designs of Norman Bel Geddes and the most successful of the later streamlined trains could match this design in unity and audacity of conception.[9] That others also had visions to be realized only much later is testified to by the "first carriage" of "The Aerial Transit Company," a dream by W. L. Walton of Britain, sometime in the mid-1800's (*Fig. 56*).

Trains completely displaced public coaches in the first half of the nineteenth century, but elegant private carriages continued in vogue during the Victorian and Edwardian eras, until the advent of the motor car. Again carriages served as models for the new kind of vehicle; the earliest automobiles resembled horseless carriages and retained some of the lightness and linear transparency of the vehicle they were about to replace (*Figs. 57–59*). But even before the turn of the century, their unique form had evolved—a body composed of circular and rectangular forms of plain surfaces and lines that once more echo the words of Maudslay as to what the components of a machine inevitably are. Today, we are accustomed to think of automobile design as being capricious and subject to frequent superficial styling changes. Though

57. *Automobile with twin-cylinder, V-type engine, and wire wheels, by Gottlieb Daimler, 1889.* (Deutsches Museum, Munich)

58. *Lady's phaeton, American, ca. 1860.* (Suffolk Museum & The Carriage House at Stony Brook, L.I., Melville Collection)

59. *First American automobile, "Duryea," 1893.* (Deutsches Museum, Munich)

60. *First Mercedes automobile, 1901, by Daimler Motor Works.* (Deutsches Museum, Munich)

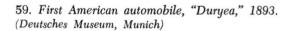

the automobile was certainly a fashionable consumer product for the affluent at the turn of the century, as the carriage had been earlier, neither the first Mercedes-Benz of 1901 (*Fig. 60*) nor the Peugeot of 1903 (*Fig. 288*), shows the slightest trace of the Art Nouveau fashion of the day in its designs. On the contrary, they are severe, abstract, geometric designs, very different from carriage design; yet, they retain the essential austerity of form that was characteristic of all transportation design throughout the nineteenth century.

Of all the means of locomotion, the ship is the noblest and purest of designs and excites the greatest enthusiasm. Even in the eighteenth century—when ships, like machines, were still often naïvely decorated in the spirit of the time by carving and gilding—the painter Hogarth remarked how "in ship-building the dimensions of every part are confined and regulated by fitness for sailing. When a vessel sails well, the sailors call her *a beauty*; the two ideas [fitness and beauty] have such a connection! " [10]

In shipbuilding, as in many other fields, the late eighteenth and early nineteenth centuries brought a change in attitude and approach to design. One was no longer satisfied to go by rule of thumb, by intuition or tradition, but began to look on ship design as a matter for scientific investigation and analysis, so that the best performance might be obtained through a form arrived at rationally. These scientific investigations had their beginnings in the eighteenth century in France and in Sweden, and found their realization in the nineteenth century in England and America. By 1865, the English naval architect John Scott Russell, writing a monumental book on the method of ship designing, could state:

The traditions of the old craft of shipbuilding have been swept away in the last thirty years by a threefold revolution, a revolution in form, for the old slow, full, round, bluff-bowed ship is now displaced by the fast, long, thin, sharp, hollow line of least resistance; a revolution in substance, for fleets of oak are being displaced by fleets of iron; a revolution in power, for the property and lives of men are no longer left to the mercy of the wind, but conducted with the regularity and security of the revolutions of fixed machinery.[11]

The famous clipper ships represent an extreme application of the changes in form, being exceedingly sharp and slim and, consequently, extraordinarily fast. The earliest and finest—though not all—clipper ships were American-made (*Fig. 61*). There is much controversy about the origins of the clipper ships, but it is clear that they were the heirs to long traditions of specialized craft, craft designed for speed, as well as the result of purposeful experiments and rational thought. In many countries, there were speedy ships that had evolved over long periods of time, and these had the essential features of the clippers, though perhaps in rudimentary form. There were, for example, the Bermuda sloop, a fast vessel developed in the eighteenth century in the West Indies for buccaneering, and the French lugger, a few of which came to America during the Revolution. Both have been considered the parent type of the Baltimore clippers, the forerunners of the more famous Yankee clippers of the 1850's. In New England, shipbuilding was a major industry long before the Revolution, and here, too, the shipbuilder, by lengthening and fining out the lines of the traditional ship, was taking steps toward the later improved form of the clippers. [12]

In America, naval architects and shipbuilders were only too eager to adopt and improve on any device that would give greater performance to their ships, but in England, this passion for innovation was not so strong. Russell relates with bitterness how his own findings and those of others,

61. *Currier and Ives:* The Flying Cloud, *extreme clipper ship, built by Donald McKay at East Boston in 1851. Her fourth voyage from New York to San Francisco was the fastest passage ever made over that course: 89 days and 8 hours, January 21–April 20, 1854. She was wrecked in 1874. (The Metropolitan Museum of Art. Bequest of Adele S. Colgate, 1962)*

as well as existing vernacular types, were ignored and improvements were delayed until the Americans had shown their efficacy. He cites the Newcastle coal keel, the Yarmouth coble, the "exquisite" Deal cutter, the London wherry, fishing sloops, yachts, privateers, smugglers, luggers, and he continues, "The long, fine entrance, the afterbody, full aloft, and fine only below, were not new in fact; they were existing forms, whose qualities were utterly unknown to our profession, or rather, they were misknown, and misbelieved, and mistaught." [13]

In both England and America, important experiments were made in the nineteenth century, with ships being pulled through bodies of water to investigate the phenomena of hydrodynamics and to determine the form of least resistance for ships. In England, these experiments range from those made by John Scott Russell in 1834 and 1835 to find the form most appropriate and functional for traversing water,[14] to William Froude's more sophisticated and more accurate experiments of 1871.[15] In America, naval architect John Willis Griffiths put shipbuilding on a scientific basis and did more than anyone else to develop the American clipper ships of the 1850's. Not only did he theorize, experiment, and document his findings, but he designed some of the great clipper ships himself, including the *Rainbow*, launched in 1845 for the China trade, and the *Sea Witch*, launched in 1846.[16]

In his book *Treatise on Marine and Naval Architecture*, Griffiths' concern with efficiency and function is matched by that for the visual aesthetic effect. In fact, *appearance* of function is as necessary to him as the mechanical exigencies. In a passage pertaining to the form of the vessel he writes:

There is more life necessary to the appearance of the bow, than is required aft; . . . This lively appearance that we sometimes see, which makes a vessel look as though she would move without the application of propelling power, is only obtained, so far as the sheer is concerned, by making the line quicker at the bow, and less so at the stern . . . The object in building ships is to compel them by application of power to move forward; and is it not perfectly clear that every effort in appearance, as well as in other things, should tend forward?

Repeatedly, he defines beauty in ships as consisting in "fitness for the purpose and proportion to effect the object designed." [17]

The ships designed by Griffiths and others—the most famous, perhaps, being those by Donald McKay, such as the *Stag Hound*, the *Flying Cloud* (*Fig. 61*), and the *Sovereign of the Seas*—were celebrated for their speed, but equally for their beauty, their litheness and gracefulness. These were the ships that also occasioned Horatio Greenough's most eloquent praise of functional form:

Observe a ship at Sea! Mark the majestic form of her hull as she rushes through the water, observe the graceful bend of her body, the gentle transition from round to flat, the grasp of her keel, the leap of her bows, the symmetry and rich tracery of her spars and rigging, and those grand wind muscles, her sails! Behold an organization second only to that of an animal, obedient as the horse, swift as the stag, and bearing the burthen of a thousand camels from pole to pole! What Academy of Design, what research of connoisseurship, what imitation of the Greeks produced this marvel of construction? Here is the result of the study of man upon the great deep, where Nature spake of the laws of building, not in the feather and in the flower, but in the winds and waves, and he bent all his mind to hear and to obey. Could we carry into our civil architecture the responsibilities that weigh upon our shipbuilding, we should ere long have edifices as superior to the Parthenon for the purposes that we require, as the *Constitution* or the *Pennsylvania* is to the galley of the Argonauts.[18]

Emerson, who knew Greenough and admired

62. *Coastal steamship* Monticello, *of the New York and Virginia Screw Steamship Company. Built by E. F. Williams, Brooklyn, L.I., 1859. (Courtesy Kenneth M. Newman, The Old Print Shop, New York)*

him,[19] also saw ship design as the exemplary way of designing, when he declared in his *Journal* (1847), "The modern architecture is ship-building,"[20] a thought taken up many years later again by Le Corbusier, who captioned pictures of ocean liners with such phrases as "An architecture pure, neat, clear, clean and healthy"; "new architectural forms, elements both vast and intimate but on man's scale . . . powerful masses and slender elements."[21]

Though the clipper was the most glamorous ship of the nineteenth century, other craft—from the whaling ship with all its gear to the simple fishing rowboat of the coastal towns—shared the nautical functional design approach, resulting in analogous though different forms because of different functions (*Figs. 62, 63*).

Steamships were beginning to replace sailing ships even before the heyday of the clippers. Very early they plied the great American rivers, and their extraordinary designs are admired by knowledgeable Englishmen, whose own river steamers were quite different, more "orthodox." In 1861, an English shipbuilding engineer who had visited America to study its river steamers, reported to the Institution of Naval Architects that an English shipbuilder's first view of an American river steamer, which he characterized as a "floating hotel,"

must always be startling. He is only conscious of beholding a large white moving house, two black chimneys, a network of iron rods and stays, and a queer looking wobbling lever in the centre of the object, and he only discovers, after some examination and study, that this phenomenon is a river steamboat, the result of years of experience, and a striking example of the best possible application of means to end (*Figs. 64, 65*).

He notes than an English river steamer is merely an altered copy of an ocean ship while "the Amer-

63. *Seine-boats in winter quarters.* "The boats used by the Gloucester fleet in the purse-seine fishery are built after a peculiar model and solely for this purpose. The present form of the seine-boat was devised about the year 1857 by Messrs. Higgins and Gifford, boat-builders, Gloucester, Mass."
From: *George Brown Goode,* The Fisheries and Fishery Industries of the United States *[Washington, 1887], III, plate 58.*

64. *American river steamer* Commonwealth, *1854, bow elevation, built by Laurence and Finches, New York.*
(From: Norman S. Russell, "On American River Steamers," Transactions of the Institution of Naval Architects, *II [London, 1861] plate 11)*

65. *Side-view of stern section of the American river steamer* Commonwealth, *1854. Note similarity of articulation of doors and windows to that of the Baltimore & Ohio railroad car in Fig. 53.*

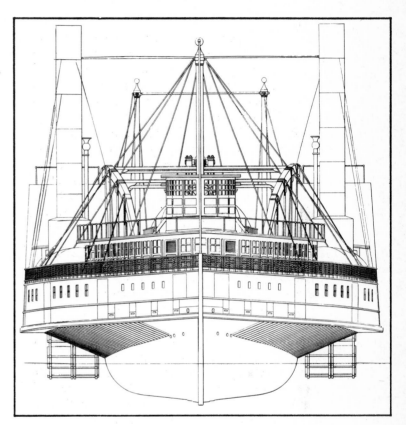

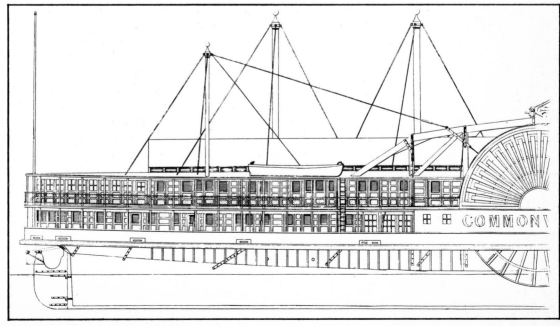

52

66. S.S. Great Britain, *built by the Great Western Steamship Company, at Bristol, 1839–43, to the designs of Isambard Kingdom Brunel. It was the first large vessel built of iron and also the first screw-steamer to cross the Atlantic.* (Photo Science Museum, London)

ican river steamer is an entirely original production." [22] British river steamers were actually largely coastal steamers that went up the rivers where they had to, whereas American river boats were built very shallow, extremely wide for their length, and on an enormous scale.

After the fame of the American clipper had passed, the British steamship excelled on the Atlantic. Iron steamships had won out over wooden sailboats and, though America had no scarcity of wood, she was at a disadvantage until later in the century in the production of large iron vessels. The large steamship owes its slim underwater form to the clippers, but in other respects it must be considered on quite a different basis. The factors determining the form were the steam engine, the iron and steel construction, and the increase in passenger capacity, comfort, speed, and safety. The hull itself was the single most effective visual form and it had to express stability, capacity, and forward thrust. Right from the start the large liners retained a high proportion of length to width, starting with about 4:1, raising that to 8:1 at mid-century, and reaching the high mark, in 1880, in the S.S. *City of Rome*, with 10.43:1.[23]

Until about 1860, passenger ships had no superstructure. Cabins, deckhouses, and other small structures for passengers and crew, as well as protective housing over the engine shaft and hatches, appeared only gradually. These are the elements from which the continuous elaborate superstructure developed, with promenade decks, tiers of cabins, and the bridge that we are used to. Dominating vertical elements above deck were, of course, the smokestacks, at first always round, later sometimes oval. Their rake often contributed to the directional force of the over-all design. Until almost the very end of the century, the appearance of the steamship was also decisively determined by masts and rigging and sails, since every steamship was also given full rigging in order to gain speed in combination with the engines, or as a safeguard against their breakdown. Color was used sparingly, usually a few good strong, sharply contrasting colors, such as red, black, and white, or black, buff, and white. It is a tradition that has been maintained to the present day.

In 1838, the *Great Western*,[24] a ship with a wooden hull and paddle engines, initiated the regular crossing of the Atlantic by steamships. It was built to the design of Isambard Kingdom Brunel, son of Marc Isambard Brunel of the Portsmouth block-making machinery fame, as were also the S.S. *Great Britain*, the first iron-hulled and screw-propelled ship to cross the Atlantic, in 1843 [25] (*Fig. 66*). The most celebrated of all iron steamships, the *Great Eastern* (*Fig. 67*), was also designed by Brunel and was built by John Scott Russell in 1858. This last was the "most spectacular conception" of the nineteenth century, the largest ship built: 680 feet long by 83 feet wide, with an engine of 4,000 horsepower driving a screw and another of 2,600 horsepower driving paddles. It was constructed on the cellular system, with a double bottom and longitudinal frames between the two skins. In addition, there were six masts to carry an ample spread of sail. She was to carry four thousand passengers and sail to Australia and back without refueling. However, the building of the ship, her launching, and her maiden voyage were beset with difficulties, technical and economical; she never did sail to Australia but was eventually put on the Atlantic run, for which she had not been designed. From contemporary pictures, it is apparent that the *Great Eastern* was majestic and gave a superlative impression of strength, enormous capacity, and driving power.[26]

Ships of steel began to be built in 1857,[27] but there were difficulties with the material, and it was not until the end of the 1870's and the 1880's that

67. The Great Eastern *leaving Southampton water for New York on her first voyage. "The stupendous, noble vessel payed off her head towards her course as if she had been the lightest cutter."*
(From: The Illustrated London News, June 23, 1860)

the era of steel in the building of ships really began. In building the *Campania* (and her sister ship, the *Lucania*), in 1893, entirely of steel, with two screws, British shipbuilding reached its highest level in the nineteenth century [28] (*Fig. 286*). These were, incidentally, the first ships to drop all vestiges of provision to set sails. With or without supplementary sails, the new ocean liners, though different in form and material from the old sailing vessels, resulted in forms of the same character: rational, logical, large simple forms, expressing "the majesty of the essential." [29]

Around 1900 and thereafter, when the functional became the ideal, carriages, trains, and ships were referred to again and again as embodying as ideal models all the principles of design that one was struggling to formulate and apply in the design of objects for everyday life. Time and time again it was demanded that furniture, lamps, and other objects be designed "like our carriages, ships, and locomotives." [30] It was not only the vehicles themselves that were admired, but also all their gear and equipment, particularly that of ships: their hardware, bells, blocks and pulleys, steering wheels, propellers, anchors, lights, chronometers, compasses, and other instruments, in all of which it was essential that function be unimpeded by superfluities (*Figs. 68–74*). Light is thrown on the character of nautical design by an occasional disparaging remark as well as by the enthusiastic ones. Edmond de Goncourt, whose taste in design lay firmly with the *ancien régime,* on seeing van de Velde's furniture at Bing's Art Nouveau in 1895, indignantly labeled it the yachting style, little realizing that he was giving it the highest possible praise in the eyes of modernists. [31]

There are other vehicles and forms of locomotion of special purposes or circumstances, such as snowshoes (*Fig. 75*), ice skates (*Fig. 76*), kayaks (*Fig 77*), and the sleigh, a carriage on runners

69. *British anchors, left to right: Martin's anchor (model), 1872; wedge-clump mooring anchor (model), 1901; Byer's anchor (model), 1903.*
(British Crown Copyright. Science Museum, London)

70. *Chronometer in form of pocket watch set in two spring-balanced containers; box with gimbal handles, ca. 1825. Inscribed: Breguet et fils.*
(Deutsches Museum, Munich)

71. *Small navigation lanterns for cutters and coastal craft, ca. 1880.*
(Courtesy Altonaer Museum, Hamburg)

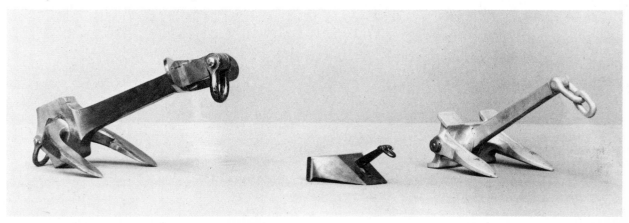

72. *Lights used on ships of the Italian navy, 1895.*
(From: Electrical World, *October 19, 1895)*

73. *Ship's screw (model), invented by the Austrian*
Joseph Ressel in 1826 (patented in Vienna in 1827),
and first used on the thirty-three-ton steamer
Civetta *at Trieste, in 1829. This was not followed up,*
but it antedates later, more successful English
experiments with ship's screws in the 1830's.
(Deutsches Museum, Munich)

74. *Ship's screw (model) of the S.S. Great Britain, 1845.*
(Deutsches Museum, Munich)

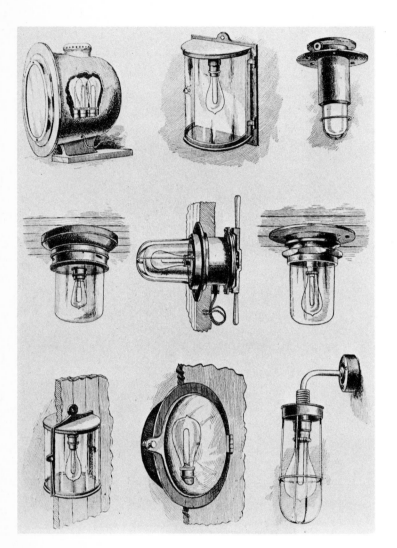

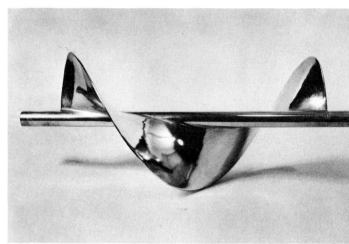

75. *Snowshoe of the Kutchin Athapascans,*
Upper Yukon, Alaska, late nineteenth century.
(Peabody Museum, Harvard University)

76. *Adjustable ice skates, 1901. From the hardware*
catalogue of W. B. Belknap & Co., Louisville,
Ky., 1901.

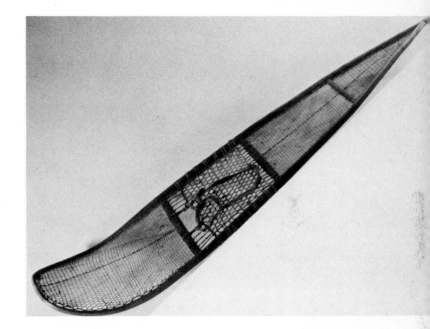

rather than on wheels. Canada sent to the Crystal Palace exhibition handsome canoes and sleighs (*Figs. 78, 79*), that had structures of curved, bent wood, very suggestive of some of the later Thonet furniture; in later decades, racing sleighs were developed, so-called skeleton sleighs, which had the same lightness and grace as the sulkies (*Fig 284*).

In contrast, there were farm carts, evolved for special uses in many variations of fine design in unassuming wood, adapted with amazing sophistication for special purposes (*Figs. 80, 81*). There were also the exciting fire engines with powerful, dramatic forms of gleaming brass, black rubber, and iron painted red (*Fig. 82*).

And, finally, there was the bicycle, the general means of individual transportation before the automobile became popular. The bicycle was an invention free of any adulteration by embellishment from the very start, and it became a prime example of industrial vernacular very quickly. The first pedal-driven bicycles appeared in the 1860's and 1870's and were devised by French and English mechanics. Interestingly, the early manufacture of the bicycle was connected with the sewing-machine industry; bicycle-making really started in the Coventry Sewing Machine Company in England, which eventually led to Coventry's becoming the capital of the world's bicycle production.[32]

Though bicycles—as well as monocycles, tricycles and quadricycles—underwent many changes and experiments in the first decades of their manufacture, at no point was any attempt made to beautify them with extraneous ornamentation, with the result that, though many of the experiments were superseded, all bicycles seem to have their own validity and authenticity (*Figs. 83–85*). Eventually, in the 1880's, the rear-wheel, chain-driven safety bicycle with the diamond frame and wheels of equal diameter became standard, and, by the 1890's, various factories were producing bicycles that embodied all the features of present-day models (*Fig. 86*). After successive discoveries and improvements, the bicycle reached a finality of form that put it in a category with the essentially unchanged and immutable tools and devices that man has used over long periods of time.

77a. *Kayak from Point Barrow, Alaska, 1888.*
(From: Edwin Tappan Adney and Howard I. Chapelle,
The Bark Canoes and Skin Boats of North America,
Washington, D.C., *Smithsonian Institution, Bulletin 230*
[1964], Fig. 187)

77b. *Kayak from Point Barrow, Alaska, 1888.*
Collected by Capt. M. A. Healy, U.S. revenue steamer
Bear, 1888, and now in the U.S. National Museum,
Smithsonian Institution.
(Photo courtesy the Smithsonian Institution)

78. *Birch-bark canoe, exhibited by Canada at*
the Crystal Palace Exhibition in London, 1851.
(From: The Art Journal Illustrated Catalogue, *p. 164)*

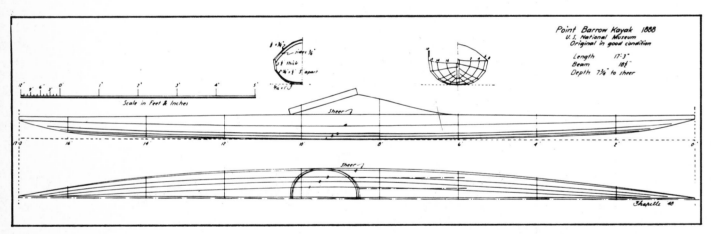

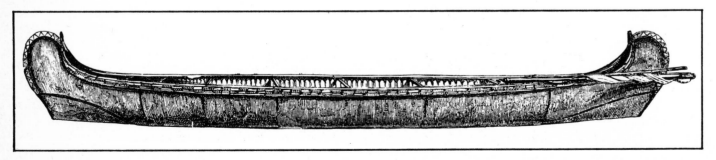

79. *Sleigh, by J. J. Saurin, of Quebec, Canada, shown at the Crystal Palace Exhibition in London, 1851.*
(*From:* The Art Journal Illustrated Catalogue, p. 119)

80. *Irish Car, by Messrs. Hutton of Dublin, Ireland. Shown at the Crystal Palace Exhibition in London, 1851.*
(*From:* The Art Journal Illustrated Catalogue, p. 227)

81. *One-horse harvest cart, made by Messrs. Ransomes and May, Ipswich, England. Shown at the Crystal Palace Exhibition in London, 1851.*
(*From:* The Illustrated Exhibitor, *October 18, 1851, p. 371*)

82. *Shand-Mason single-cylinder steam fire engine (model) for the London Fire Brigade, ca. 1876. (Lent to the Science Museum, London, by Col. J. D. K. Restler)*

83. *Tricycle with wrought-iron frame, English, ca. 1850.*
(British Crown Copyright. Science Museum, London)

84. *High-wheel bicycle of steel, 1882, built by the Coventry Machine Company Ltd., Coventry, England.*
(Deutsches Museum, Munich)

85. *Bicycle by E. C. F. Otto, ca. 1881, built by the Birmingham Small Arms Co.*
(Deutsches Museum, Munich)

86. *Singer safety bicycle, 1890, built by Singer & Co., England; the diamond frame was patented in 1888 by G. Singer.*
(British Crown Copyright. Science Museum, London)

NOTES TO CHAPTER 2

1. R. J. Forbes, "Roads to c. 1900," in Charles Singer *et al.*, *A History of Technology* (Oxford: Clarendon Press, 1958) IV, 520 ff. See also *Felton's Carriages, Being a Selection of Coaches, Chariots, Phaetons, etc., from a Treatise on Carriages by William Felton, Coachmaker* (first published in 1794; London: Hugh Evelyn, 1962). See unpaged Introduction.

2. *The Edinburgh Review*, XXXII, No. 64 (1819), 365. The book under review was by Chaptal, *De l'Industrie Française* (Paris: 1819).

3. John Tallis, *History and Description of the Crystal Palace, and the Exhibition of the World's Industry in 1851* (London and New York: n.d.), I, 67, 161; III, 38.

4. Horatio Greenough, *The Travels, Observations, and Experience of a Yankee Stonecutter* (1852; Gainesville, Fla.: Scholars' Facsimiles & Reprints, 1958), p. 33.

5. Henry van de Velde, "Vernunftgemässe Schönheit," in *Essays* (Leipzig: Insel-Verlag, 1910), pp. 114–21.

6. August Mencken, *The Railroad Passenger Car* (Baltimore, Md.: The Johns Hopkins Press, 1957), pp. 6–12; *The Catalogue of the Centenary Exhibition of the Baltimore & Ohio Railroad 1827–1927* (Baltimore, Md.: The Baltimore & Ohio Railroad, 1927), plate facing p. 110, figs. 1–3, pp. 12 ff. and p. 68; C. Hamilton Ellis, "The Development of Railway Engineering," in Singer, *op. cit.*, V, 341–44; Wulf Schadendorf, *Das Jahrhundert der Eisenbahn* (Munich: Prestel Verlag, 1965), pp. 48–58; *idem, . . . von Europas Eisenbahnen* (Munich: Prestel Verlag, 1963), pp. 87 ff.

7. Mencken, *op. cit.*, pp. 42 ff., 21–34; and Sigfried Giedion, *Mechanization Takes Command: A Contribution to Anonymous History* (New York: Oxford University Press, 1948), pp. 439–68; and *idem*, "Railroad Comfort and Patent Furniture," *Technology Review*, XLVII (November, 1944), 25–31.

8. One of our greatest railroad buffs, the late Lucius Beebe, in his *Mr. Pullman's Elegant Palace Car* (Garden City, N.Y.: Doubleday, 1961), furnishes a wealth of illustrations.

9. Samuel R. Calthrop's patent was No. 49,227, taken out on August 8, 1865. Quotes in the text are from the patent specifications. See also the *Annual Report of the Commissioner of Patents for the year 1865* (Washington, D.C.: Government Printing Office, 1867), II, 605. Mencken, *op. cit.*, pp. 85–86, reports of one other experiment at the very end of the century: Frederick Upham Adams made experiments and studies on the retarding effect of the atmosphere that resulted in a book published in Chicago in 1892: *Atmospheric Resistance in its Relation to the Speed of Trains*. This book included plans for a streamlined train, which was actually built by the Baltimore & Ohio and tested on May 8, 1900. Adams's design had included a streamlined locomotive, but since its importance was not realized, ordinary locomotives were used in the tests. They proved unsatisfactory and the train was consequently dismantled. For later streamlined trains, see Norman Bel Geddes, *Horizons* (Boston: Little, Brown, 1932), pp. 64–78, plates 57–67; Raymond Loewy, *The Locomotive (Its Aesthetics)* (London: The Studio, 1937), presents a world-wide survey of locomotive designs, with emphasis on the efforts at streamlining.

10. William Hogarth, *The Analysis of Beauty* (1753; Oxford: Clarendon Press, 1955), p. 33.

11. John Scott Russell, *The Modern System of Naval Architecture* (London: Day & Son, 1864–65), I, xxiii–xxv; Peter Kleine, *Die Architektur der Nordatlantik-Passagierdampfer 1837 bis 1914* (No. 3 of *Technikgeschichte in Einzeldarstellungen*) (Düsseldorf: VDI-Verlag, 1967), pp. 9–10.

12. Howard Irving Chapelle, *The Baltimore Clipper* (Salem, Mass.: The Marine Research Society, 1930), pp. 4 ff.; Arthur H. Clark, *The Clipper Ship Era* (New York: G. P. Putnam's Sons, 1911), pp. 6 ff.; Carl C. Cutler, *Queens of the Western Ocean* (Annapolis, Md.: United States Naval Institute, 1961), p. 58 and pp. 14–15.

13. Russell, *op. cit.*, p. xxvi.

14. His paper on these researches, "Experimental researches into the laws of certain hydrodynamical phenomena that accompany the motion of floating bodies and have not previously been reduced into conformity with the known laws of the resistance of fluids," was read before the Royal Society of Edinburgh on

April 3, 1837, and published in the *Transactions of the Society* (1840), XIV, 47–109. In his book *The Modern System of Naval Architecture,* p. xxvi, Russell claimed that these researches in their published form were responsible for the great designs of the American clipper-builder McKay, but such a claim cannot be taken seriously.

15. Kleine, *op. cit.,* pp. 10 and 21–22; A. M. Robb, "Ship-Building," in Singer, *op. cit.,* V, 386 ff.

16. John Willis Griffiths first attracted attention by a series of articles on naval architecture that were originally published in 1836 in the Portsmouth *Advocate* and later published in book form under the title *A Treatise on Marine and Naval Architecture or Theory and Practice Blended in Shipbuilding* (New York: 1850). See also article on Griffiths, *Dictionary of American Biography* (New York: Charles Scribner's Sons, 1959), IV, 626–27; Clark, *op. cit.,* p. 65 ff.

17. Griffiths, *op. cit.,* pp. 142, 104, and 384.

18. Greenough, *op. cit.,* pp. 139–40.

19. Nathalia Wright, *Horatio Greenough: The First American Sculptor* (Philadelphia: University of Pennsylvania Press, 1963), pp. 279–80, 288–90, 300; see Charles R. Metzger, *Emerson and Greenough* (Berkeley and Los Angeles: University of California Press, 1954).

20. Ralph Waldo Emerson, *Journals* (1847; Boston: Houghton Mifflin, 1912), VII, 333.

21. Le Corbusier, *Towards a New Architecture* (originally published as *Vers une Architecture* [Paris: Editions Crès, 1923]; New York: Praeger, 1959), pp. 93–94.

22. Norman S. Russell, "On American River Steamers," *Transactions of the Institution of Naval Architects,* II (London: 1861), 106, 110.

23. Kleine, *op. cit.,* p. 22.

24. *Ibid.,* pp. 62–65; L. T. C. Rolt, *Isambard Kingdom Brunel* (London: Longmans, Green, 1957), pp. 191 ff.

25. Kleine, *op. cit.,* pp. 73–76; Rolt; *op. cit.,* pp. 200 ff. The *Great Britain* has recently been rediscovered, still in existence and in use as a warehouse in the Falkland Islands. Though in sad condition, with one large crack in its hull, it is hoped that it might be repaired, and efforts are under way to bring this historic ship to San Francisco as part of the collection of the Maritime Museum. *San Francisco Chronicle,* November 11, 1968.

26. Kleine, *op. cit.,* pp. 76–82; Rolt, *op. cit.,* pp. 234 ff.; Robb, *op. cit.,* pp. 361–65; James Dugan, *The Great Iron Ship* (New York: Harper & Bros., 1953); Russell, in the two volumes of plates of his *The Modern System of Naval Architecture,* has many magnificent engravings of details, plans, and sections of the ship.

27. Kleine, *op. cit.,* p. 133, note 87; Robb, *op cit.,* pp. 372–73.

28. Kleine, *op. cit.,* pp. 98–101; Robb, *op. cit.,* pp. 374–78.

29. A phrase of Horatio Greenough's, *op. cit.,* p. 202.

30. Julius Lessing, "Neue Wege," *Kunstgewerbeblatt,* N.F. VI (1895), pp. 3–4; *idem,* in *Amtlicher Bericht über die Weltausstellung in Chicago, 1893,* erstattet vom Reichskommissar (Berlin: 1894), II, 766; Adolf Loos, "Das Luxusfuhrwerk" (1898), in *Ins Leere Gesprochen* (Innsbruck: Brenner Verlag, 1932), pp. 63–71; Henry van de Velde, "Ein Kapitel über Entwurf und Bau Moderner Möbel," *Pan,* III, No. 4 (1897), 263. Kleine, *op. cit.,* pp. 37–48, has additional quotations and references.

31. *Journal des Goncourt, Année 1895* (Paris: 30 Décembre, 1896), IX, 382. See also Henry van de Velde, *Geschichte meines Lebens* (Munich: R. Piper, 1962), p. 109.

32. C. F. Caunter, *The History and Development of Cycles, as Illustrated by the Collection of Cycles in the Science Museum* (London: Her Majesty's Stationery Office, 1955–58), pp. 7 ff.

3   *Consumer Goods*

One may argue that machines and instruments and vehicles are special, technically oriented and not really within the realm of everyday things, and that in citing them one is indulging in special pleading. However, precisely what makes the character of the age is that these things do become part of the realm of everyday design in so far as they reflect their design values on objects of more mundane purposes. But it is, of course, the area of consumer goods that determines our picture of the design of any period and has determined our notion of the history of design since the Industrial Revolution. We have allowed ourselves to be persuaded that only the tortuously artistic and the falsely refined determined that history. We have not generally seen that the modest vernacular strand, with long and deep links to the past, was also part of the picture. It performed the tremendously important task of transmitting the functional approach to design from an earlier, more settled society—in which it was used as a matter of course —over the hiatus of the nineteenth century, to the twentieth century, in which the functional approach was again particularly prized.

That we lack knowledge of this vernacular strand is in part due to its absence from those cultural storehouses, our museums, where we go to learn about the past. Almost all museums dedicated to the minor arts were founded in the nineteenth century as didactic institutions with the express purpose of improving taste and design. However noble the intention, these museums all reflected the prejudices of the time, and their roles in supplying models became nefarious: They collected the precious, ornate, aristocratic objects of the past, often merely the decoration itself, thereby fostering the taste for decoration and the weakness for imitation.

The first of these was the Victoria & Albert Museum in London, and it was the model for many others such as the museums for applied arts in Vienna and Berlin.[1] In these museums, the simple objects of use, which were also part of the past and more pertinent for the present, were almost entirely ignored, because they lacked artistic and social repute. One finds them in another kind of museum, in the local and national museums of historical and general cultural interest all over Europe and America. This occurs in most cases not because these objects were beautiful examples of the vernacular tradition but because they were bits and pieces of the past that the museums were dedicated to record and preserve. I have listed some of these museums in an appendix to the Bibliography at the end of this book.

The vernacular tradition represented by everyday useful objects—the simple, unpretentious utensils, tools, and furniture of everyday living—constitutes a large but submerged stratum in the nineteenth century because it was neither "refined" nor "artistic," and because its products were good enough only belowstairs, out of sight, or for the lower-class and simple country folk who didn't count. William Morris once said that well-to-do houses are filled with tons upon tons of unutterable rubbish, and the only acceptable things are usually in the kitchen, because they alone are honest, simple, and useful.[2]

Even the wealthy and fashionable sometimes required functional simplicity with minimum bulk, for example when they traveled. Travel kits, which have a long tradition, included all articles for personal use, toilet articles as well as eating implements (*Figs. 149, 150, 171*). The needs of sports and travel are combined in picnic sets, telescoping drinking cups, shooting seats, and so on. During the nineteenth century, England, as the center and supplier of Empire, developed not only the finest luggage but also campaign chests, captains' chests, safari chairs, deck chairs—the kind of thing Giedion called "nomadic" furniture [3]—all neat, trim, "nautical," often demountable. When we find these things today, they always give the impression of modernity because of their directness, their honesty—a chest is a chest and not disguised as a knight's tomb, a jug is a jug and not a bower of roses—and they often surprise by the elegance of their proportions, the beautiful treatment of their materials, and the aptness of their forms for use.

Such vernacular design came directly out of the older, pre-industrial world, and its forms and habits continued into the new industrialized world, both in machine-produced goods and in hand-crafted things, where its techniques survived. Anonymous utilitarian design made by craftsmen characterized all objects of use, whether for nobleman or peasant, during the Middle Ages. The Renaissance created not only the concept of the individual artist who rose from the ranks of craftsmen, but it introduced the concepts of art and beauty into the sphere of the everyday object for the prince and aristocrat, as a symbol of the leisure and elevated culture of a privileged ruling class. Artists then designed the aristocratic environment and gave it all the pomp and circumstance of "style," creating an environment as stage-setting for rulers rather than for use in real life. It received all the characteristics of the succession of "styles" that have formed the history of art since the Renaissance, and it was characterized by elaboration of form and virtuosity of decoration, by wealth, variety, and preciousness of materials designed for the enjoyment, glorification, and ceremonial use of a ruling class. Below this level, the ordinary craftsmen worked for the ordinary man in town and country in the older tradition of simpler, more functional forms that we call vernacular, sometimes arriving at more inspired, more felicitous results than at others, but always within fine traditions of form, and, above all, giving in

all their products that satisfaction that comes from evidence of good craftsmanship and a sense of fitness for purpose (*Fig. 87*). In this milieu, forms varied surprisingly little from century to century, evolving slowly by adjustment and refinement, giving objects and utensils a "timeless" quality. It is often difficult to date a piece of pottery or pewter precisely, in contrast to objects of high style, where the ornamentation dates an object very closely. There are silver and silk, ormolu and marquetry here, and wood and wool, pewter and pottery there.

The existence of a "two-track" production—the one utilitarian, functional, matter-of-fact, the other a matter of prestige, of aesthetic, and social differentiation—is strikingly documented in the eighteenth century by the many paintings of Chardin and Roland de la Porte (*Fig. 88*), on the one hand, and by the work of a painter like Boucher on the other. The artificiality of the style-form is castigated by Rousseau, who wrote in *Emile:*

Those who set the styles are the artists, the lords, and the very rich; and what sets their standards is their self-interest or their vanity. The latter in order to show off their wealth, and the former, in order to take advantage of it, are constantly seeking for new ways to spend money. So luxury takes hold, and sets up the cult of the difficult and the expensive.[4]

In the nineteenth century, Augustus Welby Pugin referred to the same phenomenon, only he is snobbishly indignant that cheap industrial surrogates make it possible for "persons to assume a semblance of decoration far beyond either their means or their station." He implies that simplicity is appropriate for ordinary mortals and that ornamentation has a prestige significance and should therefore be costly and reserved for the upper classes. This would mean that acceptance of the simple, functional form as the basis for modern design is, in a sense, a democratization of design.[5]

This is also the underlying idea in Thorstein Veblen's *Theory of the Leisure Class,* first published in 1899, in which he coined the term "conspicuous consumption" for all the useless finery and trumpery so ubiquitous in the Victorian era, acidly analyzing the distinction between design for the rich and for the rest. Like Rousseau, Veblen writes of the substitution of ingenuity and expense for beauty and serviceability; he distinguishes between "pecuniary beauty," which lends reputability to the rich by its uselessness and honorific waste, and "aesthetic beauty," which, in an object of use, is

best served by neat and unambiguous suggestion of its office and its efficiency for the material ends of life . . . Most objects alleged to be beautiful, and doing duty as such, show considerable ingenuity of design and are calculated to puzzle the beholder—to bewilder him with irrelevant suggestions and hints of the improbable—at the same time that they give evidence of an expenditure of labour in excess of what would give them their fullest efficiency for their ostensible economic end.

"Pecuniary beauty" lends reputability, and, by the same token, the cheap, useful, and undecorated is indecorous; it suffers from ceremonial inferiority or uncleanness.

What is common is within the [pecuniary] reach of many people. Its consumption is therefore not honorific, since it does not serve the purpose of a favorable invidious comparison with other consumers . . . It follows not infrequently that the marks of cheapness or commonness are accepted as definitive marks of artistic unfitness, and a code or schedule of aesthetic proprieties on the one hand, and of aesthetic abominations on the other, is constructed on this basis for guidance in questions of taste.[6]

The ceremonial and honorific form, as distinct from the simple utilitarian form, perhaps had its justification in a hierarchical society—though challenged at its end by Rousseau—but in a democratic society, its premises are false, and Veblen's analysis contributes much to an understanding of the design malaise of the nineteenth century.

The peculiar social and artistic climate in late-eighteenth-century England resulted, for a brief moment, in an almost perfect fusion of the inspirations of high style and the quiet, self-assured utilitarian and functional forms of the vernacular. This created an environment of such refinement and, at the same time, such convincing fitness and sound validity that its qualities and forms were admired and eagerly copied and imitated all over Europe and America. The gap between "high style" and vernacular had, in fact, never been as wide in sensibly minded England as on the Continent. However, toward the end of the eighteenth century, when the neoclassic style demanded plainer forms, uncomplicated straight lines, and tectonic design, the innate English common-sense approach coincided with the aspirations of the "high style" and permitted the national virtues of the English to triumph and to make the most significant design contribution of their history, in the work of Adam, Hepplewhite, Sheraton, Shearer, Wedgwood and a host of others, known and unknown. The vernacular was given the refinement that raised it to the level of "high style"; "high style," on the other hand, was designed with a purity of form, a noble understatement, and a careful fitness for purpose that lent it the anonymity and timeless quality of the vernacular and made it the model for the world.

This refined utilitarian design, the *style anglais*, was, in fact, admired, imported, and imitated all over the Continent in the last decades of the eighteenth century and into the nineteenth century. It formed the basis in central and northern Europe of a style of living in middle-class circles, of an environment that is often called *Biedermeier* but that one may call more broadly refined vernacular. This restrained, simple, uncluttered environment, derived from a fusion of simple classic forms and the functional forms of the vernacular, characterized burgher houses, furniture, and utensils for a few decades at the beginning of the nineteenth century until about 1840 (*Figs. 89, 90*), in most of Europe and America, and, in the less heavily industrialized countries, perhaps somewhat longer.[7] But then the impact of industrialization brought confusion of taste and habits. The growing affluence, the love for show and romance, and the passion for "artistic" things and forms of the past swept simplicity aside and supplanted it with the ornate and imitative. True, this could and did also result in genuine cultivation of the past. It included connoisseurship and collecting of antique furniture and works of art by more knowledgeable wealthy patrons, but it led more often to imitations and copies—not to speak of fakes and forgeries—of the admired objects of the past. Imitation of the ornate could range from electroplating and crude casting in a variety of materials for everyman to the copying, with consummate skill and craftsmanship, of such pieces as the Oeben-Riesener *Bureau du Roi* for Lord Hertford, founder of the Wallace Collection, at a cost of 90,000 francs.[8] "Victorian" taste became the ruling taste, and the vernacular again disappeared under the surface. Only occasionally were its simple charms and beauty seen by artists, such as Anker in Austria or Harnett in America, who, with their devotion to the vernacular are spiritual descendants of Chardin and de la Porte.

The change in the production of everyday consumer goods from hand to machine had been sporadic since the middle of the eighteenth century. However, it gained momentum in the first few decades of the nineteenth century, and by 1840 or 1850, most products for daily life were mechanically produced in factories. The change was one of technique and tool and, in many cases, also of material. It was essentially a change from the natural and organic to the mechanical and inorganic. What had been produced individually by craftsmen, with all the marks of humanity on it—the imperfections, variations, and idiosyncrasies of each maker—was now produced mechanically and perfectly by a machine, an instrument for the endless reproduction of forms through casting, stamping, pressing, and printing. And, in many cases, what had been made of wood, ivory, leather, or some other organic material, was made of harder, longer-lasting metal, which could also be cast more easily and worked more exactly by machines. The industrial processes of reproduction characterized the products of the new age not only in their outward form and in the materials employed but also in their being made available to the masses at low prices. We know how often the new industrial tools were abused to produce outrageous or silly imitative forms, but we also know that the vernacular survived. Not only were its old forms hap-

pily adapted to machine production, but, more importantly, it also proved a point of departure for new forms peculiar to machine mass production, so that we may speak of the traditional vernacular and a vernacular of industrial forms.

While the ruling taste called for ornamentation and embellishment, a few articulate men even in the mid-nineteenth century, expressed their enjoyment of the fitness of things in their functional form and put a moral connotation on the relation of form to function. No one did this with greater force and clarity than Horatio Greenough, whose praise of ships has already been cited. As an indifferent classical sculptor and an expatriate during his entire adult life, he seems an unlikely person to be a seer of American design; yet he expressed his ideas concerning design more eloquently than any other American of the nineteenth century. His ideas were bold and consistent. Once he had seen the validity or what he called the "justice" of the functional form, he was able to see everything else in the light of this fundamental principle. He did not speculate and theorize in the abstract but illustrated his principles with concrete examples that were common enough at the time. His shining examples were the clipper ships, the bridges, the yachts, and the trotting wagons, and, equally, "the old, bald, neutral-toned, Yankee farmhouse which seems to belong to the ground whereon it stands." [9]

Greenough's thoughts on design are derived from a combination of his Puritan-Protestant ethic and his inherited Anglo-Saxon common-sense approach to solving problems. He seems also to have been aware of the utilitarian aesthetics of late-eighteenth-century England, as in Alison's *Essays on the Nature and Principles of Taste*, where, as was stated above, fitness and utility were named as the chief sources of beauty. Alison's book was very popular in Greenough's student years, and similar

principles were expressed by other writers whose books are known to have been used by Greenough as texts when he was at Harvard.[10] Most important is his relation to nature as derived from the New England transcendentalism of his time. He shared with Emerson the enthusiasm for nature and saw in it correspondences and analogies with design. To him, nature was the divine spirit that was perfect in all its manifestations, and its perfection was expressed in its universal and undeviating adaptation of form to function.[11]

He places design in the context of nature and demands of it the same logic that is inherent in every form of nature. "If there be any principle of structure more plainly inculcated in the works of the Creator than all others, it is the principle of unflinching adaptation of forms to functions." To him "beauty is the promise of Function," and decoration an "opiate and deadening stimulus." [12] This anticipation of Louis Sullivan's ideas and phrases is startling, and it is therefore not surprising to find that there was a possible line of descent from Greenough to Sullivan. Emerson was much impressed by Greenough's ideas, which he mentioned repeatedly in his subsequent writings, and this gave wider circulation to them than Greenough's own writings had managed to do. One of Emerson's friends was W. H. Furness, whose son Frank Furness was an architect. The young Furness might easily have learned of Greenough and his ideas, either directly from Emerson or through his father. It was in Frank Furness's firm in Philadelphia that Sullivan was first employed.[13] Even more striking is his anticipation of Le Corbusier's famous phrase "The house is a machine for living in": Greenough termed domestic buildings "organic, formed to meet the wants of their occupants," and their "laws of structure and apportionment, depending on definite wants, obey a demonstrable rule. They may be called machines."[14]

To Greenough, in contrast to the then prevailing sentiment, embellishment is the original sin:

The invariable development of embellishment and decoration is more embellishment and more decoration. The *reductio ad absurdum* is palpable enough at last; but where was the first downward step? I maintain that the first downward step was *the introduction of the first inorganic, non-functional element, whether of shape or color.* If I be told that such a system as mine would produce *nakedness*, I accept the omen. In nakedness I behold the majesty of the essential, instead of the trappings of pretension. . . . The redundant must be pared down, the superfluous dropped, the necessary itself reduced to its simplest expression, and then we shall find, whatever the organization may be, that beauty was waiting for us. [Italics in original.]

He knew, too, that this beauty was created not by artists but by mechanics and engineers, who make "manly use of plain good sense." But the bare functional form was nothing cheap and easy.

Far be it from me to pretend that the style pointed out by our mechanics is what is sometimes miscalled an economical, a cheap style. No! It is the dearest of all styles! It costs the thought of men, much, very much thought, untiring investigation, ceaseless experiment. Its simplicity is not the simplicity of emptiness or of poverty, its simplicity is that of justness, I had almost said, of justice.

With this almost cosmic view of the rightness of functional design, it is not surprising that Greenough would be indignant over the growing corruption of American taste, which he blamed on the English who "have overwhelmed us with embellishment, . . . catch-penny novelties of form, steam woven fineries and plastic ornaments, struck with the die or pressed into molds." He saw the conflict between the rational "plain good sense" of the best of American design and its petty perversion by an invasion of goods with "ill-digested and crowded embellishment." [15]

Though Greenough's thoughts and phrases have of late become well known, he was not alone in America in his admiration for functional form. Among others, there was James Jackson Jarves, renowned for his collection of Italian primitives now at Yale, who wrote in 1869, apparently without knowledge of Greenough's writing that,

the American, while adhering closely to his utilitarian and economical principles, has unwittingly, in some objects to which his heart equally with his hand has been devoted, developed a degree of beauty in them that no other nation equals. His clipper-ships, fire-engines, locomotives, and some of his machinery and tools combine that equilibrium of lines, proportions, and masses, which are among the fundamental causes of abstract beauty. Their success in producing broad, general effects out of a few simple elements, and of admirable adaptation of means to ends, as nature evolves beauty out of the common and practical, covers these things with a certain atmosphere of poetry, and is an indication of what may happen to the rest of his work when he puts into it an equal amount of heart and knowledge.[16]

One of Jarves's books, *The Art-Idea*, first published in 1864, was recently republished. In his introduction to the new edition, Benjamin Rowland, Jr. indicates that, like Greenough, Jarves admired the simple beauty of the New England farmhouse, and he quotes Jarves as saying that it was suited to the land "as the caterpillar to the leaf that feeds him." He further quotes a passage from Jarves paralleling Greenough's praise of ships, which, Rowland says, "serves to indicate to what extent Jarves moved in the ambient of functionalism that prevailed in mid-century New England."[17]

These enthusiastic pronouncements of the mid-century praising functionalism are occasionally coupled with laments at the invasion of tawdry ornate design, and there is no question but that much of the simple, practical design was overlaid by the pretentiousness of the "cultivated tradition," as John A. Kouwenhoven put it, in America as well, particularly in the latter half of the century.

However, the functional tradition had a broad base in America and was nurtured by the particular circumstances of the country, the absence of traditional forms of the past, a scarcity of labor coupled with a genius for invention, and a virtually classless society eager to better the material circumstances of its life. From the early introduction of mass production at lower prices through standardization of parts, it was the aim of American manufactures to satisfy everyday needs, and the result was that "probably in the United States more people relative to the whole population than in any other part of the world lived in frame houses, with cabinet furniture, stoves, carpets, china, glassware, clocks, and watches; rode in carriages; and performed their ordinary labors with the facilities of improved machinery."[18]

Kouwenhoven, who stresses America's predisposition for the simple, practical vernacular form, states that "it is essential to realize that in the very decades which our cultural historians have called the ugliest and bleakest in our history . . . American people had developed skills and knowledge which enabled them to create patterns of clean, organic and indigenous beauty out of the crude materials of the technological environment."[19]

1. The Museum for the Arts of Decoration of the Cooper Union in New York was the ultimate in its exclusive emphasis on decoration.

2. William Morris, "The Lesser Arts" (a Lecture delivered before the Trades' Guild of Learning, December 4, 1877), in *Hopes and Fears for Art, Collected Works* (London: Longmans, Green, 1914), XXII, 23–24.

3. Sigfried Giedion, *Mechanization Takes Command: A Contribution to Anonymous History* (New York: Oxford University Press, 1948), pp. 469–79.

4. Jean Jacques Rousseau, *Emile ou de l'Education,* Book IV (Paris: Pourrat Frères, 1841), II, 320. Werner Sombart, the great social and economic historian, documents this development since the Renaissance, and especially for the eighteenth century, in voluminous and fascinating detail in *Luxus und Kapitalismus* (Munich: Duncker & Humblot, 1913).

5. Augustus Welby Pugin, *The True Principles of Pointed or Christian Architecture* (London: John Weale, 1841), p. 30.

6. Thorstein Veblen, *The Theory of the Leisure Class* (New York: Macmillan, 1912); the passages quoted are from pp. 152–61. The whole chapter in which these passages occur, "Pecuniary Canons of Taste," pp. 115–66, is very pertinent to this discussion.

7. Publications about this period are often heavily weighted in favor of aristocratic and princely interiors and furniture that are more ornate and more committed to traditional forms than the truly Biedermeier from the burgher sphere. But, even so, in almost every illustration one finds astonishingly simple and functional pieces. Cf. Paul Mebes, *Um 1800* (2 vols.; Munich: F. Bruckmann, 1908); Joseph August Lux, *Von der Empire– zur Biedermeierzeit* (Stuttgart: Julius Hoffmann, 1906); Josef Folnesics, *Innenräume und Hausrat der Empire– und Biedermeierzeit in Oesterreich-Ungarn* (Vienna: Anton Schroll, 1922); Hermann Schmitz, *Vor hundert Jahren* (Berlin: Verlag für Kunstwissenschaft, 1920). Georg Hermann, *Das Biedermeier* (Oldenburg: Gerhard Stalling Verlag, 1965), is more properly concerned with the burgher milieu and illustrates a number of very fine Biedermeier interiors. However, the finest interiors of the period occur in paintings, and, of

these, the best are by Georg Friedrich Kersting. See Gustav Vriesen, *Die Innenraumbilder Georg Friedrich Kerstings* (Berlin: Deutscher Verein für Kunstwissenschaft, 1935); Mario Praz, *An Illustrated History of Interior Decoration* (London: Thames & Hudson, 1964), plates 175–78. Hans Sedlmayr, *Verlust der Mitte* (Salzburg: Otto Müller, 1948), pp. 38–40.

8. F. J. B. Watson, *Wallace Collection Catalogues, Furniture* (London: 1956), pp. 235–37 and plate 71.

9. Horatio Greenough, *Form and Function,* ed. Harold A. Small (Berkeley: University of California Press, 1947), p. 105. Greenough's writings consist of only a few essays, most of which were written in 1851–52, the last year of his life, and published as *The Travels, Observations, and Experience of a Yankee Stonecutter* under the pseudonym Horace Bender (New York: G. P. Putnam, 1852). Only one copy is known to exist of this original edition, but it has been reissued in facsimile (Gainesville, Fla.: Scholars' Facsimiles & Reprints, 1958), with an introduction by Nathalia Wright. She has also written the only full-length biography of Greenough, *Horatio Greenough, The First American Sculptor* (Philadelphia: University of Pennsylvania Press, 1963), other than the account of his life published within one year of his death by Henry T. Tuckerman in *A Memorial of Horatio Greenough* (1853), which also contained essays by Greenough. It was a selection of Greenough's writings, as they pertain to design, that was published under the title *Form and Function* by the University of California Press.

10. Nathalia Wright, *op. cit.,* p. 184 and *idem,* "Horatio Greenough's Borrowings from the Harvard College Library," *Harvard Library Bulletin,* IX, No. 3 (1955), 406–10.

11. F. O. Matthiessen, *American Renaissance; Art and Expression in the Age of Emerson and Whitman* (London: Oxford University Press, 1941), and Charles R. Metzger, *Emerson and Greenough, Transcendental Pioneers of an American Esthetic* (Berkeley: University of California Press, 1954).

12. Greenough, *Travels,* pp. 162, 203, 212 respectively.

13. Richard P. Adams, "Architecture and the Romantic Tradition: Coleridge to Wright," *American*

Quarterly, IX (1957), 46–62, was first to see this possible connection. See Nathalia Wright, *Horatio Greenough,* p. 191.

14. Le Corbusier, *Towards a New Architecture* (London: The Architectural Press, 1946), p. 10; Greenough, *Travels,* p. 143.

15. For the series of quotes: Greenough, *Travels,* pp. 202, 172, 139, 172, 170, and 171 respectively.

16. James Jackson Jarves, *Art Thoughts* (New York: Hurd & Houghton, 1869), p. 323.

17. James Jackson Jarves, *The Art-Idea* (1864; Cambridge, Mass,: Harvard University Press, 1960), pp. xxiii and xxiv.

18. Victor S. Clark, *History of Manufactures in the United States,* Vol. I, *1607–1860* (New York: McGraw-Hill, 1929), p. 436.

19. John A. Kouwenhoven, *Made in America* (Garden City, N.Y.: Doubleday, 1948), p. 30.

4 Metalware

91. *Revolver, Colt Firearms Company, Hartford, Conn., ca. 1868.*
(Courtesy of The Henry Ford Museum, Dearborn, Michigan)

Almost all the products of early American industry were anonymous and, though many were ingenious devices and had interesting and unusual shapes, they were appreciated only locally. However, in the first half of the nineteenth century, two categories were noted for their technological achievement and their consequent conquest of world markets: namely, American firearms and timepieces.

The earliest rifle of fame in America was the Kentucky rifle, which developed from the German Jaeger, or hunting rifle, brought to Pennsylvania in the seventeenth and eighteenth centuries. It had a longer, narrower barrel, was more accurate, lighter in weight, and used less lead and powder; therefore it was of greater use in the frontier forests and wilderness to kill game and hold off the Indians. By the 1840's with the opening of the Great Plains, a new type was needed, and the Plains rifle was developed. It was shorter, heavier, more rugged and effective for large game, such as the buffalo.[1]

Of greatest renown, however, was the repeating firearm perfected by Samuel Colt (*Fig. 91*). His revolver was patented first in England, in 1835, and then in America, in 1836. Initially, it was manufactured in the Whitney Works, until Colt, with the important help of Elisha Root, a skilled mechanic, established his own factory in 1854–55 in Hartford, Connecticut, where the most advanced manufacture was adopted, based on standardized interchangeable parts. "Colt" became a generic term, in both America and Europe. The revolver was used in the West and the Southwest and in the Mexican War, and it enjoyed great popularity with the Texas Rangers.[2] The success of Colt's and other American armories spurred British efforts to adopt the system of interchangeable manufacture for their own armories. This was, in fact, the sole area in which the "American sys-

tem" was applied abroad during most of the nineteenth century.[3]

Until the last quarter of the eighteenth century, American clocks had movements of cast-brass parts, cut and filed by the local clock-maker. About 1780, wooden-wheel clocks began to be made in quantity (though they had apparently been made much earlier on a smaller scale). By 1800, many clocks were made with wooden movements; they sold very cheaply because they could be quickly produced and assembled with little trouble. Eli Terry conceived the idea of mass-producing clock movements of wood with the aid of water-powered machinery and the assembly of standardized parts. By 1809, he was making 3,000 clocks a year. In the 1790's, another innovation was introduced in the form of the printed paper dial, which could be glued onto a sheet of iron or a wooden panel, a cheaper and quicker method than the earlier ones of engraving the brass dial or enameling it. Though there are many fine simple clocks from the first half of the nineteenth century, as well as many ornate ones, almost all have admirably clear dials with either Arabic or Roman numerals and nothing extraneous on the dial itself to distract from reading the time.

Power machinery, interchangeable parts, and simpler processes of manufacture had already considerably reduced the price of wooden clocks

92. *Powder flask of brass and steel, England (?), ca. 1855.*
(Courtesy of The Henry Ford Museum, Dearborn, Michigan)

93. *Pocket watch, ca. 1880, American Watch Company, Waltham, Mass.*
(Courtesy of The Henry Ford Museum, Dearborn, Michigan)

when, in the 1830's, Chauncey Jerome introduced a cheap, small, one-day brass clock. In it, he substituted rolled brass for the earlier cast-brass parts by making wheels thin instead of thick and stamping them out of sheet brass. Clockfaces were printed directly on zinc at 1,200 to 1,500 a day in one factory, and octagonal cases were prefabricated of wood on a mass-production basis. It had been impossible to export wooden clocks from New England, where most of them were made, especially on overseas voyages, which would swell the wood of the wheels and ruin the clock; but clocks of brass could be exported anywhere and were also cheaper. The result was that, by 1842, these clocks could be sent to England for as little as $1.50. So low was this price that the clocks were seized (though compensation was paid) by the British customs authorities, in the belief that they were fraudulently undervalued and represented unfair competition. Only the sustained offer at the same price convinced them of the genuineness of the low price.[4] Before 1843, a single firm had sold 40,000 clocks in foreign countries.[5]

It was only a step from clocks to watches, though far finer parts were needed. England and Switzerland had been the traditional suppliers; but in 1850, Americans began to make watches by machinery at Waltham, Massachusetts, and eventually watches were not only manufactured more cheaply but were also of superior accuracy to all but the most costly luxury watches of European manufacture. By 1876, at the Centennial Exhibition in Philadelphia, and again at the Paris Exposition of 1878, the American Watch Company of Waltham was alarming the English and Swiss watch-makers by the excellence of their machine-made watches as well as by their low prices.[6] The "dollar watch" made in Waltham could not be surpassed anywhere in the world for high quality and low cost. It was a watch that perfectly served its purpose,

with reliability of performance, clarity of face and numerals, and simplicity of shape (*Fig. 93*).

The change-over from wood to metal in the manufacture of clocks is a typical one, because metal is the industrial material *par excellence.* Victor S. Clark, a historian of American industry, says "No single thing better measures the industrial standing of a nation than its use of metal."[7] Just as in the making of large machinery itself the original wooden structure was soon replaced by metal, so, too, was almost everything that was touched by the process of industrialization, from clocks, farm tools, and household gadgets to wheels, rails, and vehicles. The beautifully hand-shaped wooden hayforks were replaced by steel forks; different, but equally beautiful, tin boxes replaced wooden boxes, and steel ships replaced clipper ships.

Many metal products of steel, iron, copper, and brass had been made in factories before 1800. Arms and cutlery had been made by forging; cooking pots, stoves, firebacks, umbrella stands, shoe buckles, doorknobs, drawer pulls, clothes hooks, various details of architectural decoration and whole pieces of furniture, as well as water pipes and rails, had been made by casting.[8] All of these and many others continued to be manufactured in very simple, sensible designs throughout the nineteenth century, right along with the increasingly popular overornate and the "style" forms (*Figs. 94–107*). Repeatedly, they appear side-by-side on pages of manufacturers' and dealers' catalogues. Just as an article could be provided in a Gothic dress, an Elizabethan costume, or with classical trappings, so could the simple vernacular forms also be provided as a further variant of production.

The same was true of cutlery (*Figs. 108–13*). Sensible, useful, undecorated knives, forks, scissors, scrapers, and razors were made, and so were

96. *Pipe-ash container of brass, nineteenth century.*
(Landesmuseum, Oldenburg)

97. *Brass coffee maker, Sweden (?), early nineteenth century.*
(The City Museum of Helsinki, Finland)

98. *Coffee grinder, made in Helsinki ca. 1845.*
(The City Museum of Helsinki, Finland)

99. *Copper measure, American, 1853–64.*
(Courtesy of The New-York Historical Society, New York City)

100. *Cast-iron stove, American, 1891. The Portsmouth Stove and Range Company, Portsmouth, Ohio. (Courtesy of The Henry Ford Museum, Dearborn, Michigan)*

101. *Puritan gas range, 1898. Manufactured by the Cleveland Foundry Company. From the catalogue of Puritan gas stoves and ranges, Cleveland, Ohio, 1898.*

102. *"Black Beauty" gas cooker, cast iron, manufactured by R. & A. Main, Glasgow, Scotland, ca. 1878. (Lent to the Science Museum, London, by R. & A. Main, Ltd.)*

103. *Hooks from a brass founder's catalogue, English,
mid-nineteenth century.
(Courtesy of the Victoria & Albert Museum)*

104. *Hooks from a catalogue of P. & F. Corbin,
New Britain, Conn., 1895, p. 311.*

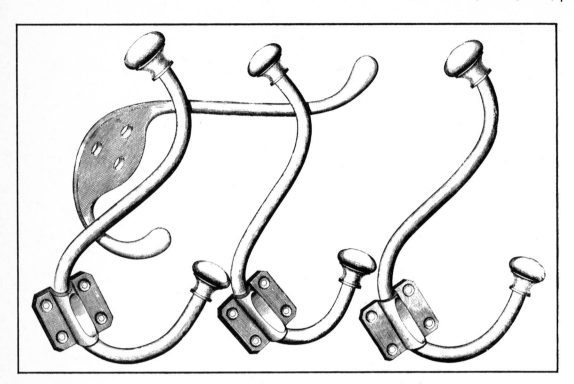

COAT AND HAT HOOKS

105. *Hooks from the same catalogue of P. & F. Corbin,*
New Britain, Conn., 1895, p. 309.

106. *Hook from the catalogue of Silber & Fleming,*
a London wholesale firm of household goods, 1887–89.

107. *Advertisement from* Iron Age, *September 6, 1883,*
p. 60.

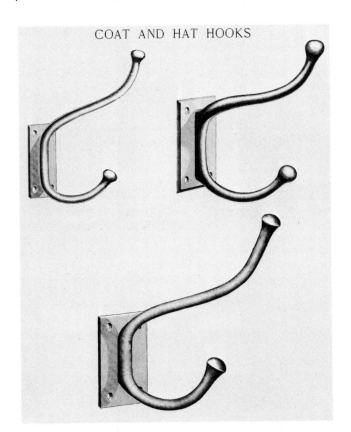

COAT AND HAT HOOKS

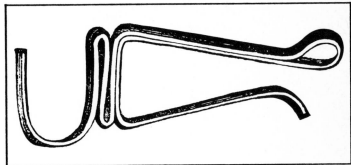

GEM

WIRE COAT AND HAT HOOKS.

EASILY PUT UP OR
REMOVED.

—

NO SCREWS OR TOOLS
REQUIRED.

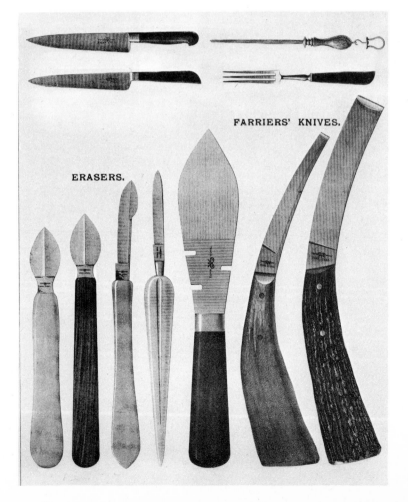

ERASERS.

FARRIERS' KNIVES.

108. *Flatware from the catalogue of Duncker &*
Maste, Iserlohn, Germany, about 1830. The catalogue
consists of a series of color lithographs,
beautifully executed.

109. *Knives for various purposes, from the catalogue of*
Silber & Fleming, 1887–89.

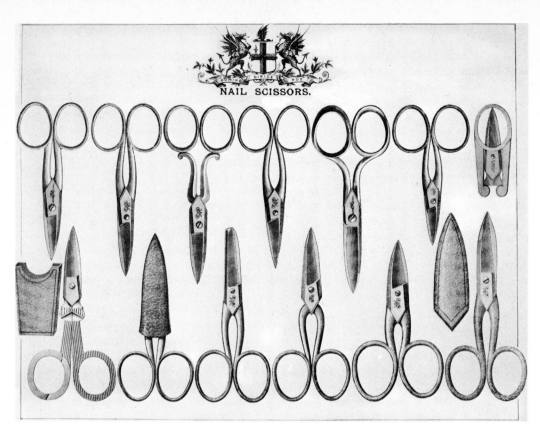

110. *Scissors, from the catalogue of Silber &
Fleming, 1887–89.*

111. *Shears and scissors, from the catalogue of
Silber & Fleming, 1887–89.*

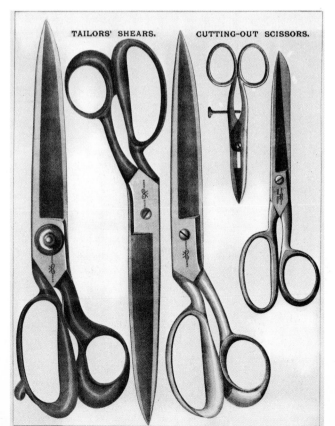

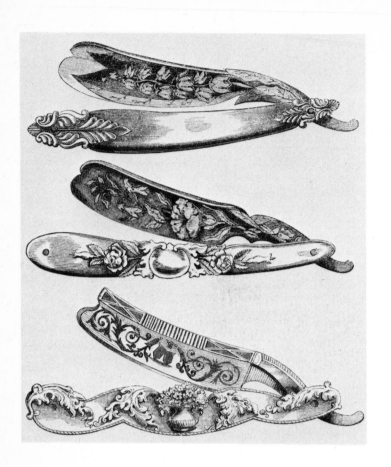

112. *Sheffield razors, shown at the Crystal Palace Exhibition in London, 1851.*
(*From* The Art Journal Illustrated Catalogue, *p. 293*)

113. *Sheffield razors, late nineteenth century; manufactured by Gilbert Brothers Manufacturers, Sheffield, England; from their catalogue of cutlery.* (*Smithsonian Institution*)

ludicrously overdecorated or excessively complex examples. Often, rational design was lost sight of through pride in the capacity for ingenuity. There were always knives and scissors that we would not hesitate to buy today, and there were knives and scissors so spiky and bulgy with extraneous forms of decoration that they were unusable even then. J. B. Himsworth, in *The Story of Cutlery,* shows many nineteenth-century knives for special uses—butchers', cooks', and camp knives, shoemakers' and glaziers' knives, and Bowie knives—all rationally shaped and only very few decorated.[9] However, even the trade observed that designs sometimes did go astray. The *Sheffield Mechanics' Exhibition Magazine* of 1840 remarks: "Many . . . articles are wonderful achievements of skill, exhibiting the most exquisite workmanship, and the greatest ingenuity in their contrivance, but they are frequently at variance with good taste, and rendered altogether useless by the extravagant forms they assume. Our mechanics pride them-

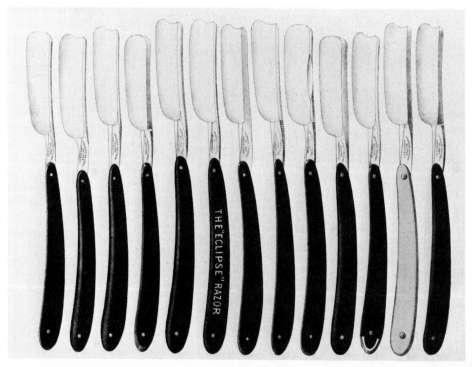

selves too much on making the largest, the most diminutive, the most costly, or the most complex articles." [10] The most flamboyant extravaganza was a "Sportsman's Knife" with eighty blades and instruments, exhibited by J. Rodgers & Sons of Sheffield at the Crystal Palace in 1851 and illustrated many times, then and now, in books dealing with the Great Exhibition.

Tinware was an important item of manufacture in the nineteenth century. In England, it was apt to strain for elegance, frequently imitating silver forms; but in America, it was more often modest and was usually referred to as "country tin." It consisted of a multitude of items for household and table use: coffeepots, trays, cannisters, spice boxes, measures, strainers, and many other necessaries. Though pieces decorated by japanning, piercing, and punching attract the attention of collectors today, advertisement of tinsmiths and surviving examples show that the largest proportion of tinware made in America was of the plain, undecorated type. [11]

In a special category are a great variety of small devices invented by ingenious Yankees as labor-saving machinery for the household. Originally of wood, many were manufactured in cast iron in interesting and unusual shapes: clothespins, cherry pitters, apple corers and peelers, meat and coffee grinders, sausage-makers, muffin tins, curling and pleating irons—most of them either long since replaced by home power tools or with all their functions relegated to the factory (*Figs. 114-20*). Particularly in America, tools of every description for farm and workshop—axes, saws, files, planes, rakes, pitchforks, and plows—were rethought and redesigned in forms more intelligent than the ancient inherited forms, with metal often replacing wood in the course of the century (*Figs. 121–35*). In 1876, a German observer reported from the Centennial Exhibition in Philadelphia that "the best of our

tools [i.e., German tools] look clumsy and antiquated next to these brilliant [American] instruments." [12] The British commissioner, in his report, noted especially the American use of steel for agricultural implements, which allowed tools to remain clean, their edges and points to remain sharp, and their weight to be reduced, while increasing the effectiveness of the tools. [13]

In the second half of the century, there was another whole group of metal products of a modest nature, made of wire. Wire was not produced in any large quantity and was unavailable for use in modest household objects until the advent of the telegraph called for unprecedented quantities. A complete new industry was founded to satisfy the demand, and eventually wire became a cheap and readily available commodity. Bent wire was used for shelf brackets, clothes hangers, and clothes hooks, which have an amazing similarity to items available today in hardware and dime stores; it was used as coiled wire for letter racks, and as woven wire for bottle racks, carriers, and baskets of many different types, most of which would be made of plastic today (*Figs. 136–38*).

After 1850, a number of factors made possible a whole new range of consumer goods. Inventiveness and manufacturing skill were coupled with business and commercial development, making large-scale manufacturing and sales a reality. During the first half of the century, entrepreneurs had been concerned primarily with manufacturing capital goods and creating the machines and factories of the industrial system itself—and particularly the building of the railway network; but in the second half, they found it possible, with the system established, to produce more consumer goods. Cheap steel, precision manufacture, and electric power were used to manufacture such items as sewing machines, typewriters, cameras, telephones, phonographs, electric irons, heaters, fans, and lamps.

114. *Patented American clothespins, nineteenth century.*
(Smithsonian Institution)

115. *Cast-iron apple parer, made by Lockey &*
Howland, Leominster, Mass., 1856.
(Courtesy of The New-York Historical Society,
New York City)

116. *"Enterprise Cherry Stoner No. 1." Made by the*
Enterprise Manufacturing Co., Philadelphia, Pa.
Patented in 1883.
(Smithsonian Institution)

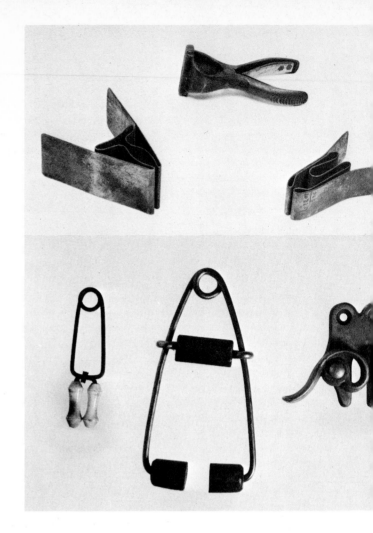

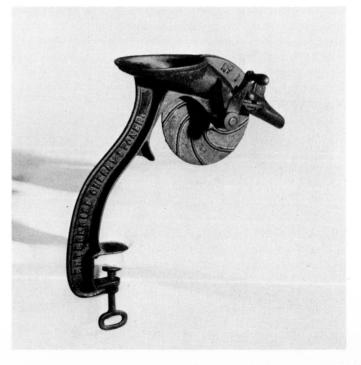

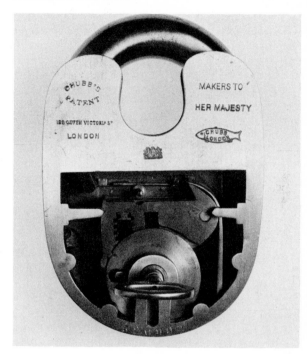

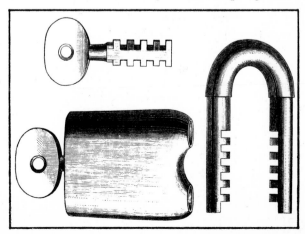

DOVER STAMPING COMPANY. 3

THE GENUINE DOVER EGG BEATERS

UNDER PATENTS

May 31, 1870; May 6, 1873; April 3, 1888 and Nov. 24, 1891.

Tumbler. Family Size. Extra Family Size. Mammoth.

No. 1. No. 2.

No. 3.

No. 4. Doz.

No. 1. For the invalid . . . .
" 2. For ordinary use . . . .
" 3. For ordinary use, but stronger, more durable and
   more effective, without Clamp . . . . . .
" 3. With Clamp . . . .
" 4. For Hotels and Restaurants . . . .

The No. 2 has found the largest sale, but experience has demonstrated that the No. 3, or extra family size, while it costs more, is more effective, more durable, and in reality much cheaper in the end. This No. 3 is specially endorsed by Miss Parloa and the cooking schools generally. It does all the small work of the No. 2, and is fitted for all the *larger* work of the kitchen.

117. *Egg beaters. From an 1895 catalogue page of Tinners' Hard Ware and Furnishings Goods of the Dover Stamping Co. Patents from 1870 on.*

118. *Lock by Chubb & Son, London, 1818.* *(Smithsonian Institution)*

119. *Cast-bronze of gun-metal spring padlock. Yale & Towne Manufacturing Co., Catalogue No. 10, 1884.*

120. *Cast-iron lock, American, 1876. Shown at the Centennial Exhibition in Philadelphia, 1876.* *(From Seelhorst,* Die Philadelphia Ausstellung, *Fig. 16)*

121. *Lawn mower, patented by Edwin Budding in 1830, manufactured from 1832 on by Messrs. J. R. and A. Ransome. Budding was an engineer in a textile factory, who studied a machine that sheared the nap off cloth and who applied the principle to a machine for cutting grass. (Photo Science Museum, London)*

122. *Plow of a type introduced into Scotland by James Small, ca. 1760. Small worked out the mathematical principle for the shape of the mold-board and was the first to make it in cast iron. (British Crown Copyright. Science Museum, London)*

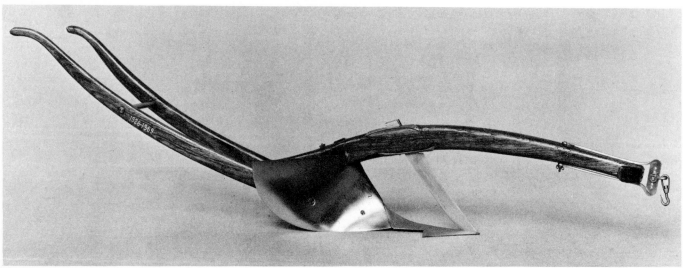

123. *Patent wheel plow, mid-nineteenth century,*
manufactured by Messrs. Howard, of Bedford, England.
(Lent to the Science Museum, London, by the
Royal Scottish Museum, Edinburgh)

124. *The McCormick Reaper at the Crystal Palace,*
1851.
(From: Tallis's History and Description of the Crystal
Palace and the Exhibition of the World's Industry in 1951,
II, after 184).

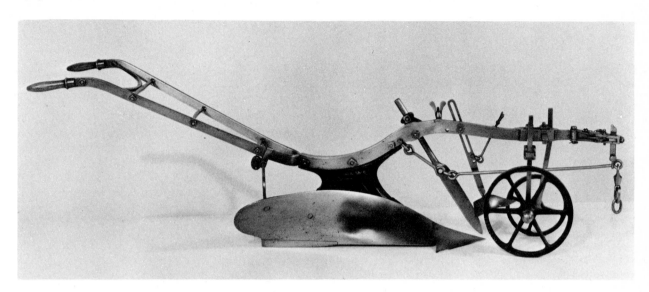

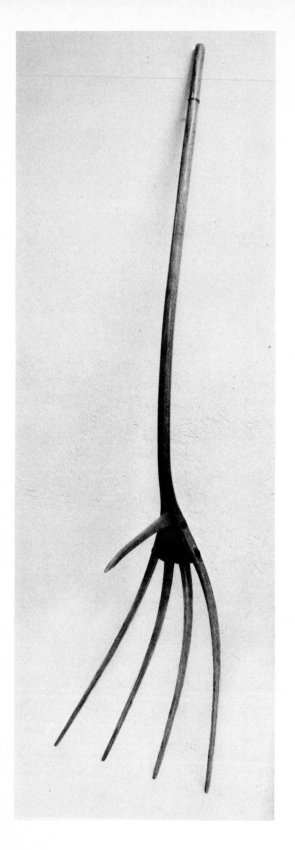

125. *American wooden barley fork, nineteenth century.*
(New York State Historical Association, Cooperstown)

126. *American cradle scythe, nineteenth century.*
(New York State Historical Association, Cooperstown)

127. *Metal cradle scythe, from the catalogue of Dinkins-Davidson Hardware Co., Inc., Atlanta, Ga.*

128. *Standard parts for metal cradle scythe, from the catalogue of Dinkins-Davidson Hardware Co., Inc., Atlanta, Ga.*

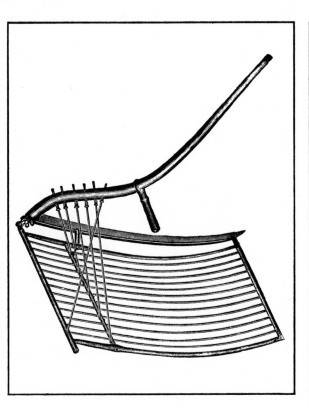

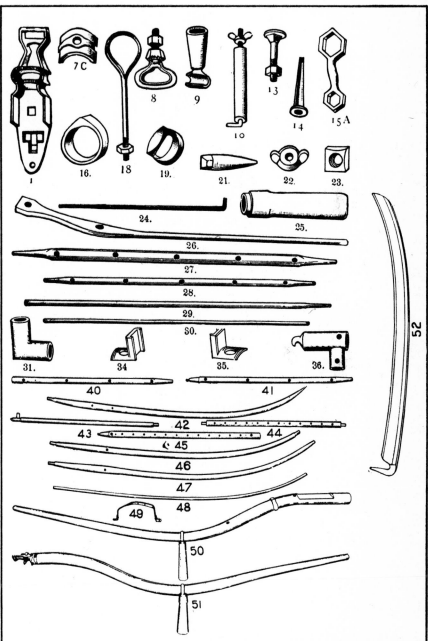

129. *Sugar tongs of forged iron, Solingen, Germany,
ca. 1800.*
*(Courtesy Deutsches Klingenmuseum, Solingen.
Photo Gnamm)*

130. *Scraping tool used by lumbermen to mark trees.
From the catalogue of Dunker & Maste,
Iserlohn, Germany, ca. 1830.*

131. *Sims's vaginal speculum, designed by
James Sims, American surgeon (1813–83).*
(Smithsonian Institution)

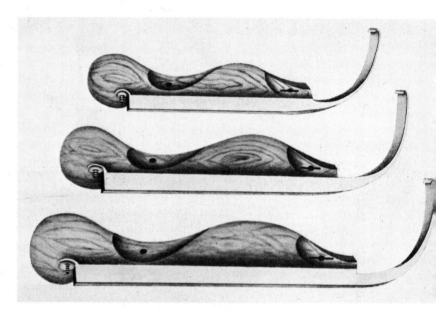

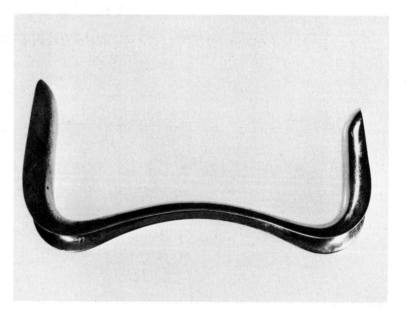

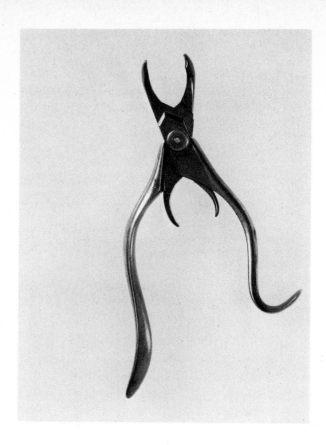

132. *All-purpose forceps, with reversible jaws, invented and patented in 1871 by Leonard G. Haskins of Newport, N.Y. (patent model).* (Smithsonian Institution)

133. *Button-hole cutter, by Samuel W. Eastren, Patent No. 116, 936, July 11, 1871.* (Smithsonian Institution)

134. *Mining safety lamps, 1815–40.* (Deutsches Museum, Munich)

135. *Miners' handlamps, with 6 v batteries and rheostat, ca. 1884.* (Photo Science Museum, London)

136. *Wire letter rack. From the catalogue of Silber & Fleming, 1887–89.*

137. *Wire bottle-carriers and baskets. From a catalogue of house and kitchen utensils of the firm of Nürnberger Metallwaarenfabrik, Gebrüder Bing, Nürnberg, 1893.*

138. *Various items from a catalogue of house and kitchen utensils of the firm of Nürnberger Metallwaarenfabrik, Gebrüder Bing, Nürnberg, 1893.*

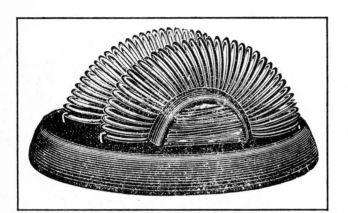

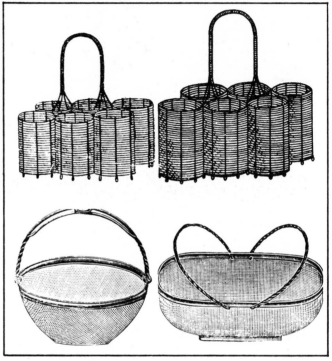

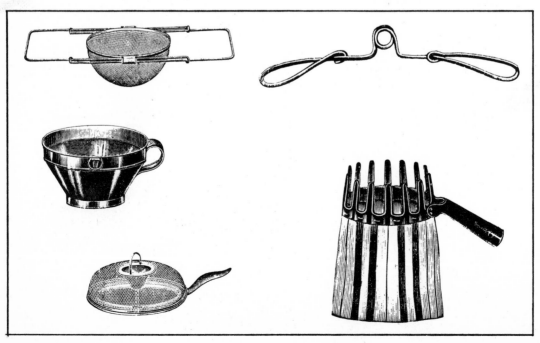

139. *Isaac M. Singer's first sewing machine, 1851.*
(Smithsonian Institution)

140. *West and Wilson sewing-machine head,*
ca. *1859. An attempt to beautify, at the same time with*
monumentality and delicacy.
(Smithsonian Institution)

141. *Willcox & Gibbs sewing machine, 1878.*
(Smithsonian Institution)

The outward appearances of these inventions were largely determined by the social circumstances of their use. The sewing machine was perfected and patented by Isaac Singer in the 1850's [14] in a form that, were it not for the crude squiggles of decoration, would remind one of the early machine tools of Maudslay and Nasmyth. It became an article of household furniture and, as such, had to be beautified to make it fit for the living room (*Figs. 139–140*). Though mechanics required skill and exactitude to produce with accuracy the many small castings and forgings for these small machines, unlike the makers of earlier, more modest gadgets, they decorated them heavily. Sewing-machine factories were the first to embellish practical machines with japanning, stenciling, gold-and-silver electroplating, and inlays of mother-of-pearl and other iridescent materials in the form of scrolls and vines and curlicues. Occasionally the sewing machine could be as direct and simple as the earlier Yankee notions and seem like a larger variant, making worthy contributions to the functional tradition (*Fig. 141*).

The typewriter went through a number of experimental stages (*Fig. 142*) and was not successfully manufactured until the 1870's.[15] The fact that typewriters were considered a woman's tool almost from the start probably contributed to considerable efforts at gentility in decorating them with gilt stenciled decoration. But the underlying form of the typewriter and other new manufactured objects was a new one and, when left unembellished could be a clear statement of its function (*Figs. 143–48*). Unfortunately in the second half of the century, even in America, a domestic object of practical use was not safe from the depredations of decorative art.

Metal products of clearly utilitarian character made of base metals would naturally tend toward simple functional forms, but silver or other precious

143. *College lantern, by George Wale & Co., Hoboken,* 97
N.J. Shown at the Philadelphia Centennial, 1876.
(From: Masterpieces of the Centennial, III, 215)

metals are in an entirely different realm. Almost universally costly materials and high social patronage mean elaborate decoration. And yet there are examples in the eighteenth century of beautiful, harmonious forms entirely without decoration, designed for the highest social circles, indeed for royal patronage.[16] It is evident that the aristocracy often preferred undecorated form, perhaps because their secure social status allowed them to choose elaboration or simplicity, as long as that security of status lasted. Some of these elegant, simple forms were created well into the nineteenth century (*Figs. 149–59*).

In the nineteenth century, silver underwent that familiar process of total elaboration, and the resources of artists, designers, and manufacturers were exhausted to produce a variety of almost totally useless, costly, and decorative objects: racing cups, table fountains, rosewater ewers, com-

memorative shields, testimonials in the form of small-scale monuments that amaze by the muliplicity and confusion of their forms and allusions, covered vases of the most astounding shapes and sizes, center pieces, and that most Victorian of table ornaments, epergnes, small-scale statuary and other such trifles and objects of virtu.[17]

Toward the end of the century, various efforts at reform of design, principally by William Morris, resulted in the setting up of small independent workshops by a number of artist-craftsmen, who produced designs in precious metals that contrasted with the stereotyped commerical production of the time. Most important was C. R. Ashbee (1863–1942), who founded the School and Guild of Handicraft in 1887. The Guild, which existed until 1908, was a workshop organization for craftsmen who executed their own and Ashbee's designs. Simple shapes derived from traditional forms

98

144. *Kodak rollfilm camera for 100 exposures. 1888.*
(Deutsches Museum, Munich)

145. *Kodak travel camera, 1888.*
(Deutsches Museum, Munich)

146. *"Victor" telegraph key. From E. S. Greeley & Co.*
Illustrated catalogue and price list of telegraph,
telephone, electric light, electric power, electric railway,
and general electrical machinery and supplies,
*New York, 1889. This catalogue is full of functionalist
statements, such as "Simplicity is strength! Complexity
is Fatal!" and "we have listened to every petition
presented to remove clumsiness, dead weight, and
false conceptions of utility and art."*

147. *Phonograph for manual operation,
by Thomas Edison, 1878.*
(Deutsches Museum, Munich)

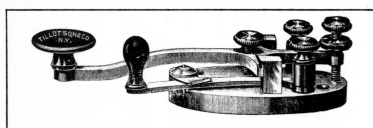

TOP CONNECTION "VICTOR" TELEGRAPH KEY, PRICE $3.00.
[PATENTED.]

148. *Electric flatiron, German, 1888.*
(Deutsches Museum, Munich)

149. *Silver travel tea service, by John Schofield,*
1786, for the fourth Duchess of Bedford. Its brass-
banded mahogany box also contained white porcelain
cups and saucers. In like manner, there was the
Duke's silver travel dinner service, also by
John Schofield, and together the two services provided
a full complement of plate for the ducal couple on
their travels. The functional simplicity of the pieces
in these services is all the more striking among the
extravagantly lush and elaborate pieces by
Paul de Lamerie, on the one hand, and those of
Paul Storr, on the other, in the ducal collection.
(From the Woburn Abbey Collection, by kind permission of
His Grace, the Duke of Bedford).

150. *Pieces of silver, ebony, and horn from a travel service belonging to a Count J. F. Hoensbroech. German, 1803.*
(Germanisches Nationalmuseum, Nürnberg)

151. *Basket of silver wire. Hallmarks: Copenhagen, 1813; Assayer: Fred. Fabricius; Maker's mark "Capricorn" not identified.*
(Museum of Decorative Art, Copenhagen)

were given some embellishment of enamel, cabochon stones, or silver wire, the latter used for handles, finials, or supports. Undecorated surfaces bore the small marks of the hammer made in beating the sheet metal into shape, and the silver was given a soft sheen by burnishing.[18] Almost all of Ashbee's pieces convey preciousness and effeminacy, qualities that have often caused his work to be classed as Art Nouveau, though it is cooler, less lush and full-blooded than most Continental Art Nouveau. They were, in actual fact, precious, not at all made for everyman (*Fig. 160*).

At the end of the nineteenth century, only the rich could possess handmade silver. What strikes one most about it is the incongruity of precious material, craftsmanship, and cost, compared to the mundane or silly purposes for which the objects were intended. The modern mind is no longer attuned to accept the rhetoric of a piece of parcel-

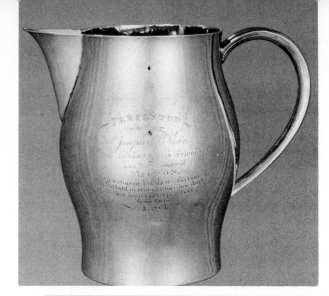

152. *Silver pitcher, by Paul Revere, 1804.*
(Courtesy, Henry Francis du Pont Winterthur Museum)

153. *Silver coffeepot, by L. Wieninger, Vienna, 1818.*
(Vienna, Austrian Museum for Applied Arts)

154. *Silver pitcher, by B. Ranninger, Vienna, 1820.*
(Vienna, Austrian Museum for Applied Arts)

155. *Silver Mocha pot, by Carl Weisshaupt, Munich,*
ca. 1840–50.
(Courtesy Wilhelm Braun-Feldweg)

156. *Silver pap boat, made by William I. Tenney,*
working in New York City ca. 1840.
(Courtesy of the New-York Historical Society,
New York City)

157. *Silver serving spoons, German, first half of the nineteenth century.*
(Courtesy Wilhelm Braun-Feldweg)

158. *"Baguette" pattern of silver flatware, by Orfevrerie Christofle, Paris. First produced sometime in the nineteenth century and not discontinued until the 1950's.*

159. *Silver spectacles, by Samuel Kirk, Baltimore, Md., ca. 1830.*
(Courtesy Samuel Kirk & Son, Inc., Baltimore, Md.)

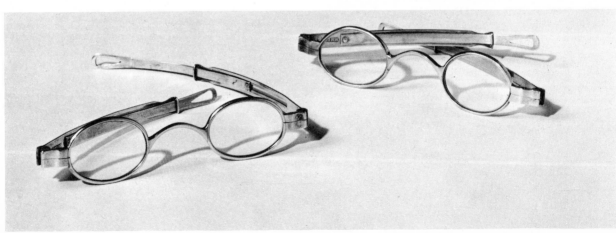

160. *Silver bowl and spoon, by C. R. Ashbee,* ca. 1900.
(Courtesy Mrs. Shirley Bury, London)

161. *Salt cellar and cover, parcel gilt and set with amber beads. London hallmark for 1899–1900; maker's mark of C. R. Ashbee.*
(Courtesy of the Victoria & Albert Museum)

gilt silver set with amber beads and shaped in the form of an angel standing on a semisphere, supporting aloft with its wings and a curious tendril-like wire a larger sphere above, which turns out to be merely a salt cellar and cover by Ashbee [19] (*Fig. 161*).

As pioneer efforts of modern design, the value of such items must be gauged against many anonymous items that appear in commerical catalogues of the time: silver cigar and cigarette cases, egg cups, flasks, tumblers, boxes, and containers in simple geometric forms (*Figs. 162, 163*). These belong to that body of truly protomodern forms cited as exemplary by Loos and other modernists and offered as living evidence of their theories of modern design.

The Industrial Revolution also brought changes in the manufacturing process of precious metals. Plating by fusing silver on copper, and thus reducing the requirement of precious metal, was already an old, established form of making silver more widely available. It was an industry associated with the city of Sheffield, since the method of fusing had been invented there about 1743, by Thomas Boulsover. But the nineteenth century brought an even cheaper and easier method in the form of electroplating. In 1840, George and Henry Elkington of Birmingham took out the first patents to deposit a film of silver on an inferior, cheaper, metallic surface through electrolytic means.[20] The Elkington firm, which was to be the dominant firm of the trade throughout the nineteenth century, maintained a monopoly for some time by engaging in constant experimentation and also by buying up patents. Not only could silver hollow-ware be produced cheaply by electroplating, but materials other than base metal could also be given a coating of silver or other metal. Actual leaves and fruit were plated for decoration, contributing

162. Silver matchboxes, from the catalogue of
Silber & Fleming, 1887–89.

163. Picnic cases with Sheffield cutlery.
From a catalogue of Gilbert Brothers Manufacturers,
Sheffield, England, late nineteenth century.

SOLID LEATHER PIC-NIC CASE.

PIC-NIC CASE AND

RAILWAY COMPANION.

PIC-NIC CASE.

to an already existing trend toward naturalism in mid-century. Famous pieces of metalwork of the past, often attributed to Cellini, were also electro-typed and, in their turn, contributed to the habit of copying and imitating older styles. Small-scale statuary could be modeled in plaster and given a coating of bronze and, therewith, the appearance of a solid-bronze piece.

Throughout the nineteenth century, there was little to redeem this branch of industry. Conceived as a cheaper way to satisfy expensive or snobbish tastes, it was quite natural that its products would partake of all the less desirable qualities of nineteenth-century design. All the more astonishing is the work of one man, Christopher Dresser (1834–1904), who designed for several silver firms in the 1870's and 1880's. His designs are startlingly simple and clearly function as useful objects and without trying to be objects of art or of virtu (*Figs. 164–65*). They are products of a commerical designer, not an artist, not an Arts and Crafts practitioner. Dresser had a probing, independent mind that sought rational solutions and shapes, and he used a new and inexpensive process to produce functional forms that are distinctly modern and alien to the ruling taste of the time.[21] Occasionally, one finds other commercially produced objects of equal clarity and purposefulness of form (*Fig. 166*)—and perhaps many more remain to be found—but, on the whole, Christopher Dresser was an exception for his time in the field of industrially produced silver-plated ware. Similar shapes based on the elementary geometric forms were also produced in other materials, such as wood and ivory (*Fig. 167, 168*).

The whole field of metalware for domestic use, ranging from cast iron, brass, and pewter to silver and other precious metals, shows the natural tendency for modest materials to be used rationally for functional purposes in clear, undecorated forms, while the precious metals often serve only the purposes of show (*Fig. 169*).

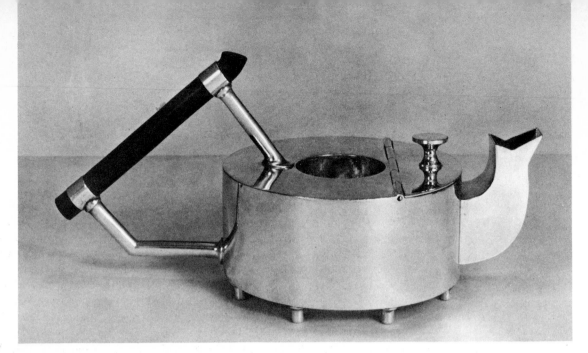

164. *Teapot, electroplate with ebony handle.
Designed by Christopher Dresser and made by
James Dixon & Sons, of Sheffield, England, about 1880.
(Courtesy of the Victoria & Albert Museum)*

165. *Tea set, electroplate. Designed by Christopher
Dresser and made by James Dixon & Sons,
of Sheffield, England. The pieces bear the registry
mark for 1880.
(Courtesy of the Victoria & Albert Museum)*

166. *Spherical silver box with cover, Sheffield, England.
Date mark is indistinct, but clearly either O or Q,
placing the piece in the period 1881–84. Maker's
mark: H. S. (Henry Stratford); bottom stamped:
Edward & Sons, Glasgow and London.
(Hessisches Landesmuseum, Darmstadt)*

167. *Spice boxes of maple and tin, made by the Patent Package Co., Newark, N.J., ca. 1865.*
(Courtesy of The Henry Ford Museum, Dearborn, Michigan)

168. *Ivory powder box, probably Paris, mid-nineteenth century.*
(Badisches Landesmuseum, Karlsruhe)

169. *Decanter, silver-mounted glass bottle set with precious stones and antique coins, designed by William Burges and made by R. A. Green in 1866. A breath-taking expenditure of materials, craftsmanship, and artistic imagination, with the result an aesthetic disaster.*
(From the collection of Mrs. A. M. H. Westland. Courtesy of the Victoria & Albert Museum)

NOTES TO CHAPTER 4

1. For the early history of the American rifle, see John G. W. Dillin, *The Kentucky Rifle* (Washington, D. C.: National Rifle Association of America, 1924), pp. 1–26; and Townsend Whelen, *The American Rifle* (New York: Century Co., 1923), pp. 3–8.

2. Joseph Wickham Roe, *English and American Tool Builders* (New Haven, Conn.: Yale University Press, 1916), pp. 137, 164–70; L. T. C. Rolt, *Tools for the Job* (London: B. T. Batsford, 1965), pp. 144–46; William B. Edwards, *The Story of Colt's Revolver* (Harrisburg, Pa.: The Stackpole Co., 1953), pp. 211–86. The last is a painfully discursive book but does have much interesting information.

3. D. F. Galloway, "Machine-Tools," in Charles Singer *et al.*, *A History of Technology* (Oxford: Clarendon Press, 1958), V, 638–39; Rolt, *op. cit.*, pp. 146–47.

4. For early American clocks, see Carl W. Drepperd, *American Clocks and Clockmakers* (Garden City, N.Y.: Doubleday, 1947), p. 46 ff., 79, 114; Brooks Palmer, *The Book of American Clocks* (New York: Macmillan, 1950), pp. 4–5; and Chauncey Jerome, *History of the American Clock Business* (New Haven, Conn.: 1860), pp. 27–39.

5. Victor S. Clark, *History of Manufactures in the United States,* Vol. I, *1607–1860* (New York: McGraw-Hill, 1929), p. 363.

6. James C. Watson, "Horological Instruments," United States Centennial Commission, *International Exhibition 1876, Reports and Awards* (Washington, D.C.: 1880), VII, 410 ff.; Edward H. Knight, "Watchmaking Machinery," *ibid.*, pp. 90–97; *idem*, "Report on Clocks and Watches," *Reports of the United States Commissioners to the Paris Universal Exposition 1878* (Washington, D.C.: 1880) IV, 405–15.

7. Clark, *op. cit.*, pp. 496, 518–20.

8. J. L. and Barbara Hammond, *The Rise of Modern Industry* (8th ed.; London: Methuen, 1951), p. 138.

9. J. B. Himsworth, *The Story of Cutlery* (London: Ernest Benn, 1953).

10. Quoted by C. R. Fay, *Round about Industrial Britain 1830–1860* (Toronto: University of Toronto Press, 1952), pp. 57–58.

11. Henry J. Kauffman, *Early American Ironware* (Rutland, Vt.: Charles E. Tuttle, 1966), p. 140. See also the many examples illustrated in Mary Earle Gould, *Antique Tin and Tole Ware* (Rutland, Vt.: Charles E. Tuttle, 1958).

12. Georg Seelhorst, *Die Philadelphia-Ausstellung und was sie lehrt* (Nördlingen: C. H. Beck, 1878), pp. 93–94.

13. Great Britain, Executive Commission, *Reports on the Philadelphia International Exhibition of 1876* (London: Her Majesty's Stationery Office, 1877), I, 139.

14. D. A. Farnie, "The Textile Industry: Woven Fabrics," in Singer, *op. cit.*, V, 588–92; Frederick L. Lewton, "The Servant in the House: A Brief History of the Sewing Machine," Smithsonian Institution, *Annual Report for 1929* (Washington, D.C.: 1930), pp. 559–83; Grace Rogers Cooper, *The Invention of the Sewing Machine* (Washington, D.C.: Smithsonian Institution, 1968).

15. George Tilghman Richards, *The History and Development of Typewriters* (2d ed.; London: Her Majesty's Stationery Office, 1964); Richard N. Current, *The Typewriter and the Men Who Made It* (Urbana, Ill.: University of Illinois Press, 1954).

16. Walter Dexel, *Das Hausgerät Mitteleuropas* (Braunschweig: Klinkhardt & Biermann, 1962), illustrates a number of silver pieces from the possession and with the monogram of Augustus the Strong of Saxony, all formerly in the Saxon Court Silver Chamber at Dresden: p. 268, fig. 485, a covered tureen; p. 272, fig. 499, a coffeepot; p. 276, fig. 511, a teapot; p. 291, fig. 564, silver-gilt flatware. Heinrich Kohlhaussen, *Geschichte des Deutschen Kunsthandwerks* (Munich: F. Bruckmann, 1955), illustrates two pieces from the Bavarian court, p. 518, fig, 486, a silver box for travel provisions and, p. 550, fig. 517, a silver chafing dish.

17. See Patricia Wardle, *Victorian Silver and Silver-Plate* (London: Herbert Jenkins, 1963), plates 1–50.

18. *Ibid.*, pp. 199 ff. and plates 57–69.

19. *Ibid.*, plate 60. For Ashbee's philosophy see: C. R. Ashbee, *Craftsmanship in Competitive Industry,* (Campden & London: Essex House Press, 1908). That William Morris himself also became painfully aware of the fatal flaw of handcraftsmanship in an industrial

society is attested to by an incident reported by W. R. Lethaby, *Philip Webb and His Work* (London: Oxford University Press, 1935, pp. 94–95): Sir Lowthian Bell, meeting Morris in an apparently upset state, inquired as to the reason: "He turned on me like a mad animal— 'It is only that I spend my life in ministering to the swinish luxury of the rich.'" That he could also accommodate himself to realities of workmanship and quietly ignore medieval fantasies was shown by Peter Floud in two very illuminating articles: "William Morris as an Artist: A New View," *The Listener,* LII No. 1336 (1954), 562–64, and No. 1337 (1954), 615–17. Morris, who lectured and wrote so passionately and indefatigably on the craftsman's pleasure in his own work being the one indispensable precondition for beauty in art, and, therefore, the necessity of the designer and craftsman being one and the same person, had more than half of his wallpapers and textiles produced by outside firms, not even under his direct supervision.

20. Wardle, *op. cit.,* pp. 29 ff. and 41 ff.; R. Chadwick, "The Working of Metals," in Singer, *op. cit.,* V, 632 ff.; Seymour B. Wyler, *The Book of Sheffield Plate* (New York: Crown, 1949), pp. 3 ff. and 80 ff.

21. Anonymous, "The Work of Christopher Dresser," *The Studio,* XV (1898), 104–14; Nikolaus Pevsner, "Christopher Dresser, Industrial Designer," *The Architectural Review* LXXXI (1937), 183–86; Shirley Bury, "The Silver Designs of Dr. Christopher Dresser," *Apollo,* LXXVI (1962), 766–70; Wardle, *op. cit.,* p. 160 and pp. 173 ff.

5 Ceramics and Glass

Considering the modest character of clay as a raw material, one might assume that pottery was unsuitable for pretentious decoration and that it should have been characterized by good sense and good shapes in the nineteenth century as it had been for many centuries.[1] However, its cheapness and ease of working led to many extravagances just as with many other materials and processes. The more modest classes were the consumers of the vernacular; and, though there were many differences of taste and consumer patterns between farmers and small townspeople in the new lands of North America and similarly placed people in European countries, who were more tradition-bound, it is interesting to see how utility and function gave similar shapes, particularly in the more modest traditional materials, to the articles of everyday use in Ohio and Finland, New England and Austria. They were formed by a taste that was assured and at the same time truly naïve, but, above all, entirely free of artistic and social pretense. In the new middle classes in Europe and America, where new wealth created new tastes, social and artistic ambitions arose that could only be satisfied by imitating and scaling down the life style of the aristocracy. The new manufacturers—middle class themselves and sharing the same tastes and ambitions—helped by supplying the demand. It was easier to apply decoration than principles of proportion and form, and anyway, the former satisfied the demand for "art" and "poetry." Decoration was a kind of ersatz art, cheaper, readily available (it could literally be bought by the yard), and lavishly applied, but it obscured form and proportion and often hampered function and utility. This was especially true of porcelain, which was expensive in proportion to its pretentious decorative affectations.[2]

Most museum collections and books on pottery and porcelain contain examples of odd productions from the nineteenth century, and the odder they are, the more they seem to appeal to some people's collecting instincts. The oddities include bottles and containers in the shapes of shoes, top hats, hands, and feet or whole figures, log cabins, flowers, and vegetables; vases and pitchers in the shapes of cows, pigs, dogs, and the presidents of the United States. Vernacular functional forms are less frequently seen; one must seek them out. Of course, it must not be forgotten that they were *used* and therefore had a natural life-span; they were discarded when broken or worn out, while ersatz art stood unused on the mantle shelf and could live to be treasured by latter-day collectors.

Writing with excusable patriotism on English vernacular ware, Geoffrey Bemrose, states, "It has invariably shown a keen grasp of those twin essentials—comeliness and utility. This plain sobriety is perhaps our truest national characteristic in the minor arts and is best seen in the work of men unaware of fashionable models. . . . Some of our best pottery has found expression in simple objects. . . . It is when we have ventured into extravaganza that we have become ridiculous."[3] The same might be said of vernacular ware anywhere, and it is not surprising that others writing on pottery in other areas use similar language: "Simple though New England redware may be, it is nevertheless sturdy and vigorous in form and it has a charm that is difficult to define . . . That its beauty is largely accidental makes it no less lovable . . . It is truly an expression of simple people—men almost without conscious thought of art. Like them their pottery is strong, direct, stripped of pretense and foolish ornamentation."[4]

It is out of this kind of background that the first industrial potteries emerged in mid-eighteenth-century England, in the five neighboring Staffordshire pottery towns later incorporated as Stoke-on-Trent. There was a better selection of raw materials, particularly in the search for a white-bodied ware to replace the more costly tin-glazed Delftware or imported Oriental and Continental porcelain; new methods and materials of glazing were tried, and the processes of manufacturing were improved; ovens were enlarged and modified in design to increase control over the product. Most significant was the change about 1740–50 from shaping each piece by hand on the potter's wheel to the use of molds, into which the clay was poured or pressed. This made possible the speedy reproduction of standard designs and increased the importance of the quality of the initial design. The standardization and mass production of shapes necessitated a like change in the method of decoration, and about the middle of the eighteenth century, transfer-printing of decoration supplanted individual hand-painting of ceramic ware.[5]

The most famous potter, and the man who contributed most to the development of the ceramic industry, was Josiah Wedgwood (1730–95). He was not only an accomplished and original potter but also an active and energetic entrepreneur; he was constantly and eagerly experimenting for the improvement of his pottery, its ingredients, and its manufacture; he himself was also active in its design and engaged leading artists, such as John Flaxman, to design for him; he interested himself in road- and canal-building, to insure the best transportation for his products to market, and he was equally concerned with the retail and wholesale disposal of his wares, not only in London but throughout the world. In his career, as well as in the form of his product, he anticipated much later industrial development.

The many earlier experiments and improvements in the production of fine white English earthenware culminated in Wedgwood's cream-colored ware, which he began to manufacture in his Burslem works in 1759–60 and later in Etruria, established in 1769.[6] He himself described his cream-ware as "a species of earthenware for the table quite new in its appearance, covered with a rich and brilliant glaze bearing sudden alterations of heat and cold, manufactured with ease and expedition, and consequently cheap, having every requisite for the purpose intended."[7] He presented a service of this ware to Queen Charlotte in 1762, and by 1765 he became Potter to the Queen, after which this product was termed "Queen's Ware."

Wedgwood designed a series of shapes for his Queen's Ware in the 1760's and 1770's that have been admired and sought after ever since (*Fig. 170*). The shapes are a refinement of vernacular forms, which Wedgwood had perfected for domestic use, and they also partake of the then current enthusiasm for classical shapes, fostered by the discovery of Pompeii and the finds of Greek vases in Etruscan tombs. This fusion of vernacular and classical forms (noted in a wider context above) here, too, produced timeless forms that were exemplary in every respect. They satisfied all the utilitarian, common-sense requirements of easy handling, good pouring, solid base, and wide openings for cleanings; at the same time, they pleased the senses by the harmonious flow of their outlines and shapes and the perfect beauty and warmth of their cream-colored glaze.

It is true that with Wedgwood's manufactured ware, perfected and standardized in shapes to be easily produced by mechanical means, the freedom and charm of hand-thrown and hand-decorated pottery was lost, and this has been pointed out and lamented.[8] But it is precisely because Wedgwood saw and understood the difference between the qualities of the old hand-thrown method and those of industrial production that he succeeded in creating exemplary industrial design. It was,

170. *Shapes developed by the first Josiah Wedgwood
in the latter part of the eighteenth century, as they
appeared in the first catalogues of the firm and as
they are still produced today.*
(From: Graham, Wedgwood, *The Brooklyn Museum*, 1948)

171. *Traveling case owned by President John Adams,
containing a coffee service and a punch bowl
of Meissen porcelain, silver spoons, wineglasses,
decanters, tumblers, and four tin cannisters, ca. 1800.*
(Courtesy of The Henry Ford Museum, Dearborn, Michigan)

114

furthermore, a necessary development in order to satisfy the daily needs of a growing population with steadily rising standards of living.

This handsome Queen's Ware has been manufactured and sold for 200 years; indeed, it is still being manufactured today. It is an early example of industrial design with the qualities defined as modern. It is also another example of that supreme moment in English design history when its innate soberness and common sense, refined by the discipline of the neoclassical style, produced a style of its own, one of reticence and elegant simplicity, based on economy and utility. Queen's Ware belonged with the best of Adam, Sheraton, Hepplewhite, and others of their time, and by its enormous popularity and widespread use in England, America, and on the Continent became a model for other manufacturers well into the nineteenth century. Again and again, one meets with types in the manufacture of various factories that are clearly derived from the Queen's Ware shapes of Wedgwood. A French traveler, writing in the early nineteenth century about Wedgwood's cream-ware, remarked,

its excellent workmanship, its solidity, the advantage which it possesses of sustaining the action of fire, its fine glaze impenetrable to acids, the beauty and convenience of its form, and the cheapness of its price, have given rise to a commerce so active and so universal, that in travelling from Paris to Petersburgh, from Amsterdam to the furthest part of Sweden, and from Dunkirk to the extremity of the south of France, one is served at every inn upon English ware. Spain, Portugal, and Italy, are supplied with it; and vessels are loaded with it for the East Indies, the West Indies, and the continent of America.[9]

The qualities of Wedgwood ware became a point of reference in unexpected contexts: In trying to define the character of Goethe, Novalis, a German poet and philosopher, wrote in 1798: "Goethe is the completely practical poet. His works are like the Englishman's [Wedgwood's] wares—extremely simple, neat, convenient, and durable." [10]

Under the influence and, often, in imitation of Wedgwood, some fine, simple shapes were produced for middle- and upper-class clientele in factories in varous parts of Europe and America (Figs. 172–76), but ceramic design on the whole, except where the vernacular survived, deteriorated in the nineteenth century. The bulk of production during most of the century was dedicated to romantic and pretentious extravaganzas, often gross and blatant in coloring, in gilding, and in decoration, stamped, molded, painted, and printed. "Reform" came toward the end of the century with the artist-potter in both Europe and America, but the superficiality of these artist productions becomes immediately and strikingly apparent when seen next to contemporary vernacular pieces of comparable form. The artist-potter's piece is affected, so easily ridiculous and so quickly out of fashion (Fig. 177), while the vernacular is full of vitality without stridency, unarguable in its devotion to function, pleasing in its lines and masses, color and surface. Only on the vernacular level was the utilitarian tradition carried on uninterruptedly, producing pitchers, bowls, covered jars, jugs, and mugs, coffeepots and teapots that could not be improved on (Figs 178–82). Their forms serve their function so directly, so naturally, and with such sureness that the momentarily fashionable artistic pottery pieces drop into complete insignificance at their side. And yet the "reform" by the "artist-potters" is usually cited as the turning point and first step toward modern design in that field too.

Glass presents a very similar picture. It was again in vernacular production by the traditional means of blowing, both free and in molds, that the simple, utilitarian, modern forms were produced throughout the nineteenth century (Figs. 183–96) in many small factories and workshops all

172. *Cream-colored stoneware coffeepot, German,
ca. 1820. Manufactured by the Stoneware Factory in
Zell am Hamersbach.*
(Badisches Landesmuseum, Karlsruhe)

173. *Teapot of white glazed stoneware, German,
ca. 1840. Wächtersbacher Steingutfabrik, Schlierbach
bei Wächtersbach.*
*(Wächtersbach Ceramics. Otto Friedrich Fürst
zu Ysenburg und Büdingen. Photo: Hessisches
Landesmuseum, Darmstadt)*

174. *Stoneware pitcher, glazed white. French, ca. 1850.
Stamped: Crail & Monthereau.*
(Courtesy Neue Sammlung, Munich. Photo: S. R. Gnamm)

175a and b. *Combined teapot and coffeepot, earthenware. Made by Wedgwood, England (Etruria) 1869. The teapot appears in precisely this form in the 1817 catalogue of the firm, which was engraved by William Blake.*
(Courtesy of the Victoria & Albert Museum)

176. *White porcelain match container, with ribbed striking surface, ca. 1870.*
(Landesmuseum, Oldenburg)

177. *Pitcher of Rookwood pottery, Cincinnati, Ohio, 1895. Artist: Kataro Shirayamadani.*
(Smithsonian Institution)

178. *American Redware pitcher, ca. 1840.*
(Courtesy of The Henry Ford Museum, Dearborn, Michigan)

179. *Pottery jug, American, New England, 1800–1825.*
(Courtesy of The Henry Ford Museum, Dearborn, Michigan)

180. *Pottery bottle, American, ca. 1825.*
(Courtesy of The Henry Ford Museum, Dearborn, Michigan)

181. *Stoneware inkwell, American, ca. 1875.*
(Courtesy of The Henry Ford Museum, Dearborn, Michigan)

182. *Pottery jar, American, ca. 1850.*
(Courtesy of The Henry Ford Museum, Dearborn, Michigan)

over Europe and America. The change from small factory or workshop to larger industrial production began in America in the 1820's, with the invention of machinery to press glass in molds. Within a few years, such machines were being exported to Europe, and there, too, the industrialization process began. As with the use of molds in pottery making, these glass-pressing machines made possible the multiple reproduction of any design and any pattern and inevitably led to large-scale factory production. The machinery was used through the nineteenth century to produce glass covered with ornamentation in imitation of cut glass, usually with extreme horror vacui. In the earlier decades, an over-all pattern was used, the so-called "Lacy pattern," that makes at least some of the glass look textured rather than overornamented, which it really is. Here, mechanization brought definite degeneration in design, because it allowed extreme virtuosity in applying ornamentation with the greatest ease and at minimal cost (*Fig. 197*).

In America, pressed glass is identified most often with Sandwich glass, the product of the Boston and Sandwich Glass Company, to whose founder, Deming Jarves, is often attributed the invention of the process.[11] However, its production and typically elaborate over-all decoration soon spread to all glass-making centers in Europe as well, including such prestigious glass houses as Baccarat, Val-Saint-Lambert, and the factories of Bohemia. Its spread was inevitable because of the fantastically low cost of production; glass prices in Bohemia fell 200 per cent, owing to the importation of English pressed glass. Gustav E. Pazaurek, director of the Württemberg Industrial Arts Museum in Stuttgart, which was actively involved in consumer education, wrote of the flooding of the world market with this "cheap and nasty" product as a "crime" and the chief cause for the degeneration of taste for decades to come.[12]

183. *Preserve jar of amber-colored glass, Stoddard glassworks, New Hampshire, 1846–70.*
(Corning Museum of Glass)

184. *Mason jar, Muncie, Ind., 1858.*
(Courtesy of The Henry Ford Museum, Dearborn, Michigan)

185. *Jar of transparent olive-green glass, with blowing spirals. America, late eighteenth–early nineteenth centuries.*
(Corning Museum of Glass)

186. *Glass teapot, Finland, near end of the nineteenth century. Manufactured by the Grönvik factory, near Vaasa, Finland. This teapot has a striking similarity to the twentieth-century glass version designed by Wilhelm Wagenfeld and manufactured in Germany for many decades by Jenaer Glaswerk Schott & Gen.*
(National Museum of Finland. Photo: P.-O. Welin)

187. *Cream pitcher of clear glass, English, nineteenth century.*
(Courtesy of the Victoria & Albert Museum)

188. *Sugar bowl, with cover of free-blown deep amber glass. America, Midwest, 1815–30.*
(Corning Museum of Glass)

189. *Writing utensils of green glass, Finland, nineteenth century. Manufactured by Berga.*
(National Museum of Finland. Photo: P.-O. Welin)

190. *Glass bottle used for smoothing clothes, dark green, Finland, nineteenth century. Manufactured by Berga.*
(National Museum of Finland. Photo: P.-O. Welin)

191. *Glass compote, American, 1810–40.*
(Courtesy of The Henry Ford Museum, Dearborn, Michigan)

192. *Glass bowl, South German, ca. 1850.*
(Badisches Landesmuseum, Karlsruhe)

193. *Jug of clear glass, pattern molded. American,*
probably late nineteenth century.
(Corning Museum of Glass)

194. *Glass pitcher and mugs, Finland, manufactured*
by Iloniemi in Uskela, 1857–90.
(National Museum of Finland. Photo: P.-O. Welin)

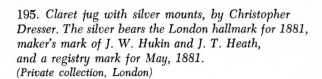

195. *Claret jug with silver mounts, by Christopher Dresser. The silver bears the London hallmark for 1881, maker's mark of J. W. Hukin and J. T. Heath, and a registry mark for May, 1881.*
(Private collection, London)

196. *Ruby-red glass tumbler, German, 1850–60.*
(Courtesy Neue Sammlung, Munich. Photo: S. R. Gnamm)

197. *Covered cake stand, pressed of colorless glass in the pattern originally marketed as "Pioneer" but now called "Westward Ho" by collectors. Made by Gillender & Sons, Philadelphia, about 1880.*
(Corning Museum of Glass)

198. *Glass tumbler, "Reeded" pattern, American, second quarter of the nineteenth century. Lead glass, pressed in one piece.*
(Corning Museum of Glass)

124

Occasionally, one does find simple, strong shapes in pressed glass (*Fig. 198*), but, generally, the older methods of blowing glass, free or in molds, carried on finer traditions of form in many workshops and factories in Europe and America. Undecorated, modern forms range from the supremely elegant and sophisticated service by Ludwig Lobmeyr of 1856—and made ever since then by J. and L. Lobmeyr of Vienna—(*Fig. 199*), to the many fine but sturdier, more practical pieces made in a multitude of factories in Europe (*Fig. 200*) and in America. Though the clear, undecorated modern forms must be culled from a majority of lavishly decorated forms (*Fig. 201*), many pieces of tableware—goblets, glasses, decanters, pitchers, covered sugar bowls, butter dishes, salt dishes, compotes, cruets, and numerous other items—were produced in simple pleasing forms and can be found in such museums as that of the Corning Glass Center. One is more apt to find these in American publications on glass, while European publications more often exclude utilitarian ware,[13] unless they are specifically dedicated to it, such as those of Dexel mentioned earlier.

In England, the architect Philip Webb designed a set of clear glassware that was manufactured by James Powell & Sons of London and was said to have been designed for William Morris in 1859 for the "Red House" (*Fig. 202*). It is of extreme simplicity, the tumbler being of straight cylindrical form, with a slight horizontal bulge in the middle, presumably for ease of holding; a stemmed goblet is slightly conical with several such horizontal bulges. There is, of course, no cutting, no engraving, no enameling on these pieces, as befits the nascent Arts and Crafts movement, with its revolt against all such treatment of glass. However, fine as these pieces are, they by no means deserve veneration as unique pioneer pieces. Commercial production, as it appears in catalogues of the

200. *Glasses from various wine restaurants in Munich,*
Germany, nineteenth century.
(Courtesy Neue Sammlung, Munich. Photo: S. R. Gnamm)

201. *Pitcher of free-blown colorless glass decorated*
with copper-wheel engraving, so-called rock crystal
engraving, by William Fritsche, working at
Thomas Webb & Sons, Stourbridge, England;
signed and dated 1886.
(Corning Museum of Glass)

202. *Group of table glasses, clear glass, designed by Philip Webb and made by James Powell & Sons at the Whitefriars Glass Works, London. English, late nineteenth century. The three pieces with bulges in the body are from a set that is said to have been designed by Webb for William Morris, in 1859, for the Red House.*
(Courtesy of the Victoria & Albert Museum)

second half of the century, shows many forms that can stand favorable comparison with the designs of Webb (*Fig. 203*). They appear in store catalogues for ordinary home use, but they were, of course, also intended for hotel and restaurant use and for railway dining cars. Dresser, whose metal designs have been mentioned above, also designed glass for James Couper & Sons of Glasgow in the 1880's. It stands somewhere between the simple, utilitarian forms of Philip Webb and the later products of James Powell & Sons of the 1890's, which are already Art Nouveau in their delicate and effeminate affectation.[14]

As one might expect, in the more strictly utilitarian pieces, particularly bottles, one finds a far larger proportion of simple, direct shapes (though here, too, there are pictorial and historical pieces inspired by sentiment and patriotism rather than function and use). Vast numbers of nineteenth-century bottles exist of wonderfully pure forms in many different shapes, among them many of superb design to which color, whether shades of green, amber, amethyst, or brilliant blue, often adds a special beauty. They are often mold-blown to produce ribs, swirls, or other simple devices to enliven the surface, by means inherent in the glass technique itself; they may be square to fit in chests, almond- or pear-shaped, bubble-shaped, flattened, or spherical. They are of infinite variety, since they were essentially a craft product (*Figs. 204–8*).

From 1859 on, patents were granted in various countries for semi-automatic bottle-making machines, but it was not until M. J. Owens patented his machine in 1898 that the first completely automatic bottle machine became a success. Five workers making bottles by hand could produce about 150 bottles an hour, while a ten-head Owens machine produced 2,500 bottles an hour.[15] As with pressed glass, the technical advance gave such enormous economic advantage that the older

203. *From the catalogue of A. M. Silber & Co., a London wholesale firm, 1882.*

204. *Glass bottle, American, Zanesville, Ohio, 1825–40.*
(Courtesy of The Henry Ford Museum, Dearborn, Michigan)

PLAIN THIN CRYSTAL TABLE GLASS.

No. 5075.—Champagne.
No. 5075.—Claret.
No. 5075.—Sherry.
No. 5075.—Liqueur.
No. 5075.—Port.
No. 5075.—Jelly.
No. 5075.—Decanter, pint.
No. 5075.—Carafe and Tumbler.
No. 5075.—Claret Jug.
No. 5075.—Finger Basin.
No. 5075.—Custard.
No. 5075.—Champagne Tumbler.
No. 5075.—Decanter, quart.
No. 5075.—Tumbler, half-pint.
No. 5075.—Soda-water Tumbler.

No. 5075.

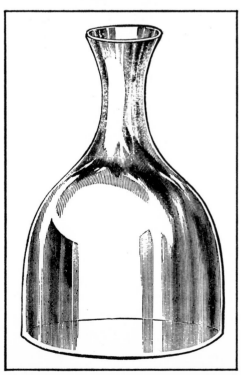

205. *Snuff bottle of green glass, New England, ca. 1825.*
(*Smithsonian Institution*)

206. *Clear glass bottle, German, eighteenth-nineteenth centuries.*
(*Badisches Landesmuseum, Karlsruhe*)

207. *Green glass bottle, nineteenth century.*
(*Courtesy Neue Sammlung, Munich. Photo: S. R. Gnamm*)

208. *Decanter offered by Silber & Fleming, London, wholesalers of household goods, from their catalogue of 1887–89.*

209. *"Verrerie du Commerce,"* 1925.
(From Le Corbusier, L'Art Décoratif d'aujourd'hui, *Paris, Editions G. Crès [1925], p. 97)*

210. *Light bulb, by Thomas Edison,* ca. *1885.*
(Deutsches Museum, Munich)

methods of making bottles had to be abandoned. It is such machines that make the millions of bottles used for milk, beer, soda-pop, and other popular beverages, and some of these are classic shapes of their kind and are in themselves trademarks for the products they contain.

A similar product, which developed directly out of old vernacular shapes, was the Mason preserve jar (*Fig. 184*). Cylindrically shaped food-preserving jars had been made of stoneware as well as of glass and had been used since the Frenchman Nicolas Appert had published his book on preserving in 1810.[16] Appert had found through experimenting that food substances placed in tight containers, hermetically sealed, and subjected to a sufficient amount of heat would keep unspoiled. He had used bottles at first, but then he had made glass jars with wider openings, which he sealed with corks of three, four, and five layers, with the pores running horizontally to hinder access of air. Screw-top jars appeared after the middle of the

century. They were mold-blown, and the threads and mouths of the jars were formed in the mold. Mason's famous patent for such jars was issued on November 30, 1858, and, with it, another vernacular type was recast for mass production in industry.[17]

In 1925, Le Corbusier published a photograph of what he called "Verrerie du Commerce" (*Fig. 209*), to demonstrate the existence and availability of modern design to "eyes that do not see." The shapes go back well into the nineteenth century and even earlier.

A completely new glass product, the electric light bulb developed by Swan, Edison, and others in the 1880's, almost immediately assumed its definitive shape, which is so perfect in its adaptation to function that we accept it as if it were a product of nature (*Fig. 210*). It is a perfect example of industrial vernacular, the product we use and have all around us but do not "see," because we take it so much for granted.

NOTES TO CHAPTER 5

1. See Bernard Rackham, *Medieval English Pottery* (London: Faber & Faber, 1948), and the many fine examples in Walter Dexel, *Das Hausgerät Mitteleuropas* (Braunschweig: Klinkhardt & Biermann, 1962).

2. See Geoffrey A. Godden, *Victorian Porcelain* (London: Herbert Jenkins, 1961).

3. Geoffrey Bemrose, *Nineteenth Century English Pottery and Porcelain* (London: Faber & Faber, 1952), p. 5.

4. Lura Woodside Watkins, *Early New England Potters and their Wares* (Cambridge, Mass.: Harvard University Press, 1950), p. 1.

5. J. L. and Barbara Hammond, *The Rise of Modern Industry* (8th ed.; London: Methuen, 1951), p. 162 ff.; and A. and N. L. Clow, "Ceramics from the Fifteenth Century to the Rise of the Staffordshire Potteries," in Charles Singer *et al.*, *A History of Technology* (Oxford: Clarendon Press, 1958), IV, 344–51 and 353–57.

6. Donald C. Towner, *English Cream-Coloured Earthenware* (London: Faber & Faber, 1957), pp. 1–4 and 33–42.

7. *The Selected Letters of Josiah Wedgwood*, ed. Ann Finer and George Savage (London: Cory, Adams & Mackay, 1965), p. 7.

8. W. B. Honey, *Wedgwood Ware* (London: Faber & Faber, 1948), pp. 1–3; Bernard Rackham and Herbert Read, *English Pottery* (New York: Scribner's Sons, 1924), pp. 119–25.

9. Quoted by George Richardson Porter, *A Treatise on the Origin, Progressive Improvement, and Present State, of the Manufacture of Porcelain and Glass* (London: 1832), p. 16.

10. Novalis (Friedrich von Hardenberg), *Gesammelte Werke* (Herrliberg-Zürich: Bühl Verlag, 1945–46), III, 131.

11. Ruth Webb Lee, *Sandwich Glass* (2d ed.; Framingham Centre: 1939), pp. 79 ff.; Warren C. Scoville, *Revolution in Glassmaking* (Cambridge, Mass.: Harvard University Press, 1948), pp. 17–19.

12. Gustav E. Pazaurek, *Gläser der Empire- und Biedermeierzeit* (Leipzig: Klinkhardt & Biermann, 1923), pp. 11, 34-37, plates 308, 309, 313-19. Lee, *op. cit.*, pp. 390 ff., plates 158-62; Hugh Wakefield, *Nineteenth Century British Glass* (London: Faber & Faber, 1961), pp. 54 ff., plates 88-96.

13. Helen and George S. McKearin, *Two Hundred Years of American Blown Glass* (Garden City, N.Y.: Doubleday, 1950); Lura Woodside Watkins, *American Glass and Glassmaking* (New York: Chanticleer Press, 1950); Pazaurek, *op. cit.*, p. 383.

14. Wakefield, *op. cit.*, pp. 52-53, plates 81A and 85-86.

15. R. W. Douglas, "Glass Technology," in Singer, *op. cit.*, V, 674-77; L. M. Angus-Butterworth, *The Manufacture of Glass* (New York: Pitman, 1948), pp. 164 ff.

16. Nicolas Appert, *L'Art de Conserver pendant plusieurs Années, toutes les substances animales et végétales* (Paris: 1810). Appert's book was translated into German in 1810, into English and Swedish in 1811, and the first American edition appeared in 1812. *The Edinburgh Review* of April, 1814, pp. 104-31, ran a lengthy and interesting review of his book. See A. W. Bitting, *Appertizing, or The Art of Canning: Its History and Development* (San Francisco: 1937), pp. 7–18.

17. Scoville, *op. cit.*, p. 17.

6 Furniture

As Wedgwood's Queen's Ware shapes became models for some of the best ceramics produced in the nineteenth century, so English furniture of the end of the eighteenth century was exemplary for the best that was to follow. It was practical and useful and yet of the utmost refinement of form, derived from the great triumvirate of the preceding decades—Adam, Hepplewhite, and Sheraton—but without the fashionable trimmings they had usually found it necessary to give their designs. One of the most influential but least-known designers was Thomas Shearer, a number of whose designs were published in 1788 under the title "The Cabinetmaker's London Book of Prices." This was meant not as an advertisement but rather as a kind of pattern book for cabinetmakers and a guide to pricing. All the designs are of a practical nature and combine utility with an economy and grace of form that is peculiarly modern. The book was republished with the original plates and some additional ones in 1793, and a third edition was published in 1803. It was again re-issued in 1811, 1824, 1836, and 1866, and was clearly of considerable influence on cabinetmaking, though more in its earlier than in its later editions (*Figs. 211, 213*).[1] Through such publications and through many actual pieces of furniture, the *style anglais* became influential on the Continent and in the Scandinavian countries, not only during the *Biedermeier* period but also at later crucial points in the development of the modern style (*Figs. 212, 214–18*). English influence was brought to Denmark, for example, in the late eighteenth and early nineteenth centuries through the so-called Royal Furniture Storehouse in Copenhagen. It was state-supported and was stocked with fine English furniture to supply local cabinetmakers with high quality designs and examples of professional craftsmanship.[2]

In England itself, the beautifully restrained functional furniture of the end of the eighteenth century was soon discarded in favor of the (by comparison) clumsy extravagances of the Regency style and, thereafter, by the confused and heavy-handed Victorian revivals of past styles. After about 1840, it was only in the vernacular and in the unseen practical and useful that simple, functional forms were continued, both in traditional materials and techniques and in more innovative practices. The continuation of the functional tradition can best be observed in the chair, that most basic piece of furniture. An English armchair of about 1800 (*Fig. 216*), of mahogany and cane, offers a sense of luxurious well-being, in spite of a total absence of prestigious trimmings. It is pure functional form, based on calculations for bodily comfort, and is given distinction by its proportions and the noble simplicity of its materials. It is a form that was taken up quite literally by the firm of William Morris in England, in 1895 (*Fig. 217*), certainly not in the spirit of the Arts and Crafts movement but in that of the emerging modern style. It was again taken up about 1930, at the height of the modern style, by the Danish architect and furniture designer Kaare Klint[3] (*Fig. 218*).

On the vernacular level there are two important types, the ladder-back and the Windsor; examples of both range from frontier rudeness and rustic naïveté to refined sophistication and even reflected spirituality. The Windsor is usually regarded as a special contribution of the Anglo-Saxon world; in many variations, it has been a favorite in England and America since the eighteenth century (*Fig. 219*). That it was not confined to the lower classes is attested to by the fact that George Washington had thirty of them for his guests on the east portico of Mt. Vernon, Jefferson used them at Monticello; and, in a painting showing the voting of the Dec-

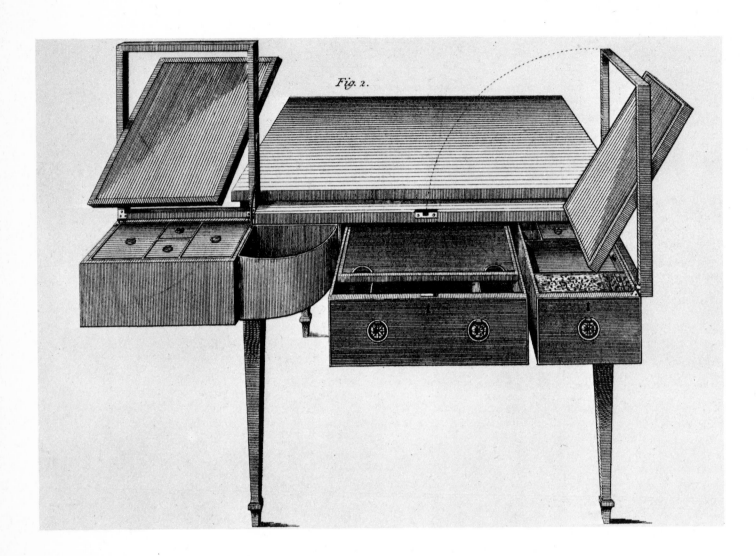

laration of Independence, in 1776, in Philadelphia's Independence Hall, several of the delegates are shown seated in Windsor chairs. But Windsor chairs of considerable refinement of form were found on almost all levels throughout the nineteenth century; they appeared in homes as well as in taverns, schools, libraries, and offices. Their con-

struction and design lent themselves to mass production. Spindles, legs, and seats could all be made efficiently, with the help of machines; the bow was shaped by steaming or boiling the wood and then pegging it in a wooden or iron plate over a block or mold, a process later industrialized on a large scale.[4]

212. *Mahogany dressing table, stamped* Gillow
Lancaster. *England, ca. 1790.*
(Photo courtesy John Keil, Ltd., London)

213. *Table desks. Plate from* The Cabinetmaker's
London Book of Prices, *by Thomas Shearer, 1788.*
*(From the 1793 edition in the library of The Metropolitan
Museum of Art)*

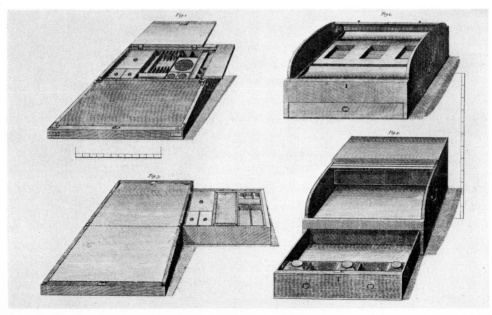

214a and b. *Portable writing desk, owned by Thomas Jefferson. Made for him from his own design by Benjamin Randolph in 1775 or 1776, and used by Jefferson in 1776, when writing the first draft of the Declaration of Independence.*
(Smithsonian Institution)

215. *Side chair of mahogany, made in Denmark by Jens Brötterup, ca. 1800.*
(Museum of Decorative Art, Copenhagen)

216. *Mahogany armchair, English, ca. 1800.*
(Museum of Decorative Art, Copenhagen)

217. *Mahogany armchair with caned back, sides, and*
seat (loose cushions not shown in this photo).
Probably designed by George Jack, made by Morris
& Co., London, ca. 1895.
(Courtesy of the Victoria & Albert Museum)

218. *Mahogany armchair with caning, designed by*
Kaare Klint in 1932 and made by Rudolf Rasmussen,
cabinetmaker, Copenhagen, since then.

219. *Stick-back Windsor chair, with cow's-horn underframing, England, ca. 1820.*
(Photo: Council of Industrial Design, London)

220. *Trade card, ca. 1870, from a firm in High Wycombe, England, illustrating variations of the Windsor-type that were made in the latter half of the nineteenth century.*
(Photo: Council of Industrial Design, London)

In England, High Wycombe was the center for chair-making, a large percentage of them Windsor chairs. Though there were so-called factories in High Wycombe, chair-making was essentially a handcraft until well into the second half of the nineteenth century.[5] But the gradual industrialization could be observed in a center of this sort. It was not a sudden change, as in some industries, because furniture-making is one of the most tradition-bound industries. At an early date, the various chair parts were usually made in different shops and assembled under one roof. Auxiliary machines, such as leg-turning lathes, mechanical saws, seat-borers, bottom-adzing machines, spindle-molding machines, and, very occasionally, a steam engine to run them, were used. A broadside type of pattern book, dating from about 1870, of the firm of Edwin Skull of High Wycombe shows one of the larger firm's range of production (*Fig. 220*). One sees a few traditional forms, infinitely varied and adapted for different purposes. Often, the traditional form has been simplified and the decoration reduced or eliminated, so that the result is a useful, economical, common-sense design that can be quite elegant in form. The Windsor chair appears as the most adaptable for every conceivable variation. There are folding chairs, revolving office chairs, deck chairs, steamer chairs, high chairs, low chairs, arm chairs, side chairs, rocking chairs, stools, and benches. It is astonishing to see how many of these commercially produced chairs have the simplicity, usefulness, and gracefulness that give them the character of modern design. By and large, these were chairs for the middle and lower classes in country and town, not for the great houses, except

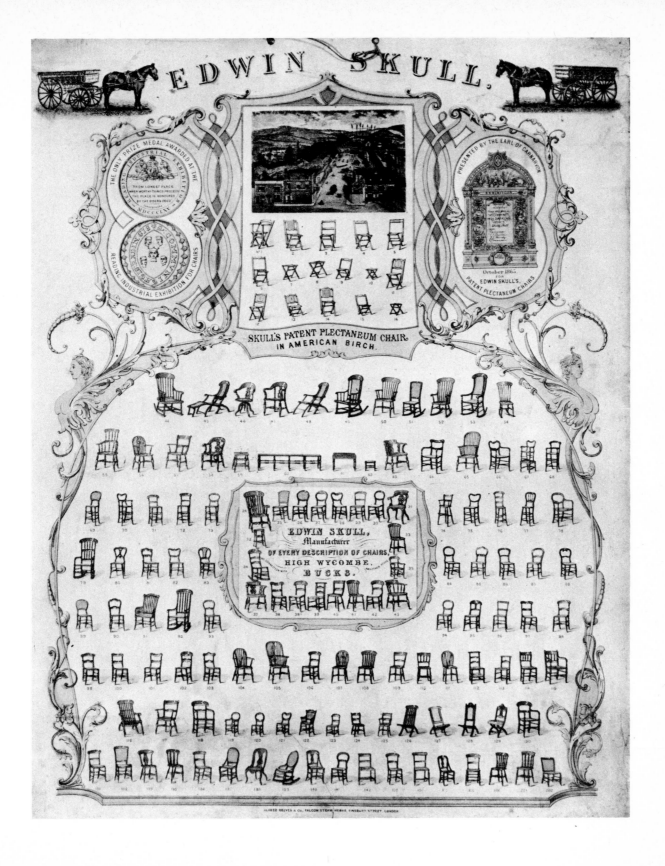

221. *Windsor chairs produced by the Sheboygan Manufacturing Co., Sheboygan, Wisconsin, in 1876.*

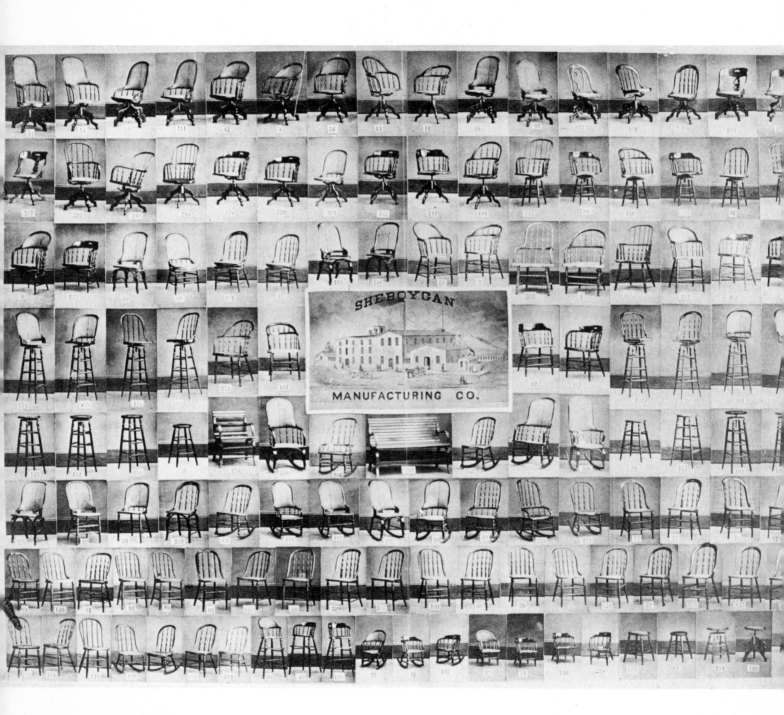

in their back rooms and service quarters, or for casual use. But the middle and working classes were an ever growing market, particularly in the rapidly expanding cities and towns, where new housing and suburbs were constantly going up.

Contemporary with the Skull broadside is a sheet from an American manufacturer, the Sheboygan Manufacturing Company of Sheboygan, Wisconsin, which is preserved in the Smithsonian Institution (*Fig. 221*). It was sent in 1876 at the Smithsonian's request by the manufacturer, and it is composed of photographs of their office chairs—all Windsor chairs. The accompanying letter states that the firm does "first-class work . . . All Bows used on our Chairs are bent and all one piece and also bent— All chairs are strong, durable, neat, tasty and easy sitting." [6] Though these chairs retained their vernacular quality by their anonymity and serviceability, they were an industrial product, and certainly the turning of the legs and spindles and the bending mentioned were machine operations. Further, many of the examples shown incorporate patented improvements that were pioneered earlier in America. Thomas Warren grasped the connection between the elegant, comfortable carriages of the day and the possibility of applying the principle to seating in general. He secured a patent for a spring-based chair in 1849, and by 1851, it was admired in London at the Crystal Palace as the latest American contribution to the cult of comfort. [7] A further advance was made a few years later, in 1853, when a patent was taken out by Peter Ten Eyck for a chair that not only rocked but pivoted and oscillated on stationary legs. It did everything the modern office chair does; the patent drawing shows these technical details applied to the form of a low-back Windsor chair. [8]

Giedion, in his *Mechanization takes Command*, concerned himself especially with such innovative furniture of the nineteenth century, furniture in which new materials and techniques were used for new purposes. He saw the work of the engineer in the multipurpose furniture, the convertible and movable pieces designed for various postures, either for ordinary comfort or for the special needs of invalids, or for special purposes, such as use in office work, typing, sewing, and in barbershops and trains. He found many examples of such American patent furniture between 1850 and 1890, some of them embodying technical innovations in an otherwise retrograde design of neo-rococo forms—as in office chairs on springs—many others finding new solutions in appropriately and uncompromisingly new forms, and still others in which there was the germ of something that came to fruition much later. At their best, these are examples of the successful fusion of technology and design and, as such, point more to the future than any of the many attempts to "wed art with industry." Where they occasionally fail is where the contrivance outruns the purpose, where the purpose could be achieved more easily and more economically without the gadget than with it, a possibility foreseen by Adam Smith, who wrote:

From a certain love of art and contrivance, we sometimes seem to value the means more than the end, and to be eager to promote the happiness of our fellow creatures rather from a view to perfect and improve a certain beautiful and orderly system than from any immediate sense or feeling of what they either suffer or enjoy. [9]

The ladder-back chair appears in as many variations as the Windsor chair, and in its simplest form it seems almost primeval. But it, too, is capable of considerable distinction. It was produced in Italy throughout the nineteenth century and was exported all over Europe (*Fig. 222*). In her admirable book on English furniture in the nineteenth century, Elizabeth Aslin reports that it was popular in England as early as the 1840's. [10] Its universal appeal can also be gauged by its appearance in the most unlikely and unexpected places. With it, the architect Karl Friedrich Schinkel furnished Charlottenhof, a small palace he built for one of the Prussian princes near Potsdam, in 1826. The princes themselves had seen the chairs in a royal villa in Naples, in 1822, on one of their stays there, and had brought the chairs to the North with them.[11] Napoleon III and the Empress Eugénie introduced it to the palaces of St. Cloud and Fontainebleau; in a series of contemporary water colors, which charmingly portray the interiors of these palaces, these light, unassuming chairs appear amidst the décor and furniture of the previous centuries, particularly of the eighteenth century, providing in the milieu of aristocratic opulence the note of simple middle-class practicality—a rather touching example of the dichotomy of the nineteenth century (*Fig. 223*). The same Chiavari chair is used in Palladio's Villa Barbaro at Maser.[12] The pedigree of locale for this modest but elegant chair is impeccable: a royal villa in Naples, a Prussian palace by Schinkel, the royal palaces of St. Cloud and Fontainebleau, and Palladio's Villa Barbaro. In a present-day version (*Fig. 224*), the Chiavari chair retains its elegant simplicity and its link with tradition.

Such traditional forms achieved a very high level of distinction and purity of form in the Shaker communities (*Figs. 225–28*). Shaker furniture had its origins in the simple country furniture of the late eighteenth and early nineteenth centuries, but it was taken beyond the ordinary utilitarian by its makers' strength of conviction. The Shakers saw in the simplicity, purity, and perfection of their environment a necessary corollary to their spiritual life. They eschewed all the ordinary luxuries and adornments of life and person and strove to live a life of order, serenity, and simplicity, imbued with moral purpose. Purity of form and perfection

of workmanship were moral obligations and reflected the spiritual. The Shakers' concern was so all-embracing that their houses, furniture, tools, and equipment have a formalized character that conveys a quiet yet cheerful serenity. The modern person feels a strange sense of peace, harmony, and well-being amidst the products of this sect, which created its finest pieces in the three or four decades before the Civil War. In spite of the separation in time, we today have a sense of kinship with the refined and perfected forms of utility, but we also feel unworthy, because we lack the purity, certainty of belief, and the disinterestedness of the makers of these objects.[13]

The true vernacular is produced and used in obscurity. The 1860's and 1870's saw the beginnings of recognition of the vernacular and its temporary rise to fashion. Even the production of the Shakers entered a new phase after the Civil War. Veritable factories were set up in several of their communities, and whereas earlier they had made furniture and utensils only for their own immediate use and always with the spiritual meaning in mind, they now enlarged their production and marketed it in the larger cities of the East Coast. A subtle difference in their forms can be discerned. The fact that they were readily obtainable, as well as light and practical, may account for their appearance in unexpected contexts. In a bedroom at *Lyndhurst*, the Gothic Villa designed by Alexander J. Davis in 1838 and enlarged in 1865, a Shaker rocker stands next to a ponderous Gothic bed. The Shaker rocker was in all probability brought there by Jay Gould, who purchased Lyndhurst in 1880. Eugene Dodd, Curator of Hancock Shaker Village in Pittsfield, Massachusetts, has written that he thinks Gould had Shaker chairs "simply because they were about the most practical kind of chair one could obtain at the time. The Shakers' own catalogues state it that way, and it's probably true." [14]

222. *The Italian side chair used by Schinkel, in 1826, in the Palace of Charlottenhof, near Potsdam.* (Deutsche Bauakademie, Berlin)

223. *Two simple Italian Chiavari chairs placed in front of the sumptuous desk created for Louis XV by Oeben and Riesener in 1760–69, in the drawing room of the Empress Eugénie in the Palace of Saint-Cloud. A water color by J.-B. Fortuné de Fournier, 1863.* (Formerly Fabius Frères, Paris. Photo courtesy Longanesi, Milano)

224. *A present-day version of the Chiavari chair, of polished cherry wood with woven cane seat. Designed by E. Rambaldi and manufactured by G. B. Marangone, Chiavari, Italy. (Courtesy Neue Sammlung, Munich. Photo: S. R. Gnamm)*

225. *Shaker ladder-back rocking chair of hickory wood, American, mid-nineteenth century. (Museum of Decorative Art, Copenhagen)*

226. *Shaker dining table, American, Hancock, Mass.,*
made before the Civil War.
(Hancock Shaker Village, Hancock, Mass. Photo:
A. J. Wyatt, Philadelphia Museum of Art)

227. *Shaker desk, American, made before the*
Civil War.
(Private collection, New York. Photo: A. J. Wyatt,
Philadelphia Museum of Art)

228. *Shaker tall chest of drawers, with cupboards,
American, Hancock, Mass., made before the Civil War.
(Hancock Shaker Village, Hancock, Mass. Photo:
A. J. Wyatt, Philadelphia Museum of Art)*

229. *Cabinet of carved oak, with panels painted in
colors on a gilt ground, probably made by
Collier and Plucknett, Warwick, England, ca. 1880.
(Courtesy Leeds City Art Galleries)*

Occasionally the simple vernacular could be made fashionable. Elizabeth Aslin has shown how an Italian marble sculpture, "The Reading Girl," by Pietro Magni, displayed at the 1862 Exhibition in London, was responsible for a vogue for simple vernacular chairs. The sculpture showed a girl sitting on a rush-bottom chair of a plain country type, made in Italy just as in England and on the rest of the Continent. The chair was commented on and recommended for use by the architect William Burges; thus, it was given approval and sanction and fashionable popularity.[15] Adolf Loos reported in 1897 that this type of chair was exported to Austria from England as an "English" chair, but he added that, of course, it was an old type also common on the Continent.[16]

In the 1860's, the firm of Morris and Co. began its production of a type of rush-seated chair found in Sussex, as well as of a simple ladder-back chair designed by Ford Maddox Brown. The Sussex chairs were copied from old village chairs and successfully retained the vernacular character; the ladder-back by Brown, though based on a cottage chair, was made into an artistic affectation by the elongation of the uprights of the back. Most of the furniture of the Morris firm did not have the light, airy qualities of these chairs but was rather solid, heavy, and embellished with painting, carving, and upholstery; it was not only very expensive and available only to a wealthy clientele but also essentially retrospective in character. Morris himself, in his writing, made a distinction between simple, utilitarian furniture and what he called ceremonial furniture:

Our furniture should be good citizen's furniture, solid and well made in workmanship, and in design should have nothing about it that is not easily defensible, no monstrosities or extravagances, not even of beauty, lest we weary of it. . . . Moreover, I must needs think of furniture as of two kinds: . . . the necessary workaday furniture . . . which should be of course both well made and well proportioned, but simple to the last degree. . . . But besides this . . . there is the other kind of what I should call state-furniture . . . I mean sideboards, cabinets, and the like . . . we need not spare ornament on these but may make them as elegant and elaborate as we can with carving, inlaying or painting; these are the blossoms of the art of furniture.[17]

The blossoms have long ago withered and proved to have had only an ephemeral life; they are today only of interest to the historian, while the workaday furniture is as useful and alive now as when it was made. That Morris himself came to regard it as too much of an aesthetic burden to be surrounded by such furniture and decoration may be gleaned from a remark he made to the poet Yeats, dispraising houses he had himself decorated: "Do you suppose I like that kind of house? I would like a house like a big barn, where one ate in one corner, cooked in another corner, slept in a third corner, and in the fourth received one's friends." [18]

Toward the end of the century, the Arts and Crafts movement produced furniture of vernacular derivation in the work of Ernest Gimson, the Barnsleys, George Walton, and Ambrose Heal, and it was then so fashionable that even Liberty's could make a chair of a refined vernacular type. The best of their work, near 1900, represents part of the more general recognition of the vernacular's qualities that marks the beginning of the modern style for the twentieth century.[19]

To this day, the furniture industry is conservative in its technology. Except for relatively few instances (such as those involving modern plastics), the industry has retained traditional materials and techniques and, often enough, traditional forms as well. There are exceptions in the nineteenth century too, particularly where metal is used. One innovator is of unusual interest because he applied new techniques to wood, the traditional material, and built an extraordinary enterprise. Just as, in the eighteenth century, Wedgwood created ceramic designs for factory production on the basis of the vernacular, giving them refined functional forms that we can only call modern, so, in the nineteenth century, Michael Thonet, a furniture-maker working in wood, took this traditional material and, using new factory techniques, created a new product. The Thonet chair was also simple, sturdy, eminently useful, and inexpensive, a product that has been in uninterrupted production since its introduction in the nineteenth century and that was as modern then as it is today. Through experimentation and development Thonet also created an industrial product, no longer with the individual charm of a hand-carved piece but with qualities of a different order, forms that were new yet so natural that they appeared timeless, and that, by virtue of their technology, were made available to countless people.[20]

Michael Thonet was born in Boppard on the Rhine in 1796 and became a furniture-maker. As early as 1830, he was experimenting with the bending of wood and making use of this technique in designing and making furniture. Long before, wood-bending had been used in the making of such furniture as the Windsor chair, as well as in shipbuilding, carriage-building, and sleigh-building, but it had in no case been turned into an industrial process.

Thonet achieved success and fame only after he moved from the Rhineland to Austria at the instigation of Prince Metternich, who had seen some of his experiments in bent wood. In 1842, the city of Vienna gave him a *Privilegium,* or patent, "to bend every kind of wood, even the most refractory, by chemico-mechanical means, into any form or curve." In establishing himself in Vienna, he was first associated with the old and famous Viennese furniture manufacturer Carl Leistler, for whom he furnished the Liechtenstein Palace in Vienna in 1842–47, his first major commission. In 1849, he severed his connection with Leistler and, with his five sons, founded his own firm. In 1853, he transferred the enterprise to them, and thereafter, it was entered under the name "Thonet Brothers."

Michael Thonet's chairs for the Liechtenstein Palace were workshop products but made with the new techniques of bending wood; the form was developed entirely out of this new technique, with a lightness and purity that puts these chairs among the most beautiful pieces of furniture in the nineteenth century (*Fig. 230*).

A set of Thonet furniture was sent to the Crystal Palace Exhibition in 1851, and, though it was handmade luxury furniture of rosewood, it also made use of wood-bending and, in its forms, foreshadows the industrial models to come (*Fig. 231*). The chairs and the settee are of an astonishing simplicity when seen amongst the more typical products shown at the Crystal Palace. There is no carving, no joining; the rods of bent wood form an open linear pattern with as few pieces as possible and these are screwed together. The seat and back are cane.

In the 1850's, Michael Thonet, the craftsman, became a pioneer industrialist. In 1856, he designed the plans for a factory in Koritschan, in Austrian Moravia, supervised its building and its equipment, and created, with his sons, the basis for mass production. He himself designed and built many of the necessary machines for a process of manufacture that is essentially simple: the strong poles of beechwood are boiled in water, then placed in the bending forms. In the forms, they are put in drying ovens for several days, until the wood is dry and retains the right shape. The factory was located not only near the raw material—beech forests—but also near cheap, unskilled vil-

230. *Chair made for the Liechtenstein Palace, Vienna, by Michael Thonet, 1843–49.*
(Photo courtesy Gebr. Thonet, Frankenberg)

231. *Armchair, bench, and chair made of bent rosewood and caning by Michael Thonet in 1851, for the Crystal Palace Exhibition in London. These pieces are of the same sparsity as some of the useful American objects displayed and had none of the grotesque ornateness of the majority of consumer goods at the Exhibition.*
(Photo courtesy Gebr. Thonet, Frankenberg)

lage labor, because professional craftsmen were no longer needed. The last technical difficulties were overcome by the use of solid wood instead of bundles of veneers, with which he had experimented earlier. The chairs were shipped knocked down, and the assembly was extremely simple by means of screws. They were light, durable, usable everywhere, and cheap.

When Michael Thonet died, in 1871, he left his sons an industry with factories scattered throughout Germany, Austria-Hungary, and Poland. By 1900, it employed more than 6,000 workers and was producing 4,000 pieces of furniture a day. Of its most famous product, the Vienna café chair, known as Chair No. 14 and first manufactured in 1859, about 50 million have been produced to date (*Figs. 232–34*).

Thonet's merit was to have designed and manufactured a mass product of undoubted aesthetic worth, a truly social product. While William Mor-

ris was expostulating about art for all the people but producing expensive pieces for wealthy patrons, the Thonet firm achieved the union of pioneering technology and a new aesthetic that resulted in an inexpensive, handsome product, truly available to the many. The Thonet chair was not usually seen in the drawing rooms of the wealthy but rather in cafés, stores, and in the homes of plain people. Where modest people might have had to make do with the "cheap and nasty," there was now made available to them furniture of enduring quality, both technically and formally.

Yet, like the Chiavari and Shaker chairs, Thonet furniture appears in the most surprising contexts. As early as about 1865, a water color by Eugène Lami shows the imposing salon in the Rothschild Château de Ferrières with a Thonet rocker.[21] The incongruity of furniture and milieu is of special irony here, because the Château de Ferrières was designed by Paxton, the designer of the Crystal

232. *Thonet production No. 14, 1859, the firm's most successful model. Here, the elements of the chair are reduced to an absolute minimum and the logic of construction made self-evident. This very inexpensive chair has been part of the international scene for over 100 years. An estimated 50 million of them have been produced to date.*
(Gebr. Thonet, Frankenberg. Photo: Pleterski Studios, Vienna)

233. *The component parts of the No. 14 chair.*
(From: Giorgio Santoro, Il caso Thonet)

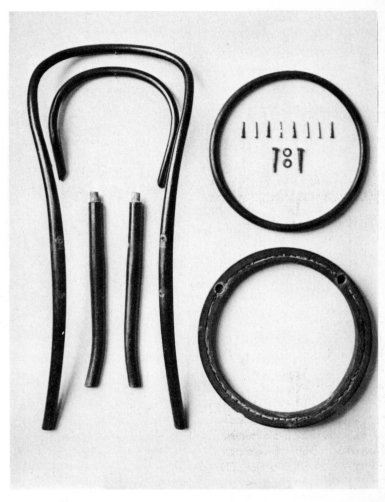

Palace, in, as Chadwick in his book on Paxton says, "an attempt to create a Third Empire clothing for a Victorian house derived from an Elizabethan plan form." [22] On the contrary, the same rocker on board ship, in a painting by J. J. Tissot called *The Last Evening* (1873), appears entirely in harmony with its surroundings (*Fig. 235*). A commentator of the Philadelphia Centennial Exhibition of 1876 writes of Thonet furniture seen there as being "exceedingly light and graceful appearing," and observes that "this furniture is especially adapted to use in summer-houses, where its lightness and coolness make it agreeable to the eye and touch." [23] Vuillard shows a Thonet rocker in a garden, in a painting (1898), in the collection of James Dugdale of Crathorne, England. [24] The appearance of the famous café chair in Toulouse-Lautrec's *Au Moulin*

Rouge (1892), in the Art Institute in Chicago, demonstrates its common use in cafés and restaurants of the time. Karl Mang, the Viennese architect and authority on Thonet history, has informed me that the two desk chairs of the Emperor Franz Joseph and the Empress Elizabeth in the summer palace at Ischl are Thonet chairs, acquired shortly before the Empress's assassination in 1898.

A catalogue sheet from about 1875 (*Fig. 236*) shows the lightness, elegance, and variety of production and, above all, the astonishing consistency of the firm's design program. Curiously, though, in the nineteenth century, this furniture was sold all over the world in great quantities, and though its designs were imitated and pirated everywhere (even the Shakers produced a bent-wood chair after they had seen one of Thonet's at the Cen-

235. *J. J. Tissot*, The Last Evening, 1873.
(Reproduced by courtesy of Guildhall Art Gallery, London)

152

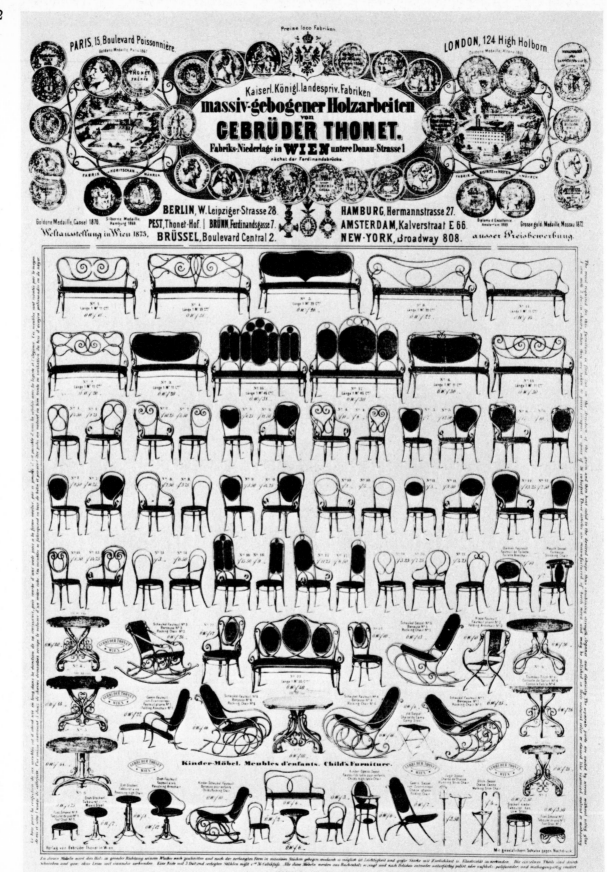

236. *From a catalogue of the Thonet firm, ca. 1875.*
This is well worth studying in detail. It shows not only
the diversity and multiplicity of the Thonet
production but also its consistency and inner logic.
Many of the models seem strikingly contemporary,
and many are antecedents of classic twentieth-
century chair solutions.
(Courtesy Gebr. Thonet, Vienna)

tennial Exhibition in Philadelphia), it stands apart from the accepted and fashionable design as well as from all "reform" design.

The premise and aim of all reform was always art and not design, and reform sought inspiration in the past, in nature, or, at most, in such exotic cultures as the Japanese,[25] but almost never in the logic of structure and use. No artistically oriented reform succeeded in producing forms of a character as timeless—or as modern—as Thonet did (*Figs. 237, 238*).

As a last comment on Thonet, it might serve to put his contribution in its proper light by comparing his work with that of John Henry Belter. Like Thonet, Belter was a German but came to America around 1844, at about the same time that Thonet went to Vienna. Belter brought with him a technique that he developed and patented in America of using bent plywood in the making of his furniture, a technique as modern and untraditional as Thonet's. However, while Thonet's designs are commensurate with his technique and have, in many cases, the timeless modern quality, the designs of Belter are of the most exuberant and luxurious rococo revival, fashionable at the time, but soon dated[26] (*Fig. 239*).

The new industrial material was metal, and it, too, was used for furniture. Cast-iron furniture, which had been made occasionally for use in the garden, was made for many uses and in many forms in the nineteenth century. Even in Prussia, where the iron industry was in its infancy, the architect Schinkel used cast iron in the first decades of the century, for both indoor and outdoor furniture, mostly in classically derived forms.[27] J. C. Loudon, in his *Encyclopaedia of Cottage, Farm and Village Architecture and Furniture*, first published in 1833, illustrated many instances of furniture and other appurtenances of the house to be made of cast iron.[28] Cheek by jowl with an ornate

"Etruscan" chair of cast iron (which he recommends be painted in imitation of oak), he illustrated a kitchen chair of a strange new form made, as was the Etruscan chair, by a Mr. Mallet (*Fig. 240a*). Its back and arms are flat, rectangular shapes of metal cast in one piece, and the arm supports and the chair legs are screwed into an iron frame under the wooden seat. Legs and arm supports are of gas tubing, used again almost exactly 100 years later by Mart Stam in the first cantilever chair.[29] As a matter of fact, the kitchen chair and a three-legged cast- and wrought-iron chair illustrated by Loudon and also made by Mallet (*Fig. 240b*) immediately evoke the 1920's and 1930's, and one cannot help but wonder whether these new forms, so different from the inherited types of furniture, were ever accepted in the 1830's. Even in the 1930's, furniture of metal tubing seemed new and, to many people, unacceptable because of the new proportions, the fear of instability, and the open linear forms so different from those one was used to in the more conventional materials. By the 1930's, the use of thin iron and steel members in building, as well as examples of metal furniture, had been in the public's eye for over 100 years; yet most people insisted on proportions and forms derived from and appropriate to the heavier, bulkier natural materials, such as wood and stone. The reporting and advocacy by Loudon in 1833 of metal furniture in new forms is therefore quite astonishing. The fact that cast-iron pieces for a multitude of purposes—from umbrella stands to chairs, tables, and other necessaries—were executed in metal and bought is not at all surprising, as long as they stayed within the accepted eclectic form language of the "ruling taste." Technology itself was enthusiastically approved and welcomed; society usually balked only when products were offered in new forms that had a kinship with technology itself.

237. *Fireplace armchair, by Michael Thonet, probably late 1860's.*
(*From the collection of John Sailer, Vienna*)

238. *A chaise-longue, by Michael Thonet, probably late 1860's.*
(*From the collection of John Sailer, Vienna*)

239. *Carved, laminated rosewood side and armchair, from a parlor suite attributed to John Henry Belter, New York, ca. 1855.*
(*Smithsonian Institution*)

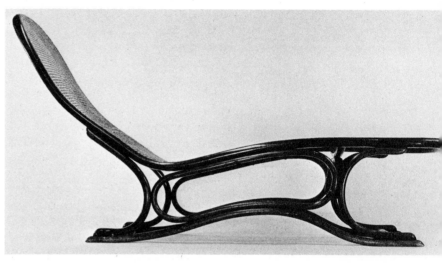

240a and b. *Two metal chairs.*
(*From: Loudon's* Encyclopaedia of Cottage, Farm, and Villa Architecture and Furniture, *London, 1833*)

241. *Rocking chair of strap brass, with gilt inlay, upholstered in plush. Made by R. W. Winfield, Birmingham, England, 1862.*
(*Courtesy of the Victoria & Albert Museum*)

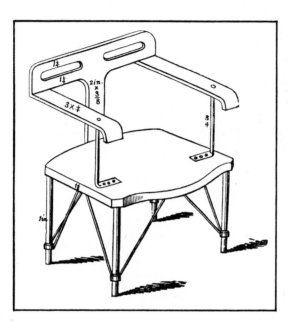

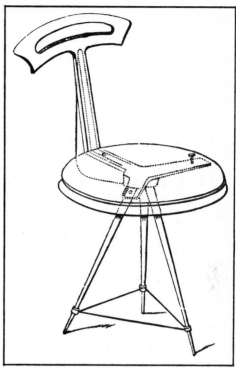

242. *Detail from a painting by Bazille,* The Artist's Family on a Terrace, *1868–69.*
(Louvre, Paris. Photo: Giraudon)

243. *Terrace of the Villa at Garches, by Le Corbusier,*
1927.
(Lucien Hervé, Paris)

Beds, in both brass and iron, are also illustrated by Loudon. Metal bedsteads were urged not only on the grounds of economy but also on the grounds of hygiene; they were therefore more easily accepted, since hygiene became an increasingly popular cause in the nineteenth century. By 1875, some 6,000 metal bedsteads were made each week in Birmingham, and their popularity became almost universal.[30] They were made in every guise, from the overornate to the most austere folding campbeds. Over many decades, until wood became popular again toward the end of the century, Heals of London, a famous bedding firm, sold very ornamental but also very simple, modern-appearing beds in brass tubing.[31] In Vienna, in 1898, Adolf Loos wrote about the English brass beds that had been imported for some years and that were liked for their "distinguished simplicity." [32]

By the mid-1800's, examples began to appear of chairs of metal straps or metal tubing and with a light, curved, linear design that had no relation to inherited forms. Since these, too, were made of a continuous, ductile material, they quite naturally often resulted in forms similar to Thonet's designs. They were obviously no longer exclusively for garden use, since many of them were upholstered; a well-known example is the rocking chair made by Peter Cooper of New York, but very similar chairs were made in England at the same time [33] (*Fig. 241*).

After the invention, in the 1860's, of the Bessemer system, which made steel economically available, this lighter, more manageable material was widely used, in the form of strap-and-sheet steel for light, graceful garden furniture, in England and particularly in France. It appears many times in its most charming forms in the paintings of the French Impressionists, and the same types have persisted in use in French gardens and public parks down to the present day [34] (*Figs. 242, 243*).

1. A copy of the 1793 edition of this exceedingly rare book is in the library of The Metropolitan Museum of Art in New York, which was kind enough to permit me to use its plates as sources of reproduction. The book was originally published by W. Brown and A. O'Neil, under the heading of the London Society of Cabinet Makers. Percy Macquoid and Ralph Edwards, *The Dictionary of English Furniture* (2d rev. ed.; London: Country Life, 1954) III, 115, report that a majority of the plates of the original edition were also issued in 1788 as *Designs for Household Furniture* under Shearer's own name. See Ralph Fastnedge, "A Leader of 18th-Century Craftsmen," *Country Life* (October 20, 1960), pp. 917–21. Fastnedge has also edited and supplied with a preface and descriptive notes a new, readily available edition of *Shearer Furniture Designs from the Cabinet-Makers' London Book of Prices 1788* (London: Alec Tiranti, 1962).

2. Ole Wanscher, *The Art of Furniture* (New York: Reinhold, 1966), p. 360; Erik Zahle, "The Arts and Crafts of the 18th and 19th Centuries," in *The Arts of Denmark,* catalogue of an exhibition organized by the Danish Society of Arts and Crafts and Industrial Design, for the United States (1960–61), p. 71.

3. The English chair of about 1800 is in the Danish Museum of Decorative Art in Copenhagen; it was acquired by the Museum in 1938 because of its similarity to Klint's, thus eliminating the possibility that it served as a model for Klint. However, I have learned from the Museum that Klint did know of another English chair of exactly the same type and date that was, and still is, privately owned in Copenhagen. (Letter of Mr. Svend Eriksen, the Museum of Decorative Art, Copenhagen, September 18, 1967.) The designer of the Morris firm chair of 1895 must have known a similar example.

4. F. Gordon Roe, *Windsor Chairs* (London: Phoenix House, 1953), pp. 21–29, 73–80; J. Stogdell Stokes, "The American Windsor Chair," *The Pennsylvania Museum Bulletin,* XXI, No. 98 (1925), 47, 55–56, plate 10; Fiske Kimball, "Thomas Jefferson's Windsor Chairs," *The Pennsylvania Museum Bulletin,* XXI, No, 98 (1925), 58–60; David Stockwell, "Wind-

sors in Independence Hall," *Antiques* (September, 1952), pp. 214–15.

5. L. J. Mayes, *The History of Chairmaking in High Wycombe* (London: Routledge & Kegan Paul, 1960), pp. 23–72. See also F. Gordon Roe, *op. cit., passim.*

6. Through the courtesy and kindness of Miss Rodris Roth, of the Division of Cultural History of the Smithsonian Institution, I received a photostatic copy of this interesting document.

7. Patent No. 6,740, September 25, 1849. *Report of the Commissioner of Patents for the Year 1849* (Washington, D.C.: 1850), p. 322; *The Industry of All Nations 1851: The Art Journal Illustrated Catalogue* (London: 1851), p. 152; *The Illustrated Exhibitor,* No. 8 (July 26, 1851), p. 140.

8. Patent No. 9,620, March 15, 1853. *Report of the Commissioner of Patents for the Year 1853* (Washington, D.C.: 1854), p. 154.

9. Adam Smith, *The Theory of Moral Sentiments* (1759; London: George Bell & Sons, 1880), Part Fourth, "Of the Effect of Utility upon the Sentiment of Approbation," p. 266.

10. Elizabeth Aslin, *Nineteenth Century English Furniture* (London: Faber & Faber, 1962), p. 26. Miss Aslin informed me by letter (April 14, 1967) that she bases her observation about the popularity of the Chiavari chair in England in the 1840's "largely on photographic evidence—chairs of this kind seem to have been stock photographer's equipment for 'carte de visite' portraits—and also on comment on the exhibitions of 1851, 1855, and 1862 when the chairs were admired but regarded as too familiar to warrant detailed criticism."

11. *Historische Möbel und Innenräume,* ed. Günther Wernitz (Berlin: Henschelverlag, 1956), p. 70, figs. 26 a-c, illustrates the chair, dates it about 1800, and locates it at Potsdam—Schloss Charlottenhof. Hermann Exner, *Kunst und Gerät* (Berlin: Verlag der Nation, 1961), pp. 48–49, illustrates the same chair and states that Schinkel furnished Charlottenhof with it. Johannes Sievers, *Karl Friedrich Schinkel, Lebenswerk: Die Möbel* (Berlin: Deutscher Kunstverlag, 1950), makes no mention of such chairs at Charlotten-

hof, but with the kind and generous help of both East and West German officials, I was able to ascertain a number of circumstances regarding these chairs. Dr. Harry Günther, of the East German administration of the State Palaces and Gardens in Potsdam, has assured me that these chairs were designed by Schinkel after Italian models. They are of palm wood, well preserved, and are at the moment in the furniture storage of the Neues Palais in Potsdam. It is presumed that they will be set up again in Charlottenhof, once restoration work in progress there is completed. Dr. Grete Kühn, of the West German administration of the State Palaces and Gardens in Berlin-Charlottenburg, was kind enough to call my attention to an article by Johannes Sievers, "Das Vorbild des 'Neuen Pavillons' von Karl Friedrich Schinkel im Schlosspark Charlottenburg," *Zeitschrift für Kunstgeschichte*, 1960, XXIII, Nos. 3–4, 227–41, which illustrates (p. 235, fig. 6) a water color of a room in the Casino Reale al Chiatamone, in Naples, with one of these Chiavari chairs very conspicuously in evidence. The Prussian king and the crown prince were visitors in this royal villa in 1822, just a few years before Charlottenhof was built, and Sievers indicates that it is likely they saw these chairs there and brought them from Italy to introduce them in their far-off Prussian palaces.

12. It appears in a series of photographs of the Villa Barbaro in the May, 1967, issue of the Swiss magazine *Du*.

13. Edward Deming and Faith Andrews, *Shaker Furniture* (New Haven, Conn.: Yale University Press, 1937); *idem, Religion in Wood* (Bloomington, Ind.: Indiana University Press, 1966).

14. The room with Gothic bed and Shaker rocker is illustrated by Nigel Nicholson, *Great Houses of the Western World* (New York: Putnam, 1965), p. 308, and also by John Pearce, "Transatlantic neo-gothic: A. J. Davis' designs for Lyndhurst, 1838–47, 1864–67," *The Connoisseur*, March, 1969, fig. 9, p. 185.

15. Aslin, *op. cit.*, pp. 39–40. The "Reading Girl" on her simple chair was again shown, though in a "diminished repetition," at the Philadelphia Centennial Exhibition in 1876: Edward Strahan, *Masterpieces of the Centennial International Exhibition 1876*, Vol. I, Fine Art* (Philadelphia: n.d.), facing p. 172.

16. Adolf Loos, "Weihnachtsausstellung im Oesterreichischen Museum" (December, 1897), in *Ins Leere Gesprochen, 1897–1900* (Innsbruck: Brenner-Verlag, 1932), p. 156.

17. William Morris, "The Lesser Arts of Life" (a lecture delivered in support of the Society for the Protection of Ancient Buildings, 1882), in *The Collected Works*, Vol. XXII, *Lectures on Art and Industry* (London: Longmans, Green, 1914), pp. 261–62.

18. In *The Autobiography of William Butler Yeats* (New York: Macmillan, 1938), p. 127.

19. W. R. Lethaby *et al., Ernest Gimson, his Life and Work* (London: Ernest Benn, 1924); Aslin, *op. cit.*, figs. 127–28; Bruce Allsopp, *Decoration and Furniture*, Vol. I, *The English Tradition* (London: Pitman & Sons, 1952), plate 116a; Gordon Russell, *The Things We See: Furniture* (West Drayton: Penguin Books, 1947), pp. 30–31.

20. Wilhelm Franz Exner, *Das Biegen des Holzes* (Weimar: B. F. Voigt, 1876); Hermann Heller, *Von der kleinen Tischlerwerkstätte zum Weltindustriehaus: Michael Thonet, der Erfinder und Begründer der Bugholzmöbel-Industrie* (Brünn: H. Heller, 1926); Giorgio Santoro, *il caso thonet* (Rome: edizioni lo scaffale, 1966). The Museum of Modern Art in New York organized an exhibition of Thonet furniture in 1953; and, in 1965, a most exemplary complete historical exhibition, entitled *Bugholzmöbel–Das Werk Michael Thonets* took place in Vienna at the Oesterreichisches Bauzentrum. The furniture in the exhibition was from the collection of John Sailer, and the exhibition itself was organized and designed by the architects Karl and Eva Mang, of Vienna. The book by Santoro is a direct result of this exhibition. A similar exhibition under the title *Form from Process—The Thonet Chair* was shown in fall and winter, 1967, at Harvard University's Carpenter Center for the Visual Arts. An excellent catalogue documenting the exhibition was prepared by Hans H. Buchwald. In 1969, Karl Mang composed a "Festschrift," *Das Haus Thonet*, in honor of the 150th anniversary of the founding of Michael Thonet's firm.

It was published 1969 by Gebrüder Thonet in Frankenberg/Eder.

21. Mario Praz, *An Illustrated History of Interior Decoration* (London: Thames & Hudson, 1964), fig. 367.

22. George F. Chadwick, *The Works of Sir Joseph Paxton 1803–1865* (London: The Architectural Press, 1961), p. 194.

23. Walter Smith, *Examples of Household Taste* (*The Industrial Art of the International Exhibition*) (New York: R. Worthington, 1880), p. 422.

24. Andrew Carnduff Ritchie, *Edouard Vuillard* (New York: The Museum of Modern Art, 1954), p. 67.

25. For example, E. W. Godwin, who has been made much of as a pioneer, has very few pieces that are simple and direct and that do not betray his exoticism as an affectation. William Watt, *Art Furniture from Designs by E. W. Godwin, and others* (London: B. T. Batsford, 1877); Dudley Harbron, *The Conscious Stone, The Life of Edward William Godwin* (London: Latimer House, 1949); Nikolaus Pevsner, "Art Furniture," *The Architectural Review*, CXI (1952), 43–50; Elizabeth Aslin, "E. W. Godwin and the Japanese Taste," *Apollo* (December, 1962), pp. 779–84.

26. See Clare Vincent, "John Henry Belter's Patent Parlour Furniture," *Furniture History*, III (1967), 92–99, plates 25, 26.

27. Johannes Sievers, *Karl Friedrich Schinkel, Lebenswerk, Die Möbel* (Berlin: Deutscher Kunstverlag, 1950), pp. 40 ff., and plates 51, 54, 56, 61–65, 228.

28. J. C. Loudon, *Encyclopaedia of Cottage, Farm and Village Architecture and Furniture* (London: Frederick Warne, 1844), pp. 318–21, figs. 640, 650, 651.

29. Variously dated as 1926 and 1927. Illustrated by Adolf G. Schneck, *Der Stuhl* (Stuttgart: Julius Hoffmann, 1937), p. 58, fig. 103; Sigfried Giedion, *Mechanization Takes Command* (New York: Oxford University Press, 1948), p. 503, fig. 329; Gustav Hassenpflug, *Stahlmöbel* (Düsseldorf, Verlag Stahleisen, 1960, p. 17, fig. 21.

30. Aslin, *Nineteenth Century English Furniture*, p. 44.

31. The firm of Messrs. Heal & Son were most kind and patient in permitting me to study their library of old catalogues of the firm, going back to the middle of the last century, and, further, in supplying me very generously with photographs of catalogue pages and actual pieces.

32. Adolf Loos, "Der Neue Stil und die Bronze-Industrie" (1898), in *Ins Leere Gesprochen*, p. 30.

33. A rocking chair of metal tubing was shown at the Crystal Palace by R. W. Winfield of Birmingham in 1851: *Official Descriptive and Illustrated Catalogue of the Great Exhibition 1851*, supplementary volume (London: 1852), plate 380. Miss Aslin, *Nineteenth Century English Furniture*, fig. 50, illustrates two examples from the 1860's. Peter Cooper's chair, which is now in the Museum of the Cooper Union in New York, is illustrated in Celia Jackson Otto, *American Furniture of the Nineteenth Century* (New York: Viking Press, 1965), fig. 307.

34. H. R. Schubert, "The Steel Industry," in Charles Singer *et al.*, *A History of Technology* (Oxford: Clarendon Press, 1958), V, 53–71, especially 61 ff.; Hassenpflug, *op. cit.*, pp. 10–12. See Vuillard's *The Park* (1894), and *Woman Reading in a Garden* (1898), Ritchie, *op. cit.*, pp. 37 and 66; Manet's *Concert at the Tuileries* (1862), Robert Rey, *Manet* (Paris: Hyperion Press, 1938), p. 98.

7 Recognition and Vindication

Submerged and obscured in the nineteenth century, the functional tradition survived as a constant, as almost a natural force, and this book has offered evidence to correct our view and estimate of the century in this respect. Though generally overlooked, the functional form was occasionally glimpsed and its virtues and values noted. However, such recognition had no important consequence until near the century's end, when function began to be seen as the basis for a new style. Nevertheless, the important point is that it *did* exist and that it transmitted, though in obscurity, to the twentieth century the values of functional fitness that became the foundation for modern design. Horatio Greenough's clarion call for functional form found little echo until taken up by Louis Sullivan and Frank Lloyd Wright. The visions of others remained hesitant, confused, and contradictory, because they lacked Greenough's independence and his ability to see principles applied unconditionally. Yet, citing occasional revolts against the Victorian ruling taste is as corrective as examples of functional design.

The most notable occasion is that of the Great Exhibition of the Industry of All Nations that took place in London in 1851 and that is usually referred to as the Crystal Palace Exhibition. After almost a century of headlong industrialization, which had brought tremendous changes in every aspect of life, this was the first moment of stocktaking; it afforded an unprecedented opportunity for observing, comparing, and criticizing. The whole dichotomy of a bourgeois society performing miracles in the rational creation of science, industry, and commerce but surrounding itself with senseless bric-a-brac and overornamented designs in the home sphere comes sharply into focus in this undertaking, which was designed to sum up the achievements of the age at mid-century.

The building in which the Exhibition took place, Joseph Paxton's Crystal Palace, afforded a striking contrast with the bulk of the material shown within. Many contemporary illustrations of the Great Exhibition show the contrast between the rational elements of the structure itself—geometric, light, thin, reduced to a minimum of bulk, perfectly clear and unambiguous in their function—and the heavy, ornate, bulky character of so much of what was exhibited. And, if one goes beyond the first impression of amusement at the quaintness of so much of the Victorian design displayed and the surprise of the totally different character of the Crystal Palace itself, one can also discover exhibited items that have the same rational, functional character as the building in which they were shown. As a group, the manufacturing machines and tools stood out for the drama of their presentation. One foreign observer called this section "a veritable acting industrial encyclopaedia"; [1] in fact, it was found the most exciting by many who came, and even Queen Victoria herself, of whom one would least expect an aesthetic appreciation of machines, wrote in her journal, after one of her visits to the Exhibition, that she had found "the machinery part . . . excessively interesting and instructive," and she was filled "with admiration for the greatness of man's mind," which could devise "the most beautiful machinery." [2]

In the transportation section, the functional forms of carriages from Britain and America caused much favorable comment, as did the locomotives, fire engines, ship models, and naval mechanisms in the same section. Some consumer goods showed rational forms—musical instruments from France and Germany, a few pieces of furniture from Vienna. Where these are illustrated in the catalogue and other contemporary publications on the Exhibition, they stand out as white ravens amid the

161

often monstrous and useless forms of the rest, giving us the feeling of recognizing their modern form over the passage of time.

Of many more modest items that one might term industrial vernacular, there are almost no illustrations. Many Sheffield razors, scissors, knives, and other utensils made totally unusable by the excess of their "artistic" decoration are illustrated in the catalogue, while the simple, useful cutlery, also sent by Sheffield manufacturers, was deemed too uninteresting, too utilitarian to be illustrated, and was merely listed in the catalogue.

Many of the modest items were American "notions"; in fact, the entire character of the American contribution differed markedly from that of most other nations. America sent simple, practical, cheaply manufactured goods—from the McCormick reaper to pails, boots, guns, axes, and other tools—while most other countries had sent their most elaborate luxury products. The very plainness of the American contribution tended at first to call for ridicule on the part of European journals and observers, until second thought toward the close of the exhibition brought forth a more just appreciation. A German observer noting the snide remarks in the British press wrote:

What's all the joking about? The American products are in harmony with the industrious people who sent them, in accord with the progressive civilization which is at home there, more directed to use than to decoration. The first task of the American is to find out how he can till the soil to his best advantage, how to cross the ocean with the greatest safety and speed, how he can furnish his home with the greatest practicality and economy, and how he can further and spread education. In all these areas our transatlantic brothers occupy an enviable position and they can afford to laugh at the criticism of those who stand still or go backward, because they will progress with tearing speed. . . . Of course the Americans don't need to rely on symbols. Their whole exhibition unconsciously shows the state of their culture. They don't pretend to be any better than they are. Just as the products are shown matter-of-factly and modestly—they give a true picture of the country and its people.[3]

In the official report of the commissioners of the Exhibition, there was a supplementary report on design, written by Richard Redgrave, in which he stated that it was "unfortunate that . . . the ornamental so largely prevails to the exclusion of the useful." Though he wrote with the understood assumption that decoration is a good and necessary part of design, he rejected the overwhelming mass of it shown at the Crystal Palace as meretricious, applied without reference to the underlying form (which he called "construction"), and with no thought to use or purpose. He wrote that this "is apt to sicken us of decoration, and lead us to admire those objects of absolute utility (the machines and utensils of various kinds), where use is so paramount that ornament is repudiated, and, fitness of purpose being the end sought, a noble simplicity is the result."[4] It is characteristic that there is no indication in his writing that he would have deemed it appropriate to apply this "noble simplicity" to anything but "objects of absolute utility."

Gottfried Semper, a German architect living as a political exile in Britain, also pointed out, in a little book of comment on the Exhibition: "Only objects in which seriousness of purpose does not permit superfluities, such as carriages, weapons, musical instruments, occasionally show more soundness in the perfection and nobility of their forms, strictly prescribed by function."[5]

The Times, of course, constantly wrote about the Exhibition while it was in progress, and some of the most interesting comments appeared in its columns. On July 1, 1851, a lengthy article appeared castigating the shortcomings in the design of pottery, textiles, metalwork, and other consumer goods, and stating that "the greatest atrocities in taste are committed; all reliance upon the materials employed and the purpose they are intended to serve, seems to be thrown overboard," but goes on to say that

some sections, and especially that of machinery, feeling their pre-eminence secure and undoubted, have been content to be plain and unpretending, in consequence of which they develop a high degree of artistic excellence. The most refined taste will gather pleasure and satisfaction from a survey of our machinery department; for there, in the forms and the arrangements, strict attention to the proprieties and requirements of each machine might be readily traced. The only beauty attempted is that which the stringent application of mechanical science to the material world can supply; and in the truthfulness, perseverance, and severity with which that idea is carried out, there is developed a style of art at once national and grand.

But after his entirely understanding and sympathetic analysis of the qualities of functional design that resulted in a style "at once national and grand," this writer did not dare, either, to expect such qualities of objects of daily use. He continued, "We do not for a moment contend that the unbending precision which produces such great results in the cases quoted, would be equally applicable to the manufactured products made available for our every day and domestic wants and comforts." [6]

After the Exhibition was over and one could look to the future, another journal had the confidence to predict that the direction "ornamental art" would henceforth take would be toward simplicity, basing its opinion "on the close alliance of *utility* and *simplicity*, and the character of our race. This character may be overlaid at times by periodical fashions and temporary influences. There is, however, the strong subcurrent beneath, that shows itself partially and occasionally, and asserts its power by its onward progress." [7]

The subcurrent of utility and simplicity was, of course, that of the vernacular, both on its traditional handcraft level and also in its permutation as industrial vernacular. Unfortunately, the overlay of periodical fashions and temporary influences remained strong for a long time to come. If one looks for the evidence of the existence of the simple utilitarian products in the catalogues of the many succeeding international exhibitions, one finds them listed, but rarely illustrated, while the fashionably elaborate, the romantically artistic, is copiously illustrated each time, right down to the Paris Exposition of 1900, and allows for very little difference or improvement over the Crystal Palace of 1851. Yet, it was at subsequent exhibitions late in the century that functional design was discovered and its principles proclaimed as exemplary for "modern" design, not only for "objects of absolute utility," but for all design.

The last decades of the nineteenth century represented an end phase and a new beginning. On a broad front and in all the arts, the inherited and still widely prevalent academic values and ideals—the formula, the dogma, narrative representation, artificiality, and sentimentality—were attacked and increasingly challenged by the new realities and the desire on the part of artists to express them truthfully and honestly. In all areas and all fields, there was a revulsion against sham and imitation and a passionate search for the essence, the real, the substantive rather than the appearance. The overriding conviction of artists was that a work of art finds its justification within itself and is independent of any other significance.

Because one of the chief demands of the time was that all aspects of life should be imbued with the new morality, the new truthfulness, design was a most important aspect of this renewal. It was felt by many that since the home and its furnishings had shown the greatest degradation in design, this was where the most improvement was needed; it was the area of greatest responsibility, because so many people were directly affected by it. So strongly did many painters feel this responsibility that they abandoned painting as "selfish" and "individualistic" and devoted their lives to the design of architecture and everyday things. Peter Behrens and Henry van de Velde are the most famous of these; Richard Riemerschmid, Otto Eckmann, and Koloman Moser are others.

A renewal of design could take two directions: It could either be the task of creative artists and result in striking, imaginative new shapes and forms designed by a small number of gifted men; or it could seek the essence in the objective functional form and thereby reveal and vindicate its existence in the vernacular and more technical realms. In the one it would mean fleeting, personal, artistic expression, individually created for a few; in the other, recognition of the validity of rational type forms, peculiarly appropriate to industry and mass production.

In the event, both approaches were used concurrently; the former resulted in the brief triumph and flowering of the style we call Art Nouveau; the latter, far less observed, quietly instated the functional tradition as the accepted norm and thereby laid the foundation for the modern style of a few decades later. The German Art Nouveau artist-designer Hermann Obrist recognized these two possible approaches and wrote about them, in 1901, in an essay significantly entitled "Functional or Imaginative?" ("Zweckmässig oder Phantasievoll?"). He championed the imaginatively creative against the functional vernacular, which to him meant English design. He found the matter-of-fact vernacular unsatisfying and asked for material and psychic luxury in design. In 1903, he wrote again about the two approaches, but by then he seemed to have recognized that the Art Nouveau had run its course and produced nothing but a flood of

"decorative art," while the functional approach had not been given a sufficient chance, though he thought it would produce "noble, enduring forms." [8] The conflict between creativity and design came out again as late as 1914, on the occasion of the meeting in Cologne of the German *Werkbund*, in what might be called a historic debate on design between Henry van de Velde and Hermann Muthesius. Muthesius argued for standardization of production, for the creation of "type-forms," while van de Velde maintained that the artist would never subject himself to standardization and would forever reject any suggestion of a canon of design.[9] It is characteristic of the critical period around the turn of the century that the two approaches sometimes overlap or contradict each other in one and the same person, and that the individuals involved are blind to the camp in which their own true nature puts them, their words praising one and their deeds demonstrating the other. Henry van de Velde, for example, wrote frequently of the functional form, of his love and appreciation of the vernacular, and of the necessity for the mass production of goods, but he was an artist first and last. He was long considered, especially by himself, a towering figure in the genesis of modern design. But, though he claimed major responsibility for the formation of the modern style—especially in his autobiography, written toward the end of his life near the middle of the twentieth century— in his heart and in reality he belonged to the Art Nouveau and to its essentially individualistic nineteenth-century outlook.[10]

The ambiguity of van de Velde's position is stressed in two recent publications: The Dutch scholar Abraham Hammacher, in his *Die Welt Henry van de Veldes,* points out that only in 1913 did van de Velde develop doubts about ornamentation and that it took another full ten years before he fought his way through to the *forme*

244. *Glass case from the barbershop Haby, in Berlin, the interior of which van de Velde designed in 1901. The base of this case is by van de Velde and shows his typically curved, expressive, dynamic line, while the top is of English manufacture and shows the plain matter-of-factness that was so admired by Muthesius. The curious circumstance of this combination thus shows, in one object, the two opposed tendencies in design in the years around the turn of the century. (Courtesy Staatliche Kunstsammlungen, Weimar. Photo: Louis Held)*

pure;[11] Karl-Heinz Hüter, in his book on van de Velde, writes about the ambivalence between the aesthetic and functional tendencies that characterized the movement around the turn of the century in general and van de Velde's work in particular. This conflict is brought out specifically, for example, in van de Velde's designs for furniture, where "the ornamental principle is the motivating force," in spite of the fact that he wished to go beyond the ornamental (*Fig. 244*); it is also brought out in his designs for ornamental textiles and wallpapers, in which there is no "functional" or "constructive" reason for ornament.[12] His intellectual considerations go in one direction, with much talk of function and construction and the rejection of added ornamentation; but, in practice, almost all his work before World War I is ornamented and artistically expressive rather than *sachlich,* or functional; he speaks about the social aspects of design, saying that something not made for all is no good at all; yet, all his practical work—as did Morris's—reached only a very small group of wealthy clients.

A design created about 1912 by van de Velde for silver flatware (*Fig. 245*) is exceptional, for this artist at this date, for its calm, pure form. It makes a fascinating comparison with silver designed about 1900 by the Munich architect and designer Richard Riemerschmid (*Fig. 246*). Van de Velde's pure form is timeless, it has the quality of much eighteenth-century silver but would also cause no surprise today; Riemerschmid's design, of unquestionable aesthetic merit, is yet inescapably marked as belonging to the fleeting moment of Art Nouveau.

If one is concerned with longer trends, it appears that the Art Nouveau was a side issue, a momentary fashion created by enthusiastic artist-designers in response to the urge to reject all imitative forms and create something new. A student of

245. *Silver flatware designed by Henry van de Velde ca. 1912. Manufactured by Court Jeweler Theodor Müller, Weimar.*
(Courtesy Neue Sammlung, Munich. Photo: S. R. Gnamm)

246. *Dinner, butter, and cheese knives. Designed by Richard Riemerschmid, ca. 1900, manufactured by the Deutsche Werkstätten. The ambivalence of design and designers at the turn of the century is demonstrated by a comparison of Riemerschmid's silver with his chair of 1899 (Fig. 275) which is perfectly timeless and shows no trace of Art Nouveau.*
(Courtesy Neue Sammlung, Munich. Photo: S. R. Gnamm)

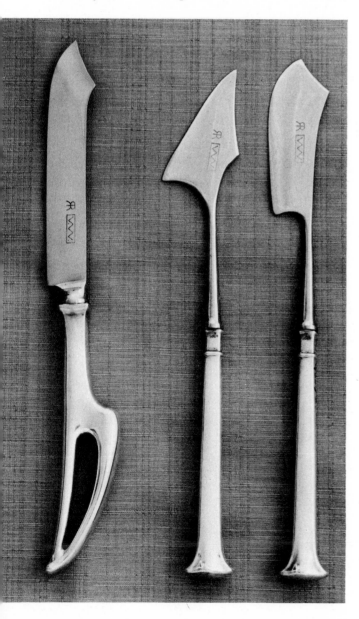

mine wrote recently, a bit naïvely but quite aptly, "The Art Nouveau was in some ways a step forward yet to the side." To say that it was a passing fashion is not to say that it did not have analogies and sources in the past—as Stephan Tschudi-Madsen, in his *Sources of Art Nouveau*,[13] and Robert Schmutzler, in his *Art Nouveau*,[14] have abundantly shown. That its fleeting and superficial character was seen by many, both then and now, may be gleaned from Jost Herman's excellently annotated bibliographical account, *Jugendstil*.[15]

It also appears that the same urge for honesty and reality and the search for the essence of things was, in the long run, even more favorable to the long-obscured functional tradition. The demand for the genuine and the real brought to light what had hitherto been glimpsed only by isolated individuals. Functional design was recognized as a constant, as valid for the coming century as for any other time, and in the early 1900's, recognition of its principles was more and more often coupled with its application in practice. It is largely the distinction of Germany to have recognized the significance of the functional tradition and to have made it the foundation of design in the first half of the twentieth century. In reaction against the successive and compulsive style-imitations and adaptations, one saw in the functional tradition the archetypes for a modern form, timeless and styleless—*beyond* style. The functional form came into honor in this brief period before World War I.

The choice between decorative and functional, between what we call Art Nouveau and the objective approach of *Sachlichkeit*, was also a social one. Those who were interested in design and were searching for modern solutions were conscious of the social aspects. They were no longer interested in romantic, individual luxury creations for artistocrats but wanted to improve the common consumer product. Machines and industry were no longer anathema to them, as they had been to the earlier reformers, but useful instruments in liberating man from the feudal pattern of privileged consumption and enabling him to tackle the problem of a just distribution of the social product. Aesthetic values were no longer exclusively looked for in art and the pseudo-art of hypercharged "artistic" design, but rather were sought in practical aspects of modern life, that is, in the functional. There is a corresponding shift in materials: Where exotic woods, gilt bronze, plush, and marble (real or fake) had been preferred, one now finds chrome, iron, glass, and simple woods. There is a socializing component in the climate of the time that finds its tasks in the betterment of the community rather than in the private satisfactions of a few. In architecture, the primary projects are no longer monuments for heroes and palaces for the rich, but workers' housing, factories, department stores, and public buildings of utility and common welfare, in which there is no room for exaggerated individualism. Rather than utopians and dreamers of the past, there now come to the fore individuals and associations whose concern is the immediate present and its actualities and needs.

One of the most important of the associations—on an ideological as well as a practical level—was the German *Werkbund,* an organization founded in 1907, on the urging and under the sponsorship of Muthesius, to promote "good design." Though its influence and importance were immeasurably greater in the decades between the two world wars, it started its career with a call for quality—material, technical, and functional quality—and the unity of these qualities in an aesthetic formal whole. From the start, it set standards by these demands and by the work of its chosen members—such men as Peter Behrens, Josef Hoffmann, Josef Olbrich, Bruno Paul, Richard Riemerschmid, later,

Walter Gropius, and eventually, every other name associated with modern design in the following crucial decades. Though marked by epoch-making modern works and words from the beginning, there was at first, in the *Werkbund,* too, a strong emphasis on arts and crafts and on the contribution of the *artist* to design. This can be seen as late as 1924 in the objects of a *Werkbund* exhibition entitled "Form." The illustrations in the catalogue, which was given the title "Form Without Ornament," show much that was truly "form without ornament" but also a surprising amount that can only be called "form *as* ornament" (*Fig. 247*). Considering the fervor of many *Werkbund* members for the pure functional form, this can only be regarded as a concession to the human frailty of weaker members. Nevertheless, the *Werkbund* was one of the most important catalyzing agents for the realization of the modern, functional style in the twentieth century.[16] Its ideas were not autogenous but grew out of the already awakened interest in, and enthusiasm for, functional design that had developed in the latter decades of the nineteenth century and around the turn of the century.

The occasions for the first pronouncements of the discovery of a "new" kind of design by Europeans on seeing English and American products in juxtaposition with European products were the Centennial Exposition in Philadelphia in 1876, the Paris Exposition of 1878, and, even more, the World's Columbian Exposition in Chicago in 1893. Observers from commercially and industrially expanding Germany were particularly impressed by the differences they saw in English and American design, which they defined as an adherence to rational derivation of form from function. Jurors, commissioners, and German museum directors were unanimous in their admiration for tools and hardware. Again and again, axes, hayforks, rakes, hoes,

247. *Tea service of brass, designed by Josef Hoffmann, made by the Wiener Werkstätte, Vienna, 1920's. (Vienna, Austrian Museum for Applied Arts)*

169

bowie knives, and other tools were praised as having been rethought and redesigned in intelligent forms that made European tools look antiquated and clumsy. The same tools evoked intense aesthetic pleasure, and their beauty was compared with that not only of sophisticated works of art but of prehistoric tools of stone and bronze.

In fact, even on the occasion of the Crystal Palace, a German visitor wrote, "The American ax with its widened grip, which makes it impossible for the handle to slip out of the hand, with its strongly curved iron blade, which will not stick even in the hardest wood, with its correct balance, this ax is decidedly a work of art." [17] At the 1876 Centennial it was again the tools that excited admiration from foreigners: "The hatchets, hoes, axes, hunting knives, wood knives, sugar cane knives, garden knives, etc., are of a variety and beauty which leave us speechless with admiration." [18] they are "instruments of genius, . . . on

every hand we are met with the results of serious research and we are astonished to see how much our own well known tools could be improved." Or, "Again and again we see examples of how American industry in its progress breaks with all tradition and takes new paths which seem to us fantastic," and then the observer cites the use of paper for barrels and for boats like the kayaks of the Eskimos. [19]

On the occasion of the Paris Exposition of 1878, Julius Lessing, director of the Berlin Kunstgewerbemuseum, wrote that, although, hitherto all nations, including the English, had tried to find new artistic forms by adapting old ones, the English were now beginning to strike out on a new path by deriving the form of their utensils strictly from modern construction. Not a few, but many, objects show this trend, he wrote and, together with spiritually related American products, they show the germ of a new and essentially modern kind of

248. *Wall telephone, with Strowger Automatic Dial, made in 1900. A. B. Strowger, of Kansas City, invented the first successful automatic telephone exchange and filed for a patent in 1889. The earliest public exchange worked on this system was opened at La Porte, Ind., in 1892.*
(Lent to the Science Museum, London, by G.P.O. London)

design. He went on to cite ships and carriages, saying that their construction was independently arrived at, without preconceptions, and was a genuine product of our time. He saw design from construction, especially in American tools, where this form principle was elevated to real linear beauty. "I can assure you that a wall showing American axes and hayforks filled me with the same intense aesthetic pleasure as highly developed works of art. I was most astonished to see how from the simplest consideration of ease of handling, from the sympathetic junction of utensil with human hand and body, a high degree of linear beauty is arrived at without a trace of ornament." He cited their similarity with prehistoric tools in stone and bronze.[20] Very similar thoughts filled him when, in an official capacity, he visited the Chicago Exhibition of 1893. In his report to the German government he wrote:

The construction of the utensil from its function means in some cases the abandonment of artistic form, but in most cases it results in pleasing new forms which correspond in high measure to the spirit of our mechanical age. This principle has for long determined completely, both in Europe and America, the design of carriages and ships in which applied decoration has been banned completely and beauty is sought for and found solely in the convincing constructive line. In America this principle has also taken over completely in the design of tools, hammers, axes, hatchets, chisels, hoes and rakes, which remind one in the most remarkable way of the finds in prehistoric graves; like them, they have the highest degree of utilitarian simplicity and thereby a singular beauty which satisfies the eye in the best sense without the help of any ornamental additions.[21]

Lessing continued to state his opinions:

Here we have utensils created in the same spirit as our iron structures, our ships and carriages; utensils whose forms are derived from material and technique with no thought to precedent. They are developed with such

249. *The Pope's telephone, ca. 1900.*
(Courtesy German Postal Museum, Frankfurt)

250. *"Grasshopper" send-receive key, 1899.*
(Lent to the Science Museum, London, by the
Marconi Wireless Telegraph Co. Ltd.)

clarity that they no longer appeal by way of the calculating reason, but directly to the senses and present to our eyes that pure and satisfying pleasure which we experience as beauty . . . Here construction has changed our concept of beauty in its innermost core [22] (*Figs. 248–58*).

Similar remarks are made by Wilhelm Bode, director of the Art Museum in Berlin, and also very much interested in design. After his own visit to Chicago, he wrote: "Common to all American design is its striving to derive form from function, to construct it entirely in accord with its use; . . . It is because American furniture is so 'practical,' because its silverware and its ironwork are so appropriate to use, that we find them beautiful, that they are beautiful." [23]

By the 1890's, America was a consumer society that had a vast array of available goods. Department stores were an established part of the urban American way of life, and now Sears, Roebuck & Co. came on the scene to supply rural as well as urban America with all its necessities and superfluities. Not long ago, the 1897 edition of the Sears, Roebuck mail-order catalogue was reissued in facsimile, and it affords a fascinating glimpse of the incredible variety of goods poured out by the cornucopia of American industry at that time. The Sears catalogue was directed at a mass market, and it contains all the best and the worst of it. In articles where "taste" was expected, one finds much that was horrendously ugly: overdecorated monstrosities that were offered to ensure gentility. But where taste did not seem to be involved, there were many marvels of pure, unaffected, functional design, praised by the huckster catalogue for quality of material, workmanship, and performance, in language worthy of the *Werkbund* (*Figs. 259–61*). Of course, the articles, while practical, were often quite modest. While Whiteley's, a similar British mail-order house in London, cater-

251. *Kenco battery fan, manufactured by Knapp Electrical Novelty Co., New York.*
(From Electrical World, 1906)

252. *Gramaphone, 1898. Parts manufactured in America by Berliner Gramaphone Co., assembled by Gramaphone Co., in England.*
(Lent to the Science Museum, London, by the Gramaphone Co. Ltd.)

253. *"Rapid" computer, 1892.*
(British Crown Copyright. Science Museum, London)

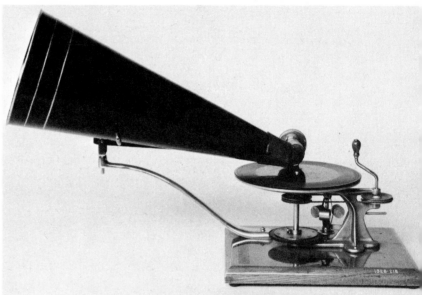

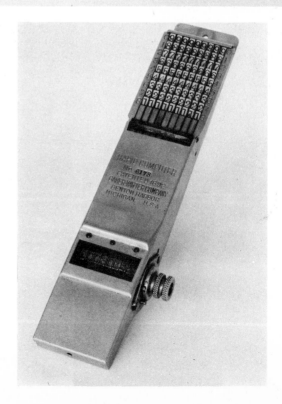

254. Two cast-bronze bell-push buttons, from a catalogue of the Manhattan Electrical Supply Co., ca. 1900.

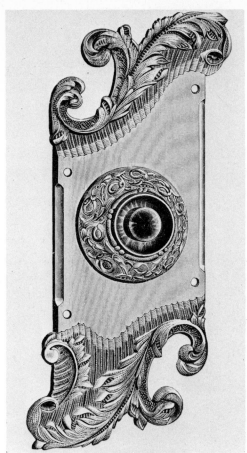

ing to the Empire, would offer, at appropriate prices, handsome, smooth silver match and cigarette boxes, Sears would offer, at 25c, a celluloid soapbox of a very similar and equally fine and simple shape. The English offered beautiful picnic sets of Sheffield cutlery in boxes of fine leather, while Sears offered equally beautiful, but differently so, light oval baskets of woven splint at 27c or whole camping outfits at $6.50. Sears's buggies of the most wonderful slimness and elegance cost $29.90 to $46.90; a Windsor bow-back kitchen chair sold at 34c, and a set of six for $2.00; the so-called Vienna dining chair cost $1.75, and a set of six sold for $10.20. While Whiteley's was the British Empire's "Universal Provider," which sounds vaguely like God, Sears called itself the "Cheapest Supply House on Earth." In the Sears catalogue there were ice skates, lemon squeezers and bootjacks, shears, scissors and pocket knives, bicycles and hunting skiffs, opera glasses, spyglasses and compasses, cameras, telephones and trombones, flutes, fifes and flageolets—all of simple, functional design, the industrial vernacular indeed.

The English background and achievement in design (*Figs. 262–66*) were studied and reported on by Hermann Muthesius, a German architect who had spent several years in England, attached to the embassy in an official capacity as observer of English architecture. He returned to Germany in 1903 and commenced to publish voluminously on English architecture and design, concerning himself directly and actively in the renewal of architecture and design in Germany. His three-volume work on the English house, *Das Englische Haus,* published in 1904–5, attests not only to his enthusiasm and understanding of the background of the modern movement as it had developed in England but also to his encyclopaedic knowledge of every aspect of design related to the house and its furnishings in England.

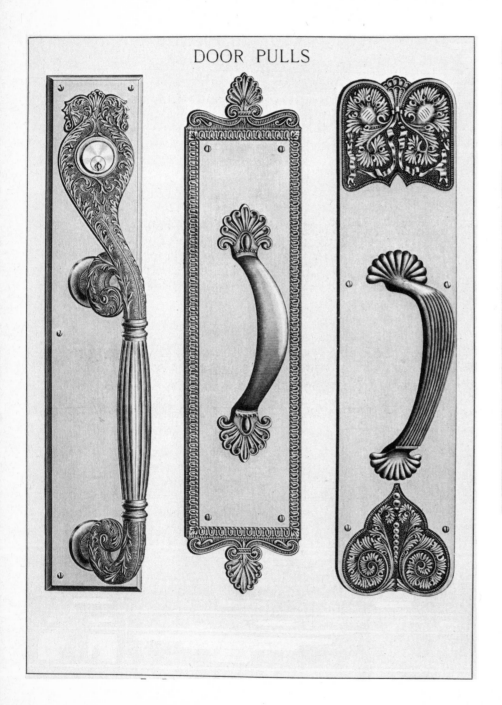

DOOR PULLS

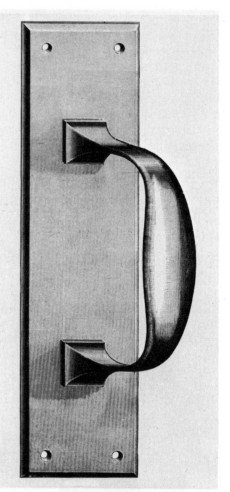

256 a and b. *From an 1889 catalogue of*
E. S. Greeley & Co., New York.

257. *Various portable and adjustable lamps that*
appeared in the Electrical World in 1906.

258. *Adjustable lamp with metallic shades, invented*
and manufactured by E. D. Cooke, Chicago.
(From Electrical World, *1894)*

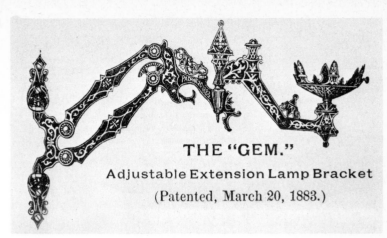

THE "GEM."
Adjustable Extension Lamp Bracket
(Patented, March 20, 1883.)

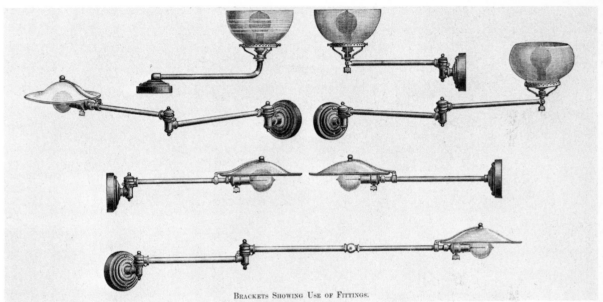

BRACKETS SHOWING USE OF FITTINGS.

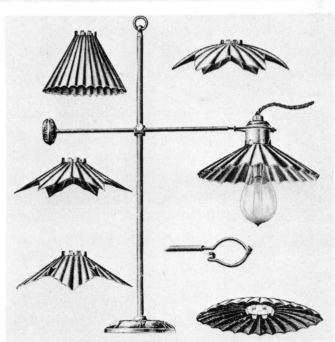

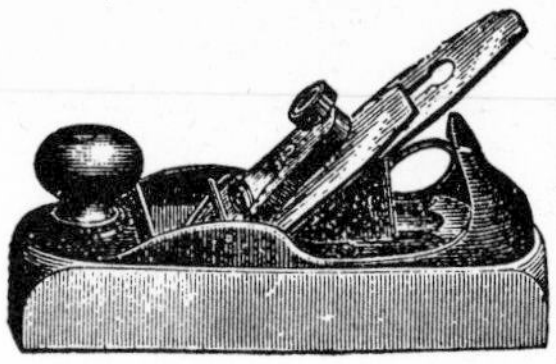

No. 12466. The Genuine Bailey Wood Smooth Plane, No. 22; length, 8 inches; 1¾-inch cutter; weight, 2¾ lbs. Price, each.......**76c**

No. 12467. An imitation of the above plane; weight, 2¾ lbs. Price, each, **70c**

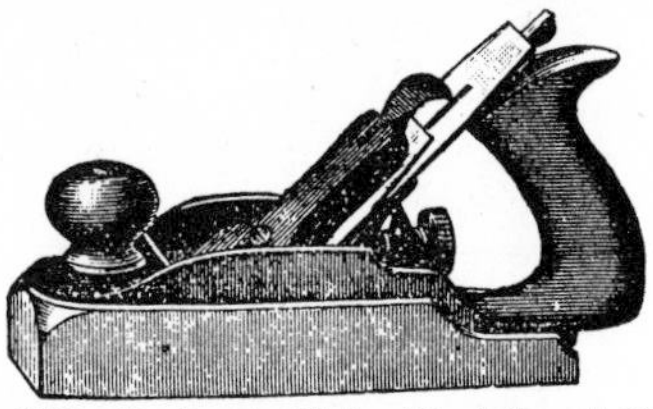

No. 12468. The Genuine Bailey Wood Smooth Plane, with handle, No. 35; length, 9 inches; 2-inch cutter; weight, 3½ lbs. Price, each.......................... **95c**

No. 12469. An imitation of the above plane: weight, 3½ lbs. Price, each.................................**90c**

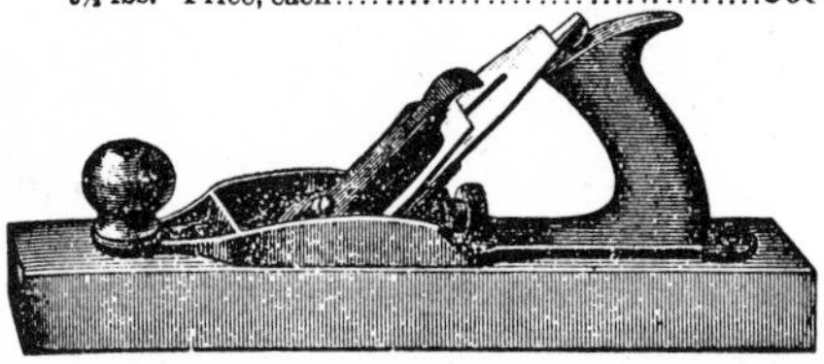

No. 12470. The Genuine Bailey Wood Jack Plane No. 27; length, 15 inches; 2⅛-inch cutter; weight, 4 lbs. Price, each...**96c**

No. 12471. An imitation of the above plane; weight, 4 lbs. Price, each...................................**90c**

No. 12472. The Genuine Bailey Wood Fore Plane, No. 29; length, 20 inches; 2⅜-inch cutter; weight, 5¾ lbs. Price, each.......................................**$1.05**

No. 12473. An imitation of the above plane; weight, 5¾ lbs. Price, each..............................**$1.00**

No. 12474. The Genuine Bailey Wood Jointer Plane, No. 32; length, 26 inches; 2⅜-inch cutter; weight, 7¼ lbs. Price, each.................................**$1.23**

No. 12475. An imitation of the above plane; weight, 7¼ lbs. Price, each..............................**$1.15**

Stanley Wood Planes.

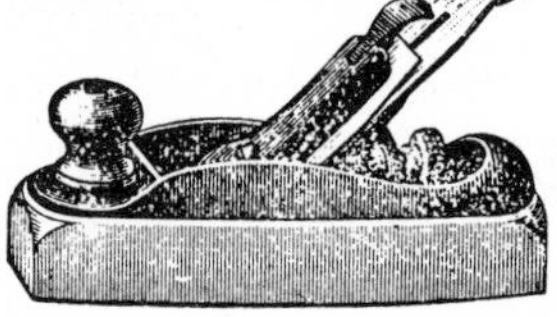

No. 12480. The Stanley Wood Smooth Plane No. 122; length, 8 inches, 1¾ inch cutter; weight, 2 lbs. Price—Each.......**57c**

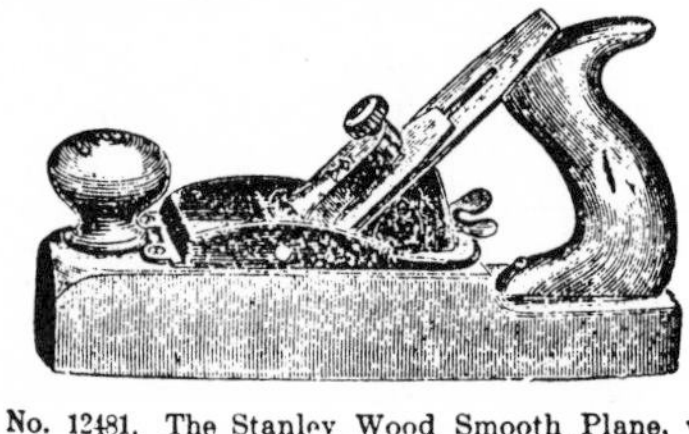

No. 12481. The Stanley Wood Smooth Plane, with handle, No. 135; length, 10 inches. 2⅛ inch cutter; weight, 3¼ lbs. Price, each..........................**76c**

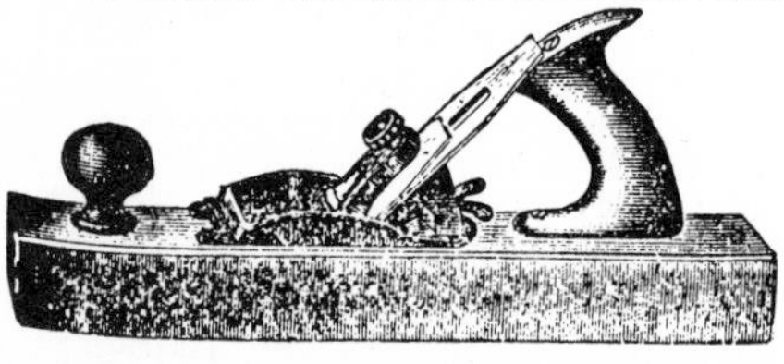

No. 12482. The Stanley Wood Jack Plane No. 127; length, 15 inches, 2⅛ inch cutter, weight, 3½ lbs. Price, each **78c**

No. 12483. The Stanley Wood Fore Plane No. 129; length, 20 inches, 2⅜ inch cutter; weight, 5 lbs. Price, each..**84c**

No. 12484. The Stanley Wood Jointer Plane No. 132; length, 26 inches, 2⅜ inch cutter; weight, 6 lbs. Price, each..**95c**

Wood Bench Planes.

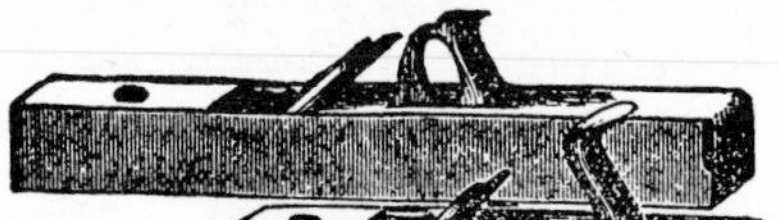

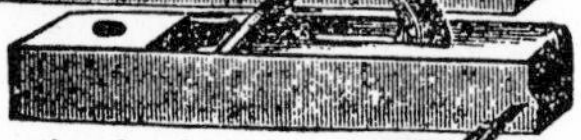

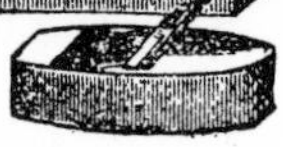

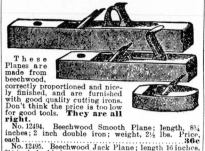

These Planes are made from beechwood, correctly proportioned and nicely finished, and are furnished with good quality cutting irons. Don't think the price is too low for good tools. **They are all right.**

No. 12494. Beechwood Smooth Plane; length, 8¼ inches; 2 inch double iron; weight, 2½ lbs. Price, each..**36c**

No. 12495. Beechwood Jack Plane; length 16 inches, 2¼ inch double iron; weight, 4½ lbs. Price, each, **40c**

No. 12496. Beechwood Fore Plane; length, 22 inches, 2½ inch double iron; weight, 6½ lbs. Price, each..**58c**

No. 12497. Beechwood Jointer Plane; length, 26 inches, 2½ inch double iron; weight, 9 lbs. Price, each....**63c**

No. 12498. Set of 4 Planes, one each of the above wood bench planes. Per set.....................**$1.90**

Block Plane.

No. 12500. Iron Block Plane; length, 3½ inches, 1 inch cutter. Not a toy, but a practical tool for light work; weight, 9 oz. Price, each.....................**8c**

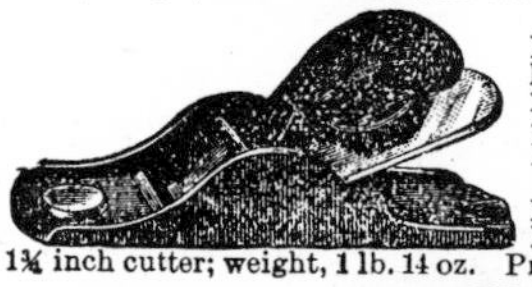

No. 12501. Iron Block Plane; length, 5½ inches, 1¼ inch cutter; weight, 14 oz. Price, each..**15c**

No. 12502. Iron Block Plane; length, 7¼ inches. 1¾ inch cutter; weight, 1 lb. 14 oz. Price, each.....**22c**

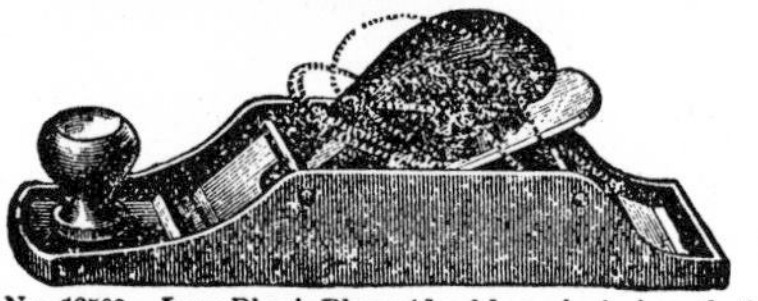

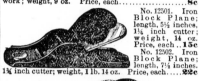

No. 12503. Iron Block Plane (double ender); length, 8 inches, 1¾ inch cutter. By reversing the cutter and clamping wedge, as shown by dotted lines in cut, this plane can be made to plane close up into corners; weight, 1 lb. 14 oz. Price, each.......................**30c**

Bailey's Block Planes, with Adjustable Mouth.

These planes are made by the Stanley Rule & Level Co. All have the lateral adjustment to set the cutting iron square with the face of the plane. The advantage of the adjustable mouth is that the mouth of plane may be made larger or smaller for different kinds of work.

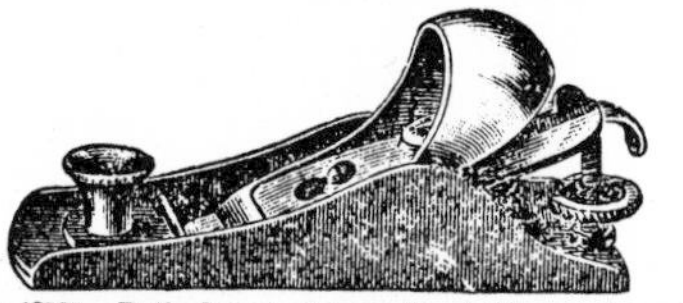

No. 12525. Bailey's patent iron Block Plane. Length, 8 inches, 1¾ inch cutter. Adjustable cutter, adjustable mouth. Weight, 1 lb. 10 oz. Price, each............**60c**

No. 12526. Same shape and adjustments as above, 7 inches long, 1¾ inch cutter. Weight, 1 lb. 14 oz. Price, each...**65c**

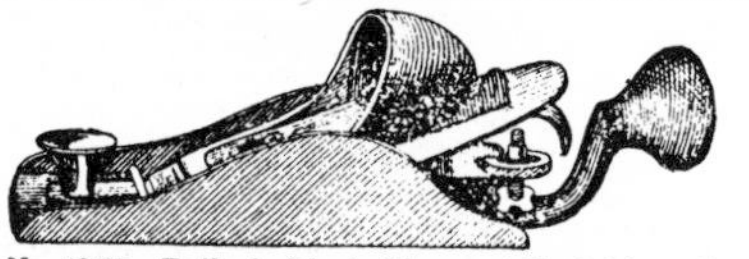

No. 12527. Bailey's Block Plane. Adjustable cutter, adjustable mouth, rosewood handle. Length, 6 inches, with 1¾ inch cutter. Price, each...................**70c**

No. 12528. Bailey's Block Plane. Same as above. Length, 7 inches, with 1¾ inch cutter. Price, each..**75c**

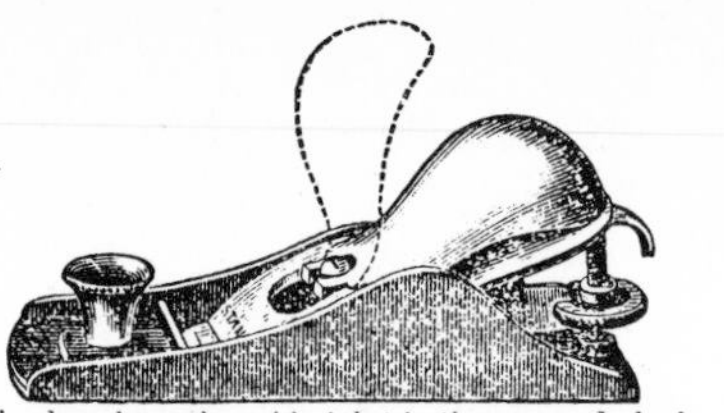

This plane has a knuckle joint in the cap, and placing the cap in position clamps the cutter securely in its seat. Has nickel-plated trimmings and all adjustments same as above planes.

No. 12532. Knuckle Joint Plane, as above. Length, 6 inches, 1¾ inch cutter. Weight, 1 lb. 10 oz. Price, each...**70c**

No. 12533. Knuckle Joint Plane, as above. Length, 7 inches, 1¾ inch cutter. Weight, 1 lb. 14 oz. Price, each...**75c**

Plane Irons.

No. 12540. **Plane Irons for Bailey or Stanley Planes.**

In ordering these plane irons BE SURE **to state the manufacturers' number of the plane for which they are wanted.**

Size, inches,	1¾	2	2¼	2⅜	2⅝
Cut Irons, each,	15c	16c	19c	23c	24c
Double Irons, each,		33c	35c	40c	42c

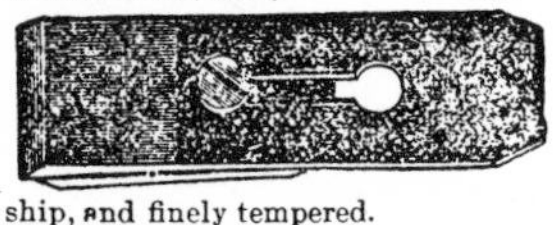

No. 12541. Extra quality Plane Irons for wood bench planes. Best of material and workmanship, and finely tempered.

Size, inches,	1¾	2	2¼	2½
Cut Irons, each,	10c	13c	15c	18c
Double Irons,	24c	25c	27c	32c

Cutters for Block Planes.

No. 12543. Steel Cutter for iron block plane No. 12443 or No. 12444. Price, each...........................**8c**

No. 12544. Steel Cutter for iron block plane No. 12445 or No. 12447. Price, each...........................**10c**

No. 12545. Steel Cutter for iron block plane Nos. 12525, 12526, 12532 or 12533. Price, each.............**12c**

Be sure to state for which plane cutter is wanted.

Stanley's Rabbet and Block Plane.

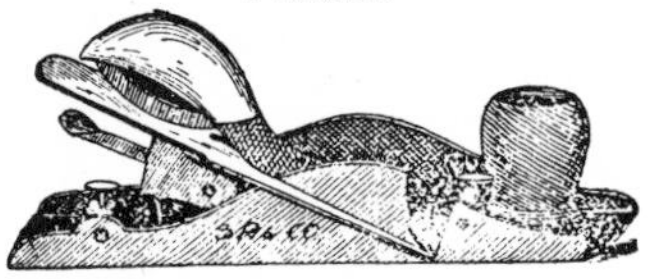

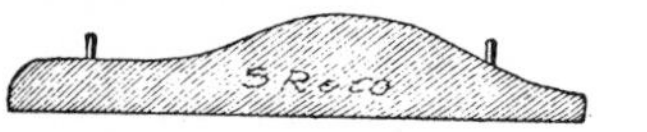

A detachable side will easily change this tool from a Block Plane to a Rabbet Plane, or vice versa. The cutter is set on a skew.

No. 12549. Rabbet and Block Plane, with detachable side, 7 inches in length, 1¾ inch cutter. Price......**85c**

Bench Plane Handles.

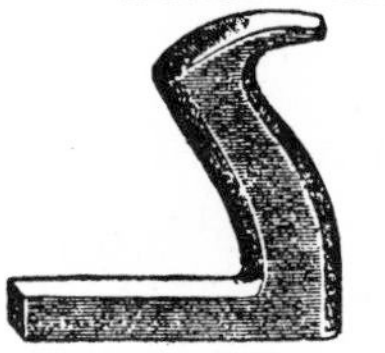

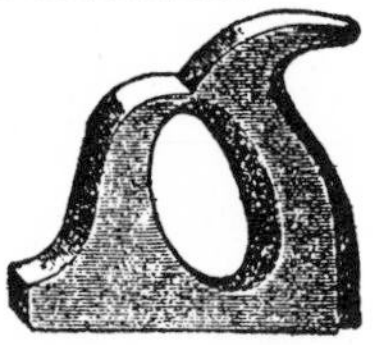

No. 12550. Jack Plane Handles, beechwood. Each, **3c**

No. 12551. Fore or Jointer Plane Handles, beechwood. Each..**5c**

Stanley's Adjustable Planes.

Stanley's Circular Plane.

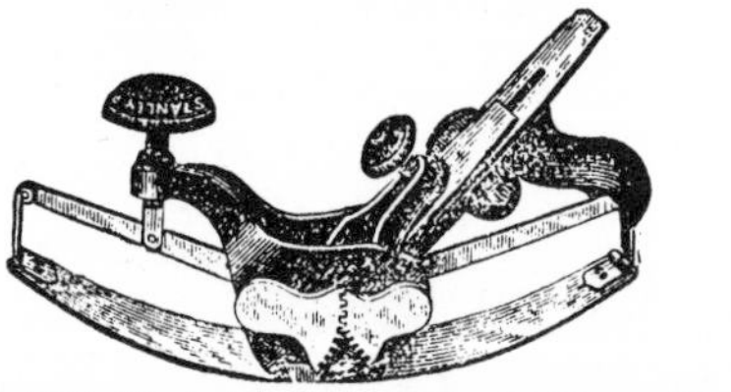

No. 12570. Stanley's Adjustable Circular Plane, with flexible steel face, which, by turning the knob on the front of the plane, can be easily shaped to any required arc, either concave or convex. Weight, 3¾ lbs. Price, each...**$1.52**

259. *Wood planes, from the Sears, Roebuck & Co. catalogue of 1897.*

260. *Stereoscopes, from the Sears, Roebuck & Co. catalogue of 1897.*

261. *Cart and carriage, from the Sears, Roebuck & Co. catalogue of 1897.*

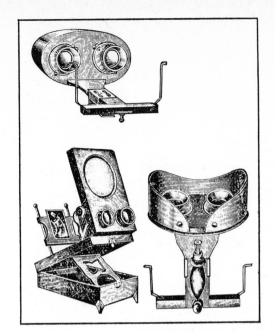

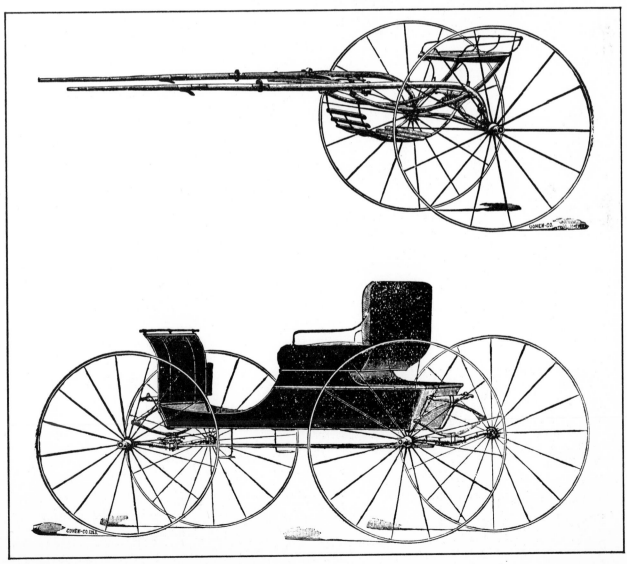

SILBER & FLEMING, Limited, 57, Wood Street, London, E.C.

LUNCHEON & PIC-NIC BASKETS.

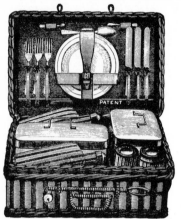

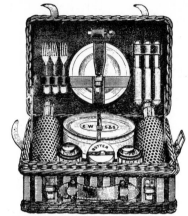

No. 12774. For 3 persons; contains 2 china provision boxes, with plated covers, 2 spirit bottles, 3 tumblers, 3 plates, and condiment bottles, nickel-plated fittings; size of basket, 19 × 12 × 7 in. Price, without cutlery, 55/-; with cutlery, 63/-

No. 12775. For 3 persons; contains 2 china dishes, with plated covers, 2 spirit bottles, 3 tumblers, 3 plates, condiment bottles and butter jar; size of basket, 16 × 14 × 7 in. Price, without cutlery, 59/-; with cutlery, 66/-

No. 12776. For 3 persons; contains 1 provision box, 2 spirit bottles, 3 tumblers, 3 plates, butter jar and condiment bottles; size of basket, 19 × 12 × 8 in. Price, without cutlery, 64/-; with cutlery, 69/-

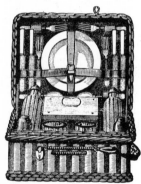

No. 12777. For 4 persons; contains 1 meat tin, 2 spirit bottles, 4 tumblers, 4 condiment bottles, 4 plates; size of basket, 16 × 13 × 8 in. Price, without cutlery, 29/-; with cutlery, 33/-

No. 12778. For 4 persons; contains 2 provision tins, 2 spirit bottles, 4 tumblers, 4 plates, and condiment bottles; size of basket, 19 × 13 × 8 in. Price, without cutlery, 34/-; with cutlery, 39/-

No. 12779.

No. 12779. For 4 persons; contains 2 provision boxes, 2 spirit bottles, 4 plates, 4 tumblers, butter pot and condiment bottles; also nickel-plated clips to hold the cutlery; size of basket, 21 × 13 × 8 in. Price, without cutlery, 84/-; with cutlery, 91/-

No. 12780. For 6 persons; contains 2 meat tins, 6 tumblers, 2 spirit bottles, 2 butter pots and condiment bottles, 6 plates; size of basket, 23 × 13 × 8 in. Price, without cutlery, 45/-; with cutlery, 51/-

No. 12781. For 6 persons; contains 2 large meat tins, 2 spirit bottles, 6 plates, 6 tumblers, butter pot and condiment bottles; size of basket, 22 × 16 × 8 in. Price, without cutlery, 41/-; with cutlery, 48/-

No. 12780.

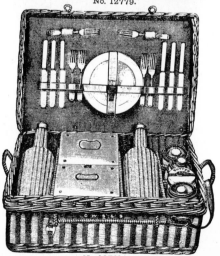

No. 12781.

263. *Field glasses, from the catalogue of Silber & Fleming, London, 1887–89.*

264. *Shooting seats, from the catalogue of William Whiteley, Ltd., London, soon after the turn of the century.*

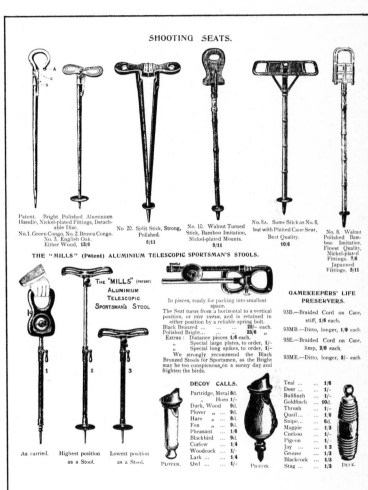

Muthesius saw the basis for England's contemporary design in the refined common-sense designs of the late eighteenth century. These had been discarded, forgotten, and overlaid by tawdry manufactured artware in the earlier Victorian period, but their principles (if not always their practice) were reinstated by William Morris and his followers in the late 1800's, with the ideal of the unpretentious, styleless country house and its qualities of commodious, friendly, homey living—in other words, the vernacular. In his writings, Muthesius examined the entire English house and its furnishings sympathetically and clearly. He admired how the English house was designed for living, carefully designed, matter-of-factly designed, so that each room was treated as an organism—not for conscious artistic purposes but to serve specific, practical purposes of living, without ostentation, without pretentiousness, to serve a natural, healthy, simple life, closely connected with garden and nature. "The actual decisive quality of the English house is its *Sachlichkeit*. It is simply a house in which one wants to live . . . It is without pomp or decoration and has that natural decency which—natural as it ought to be—is so rare in our present culture. It embodies a quality which is a precious part of the English character: unassuming naturalness." [24]

Muthesius saw that, by retaining this position, England placed itself in opposition to many of the aspirations that were exciting the Continent. While Art Nouveau artists on the Continent conceived of an interior—in fact, the entire house—as a necessarily integrated work of art, the English were content to satisfy the real needs of comfort and convenience in a direct, unaffected way. The result, he conceded, was more natural, perhaps also more "modern," that is, more *sachlich*, matter-of-fact, less affected, than the often high-flown artistic aspirations on the Continent, which, more-

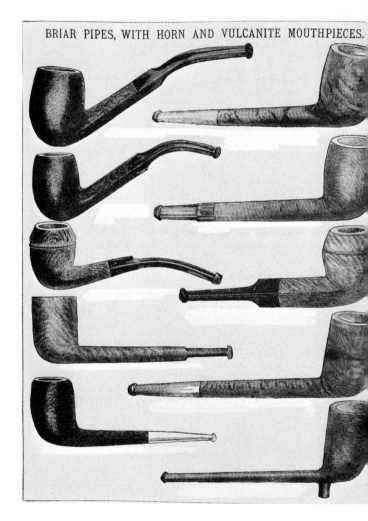

BRIAR PIPES, WITH HORN AND VULCANITE MOUTHPIECES.

266. *Various objects from the catalogue of William Whiteley, Ltd., London, soon after the turn of the century.*

181

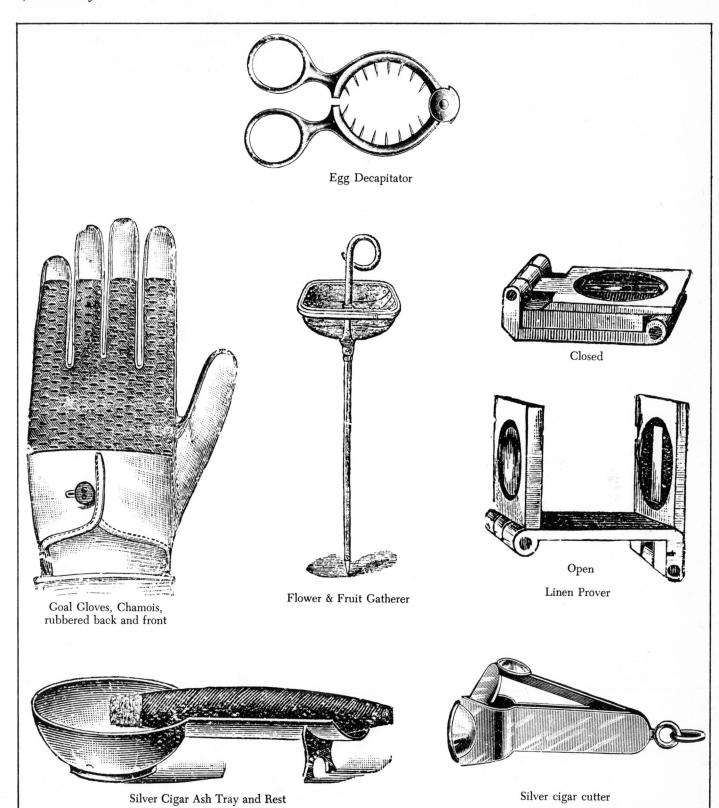

Egg Decapitator

Goal Gloves, Chamois, rubbered back and front

Flower & Fruit Gatherer

Closed

Open

Linen Prover

Silver Cigar Ash Tray and Rest

Silver cigar cutter

over, appeared more often at exhibitions than in common use.[25]

The relation of function to a new aesthetic is nowhere more clearly expressed than in his analysis of the English bathroom and its plumbing:

Water pipes for bringing and disposing of water, pipes of various kinds for hot water, for heating, for electric light, for communication, began to permeate the house and to give it the character of a refined organism with arteries, veins, and nerves, like the human body. The aesthetic beauty of an earlier ideal had to give way. But perhaps in time a new kind of beauty will take its place, the beauty of spiritualized functionalism.

He admired the English use of chrome (*Fig. 267*) whenever possible in the bathroom:

This principle creates a style of bathroom which is in the best sense artistic: the absolute denial of any ornamentation which always mars the effect, achieves genuine modernity. It is genuine and will be durable because it is developed with strict logic and does not depend on sentimental or artificial mood values. Such a bathroom is like a scientific instrument, in which intelligent technology triumphs and in which any added "art value" would only be disturbing. The form developed purely from function is so brilliant and significant that it creates aesthetic pleasure which is in no way different from artistic enjoyment. Here we have a really new art which has no need of sentiment in order to convince, an art based on actual modern conditions and modern achievements. Perhaps one day, when all the fleeting fashions of artistic movements which deem themselves modern will have blown over, it will be seen as the most telling expression of our age.[26]

In characterizing English design, Muthesius repeatedly uses the word *Sachlichkeit*, which while not entirely translatable, means matter-of-factness, attention to function, practicality, objectivity. The word and its meaning were the key concepts in the recognition and appreciation of the functional and vernacular traditions. *Sachlichkeit* constituted the reaction and opposition to Art Nouveau, and its victory meant that the future belonged to design of functional sobriety. The years up to World War I are characterized by its ascendency and the retreat of the romantically artistic, which had had its high water mark in the Art Nouveau (*Figs. 268–71*).

Though Sullivan and Wright stand in direct descent from Horatio Greenough and share his concepts and occasionally his vocabulary, neither Sullivan nor Wright, both architects, were involved or interested enough in the design of objects to be pertinent here. To be sure, Sullivan's creed was applicable to design on more than one level, as was Wright's, but their own thinking and their activities were centered on architecture and those objects necessary to create an artistic ensemble within a particular piece of architecture. Greenough's true counterpart at the turn of the century was an Austrian, Adolf Loos (1870–1933), who was an architect but also passionately interested in design as it affected all aspects of the environment, from a man's clothing to the cityscape.

An acquaintance with the writings of Greenough and Loos reveals their common point of view; indeed, as one reads, one is struck by a congruence of specific ideas and the use of similar analogies that make one wonder whether Loos knew the writings of Greenough. He did spend several years in America and conceivably could have been introduced to them, but that has, to my knowledge, never been suggested.[27]

Loos visited the World's Columbia Exposition in Chicago in 1893 and thereafter spent several years in America and England; he returned to Vienna in 1896 and began writing a series of articles full of wit and enthusiasm and always emphasizing the modern. He explicitly pointed out that it was America and England that had opened his eyes to the forms of the new age and

"SILUMIN" is White all through and will not Rust.

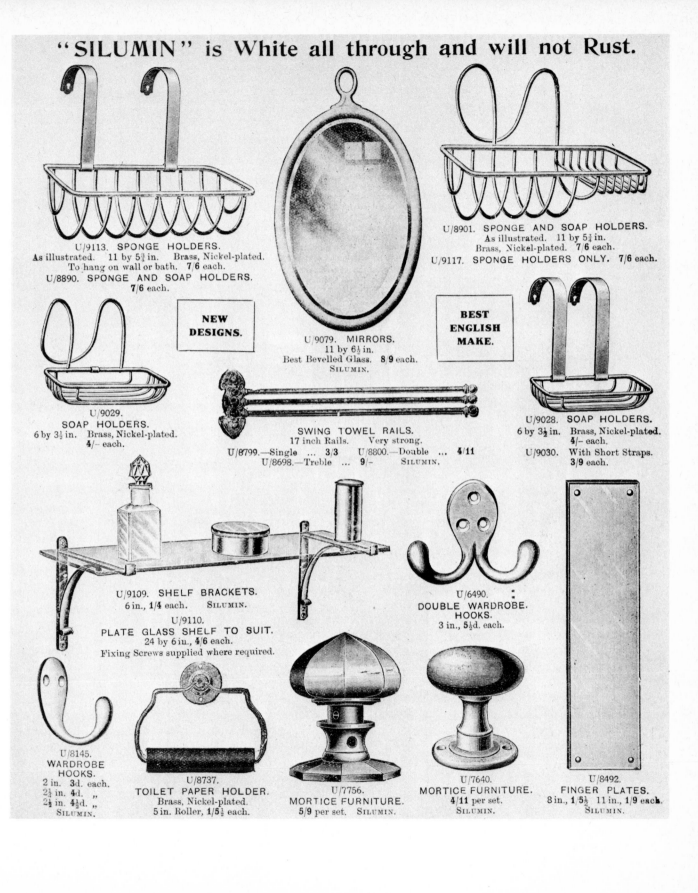

U/9113. SPONGE HOLDERS.
As illustrated. 11 by 5¾ in. Brass, Nickel-plated.
To hang on wall or bath. **7/6** each.
U/8890. SPONGE AND SOAP HOLDERS.
7/6 each.

NEW
DESIGNS.

U/9079. MIRRORS.
11 by 6½ in.
Best Bevelled Glass. **8/9** each.
SILUMIN.

BEST
ENGLISH
MAKE.

U/8901. SPONGE AND SOAP HOLDERS.
As illustrated. 11 by 5¾ in.
Brass, Nickel-plated. **7/6** each.
U/9117. SPONGE HOLDERS ONLY. 7/6 each.

U/9029.
SOAP HOLDERS.
6 by 3½ in. Brass, Nickel-plated.
4/- each.

SWING TOWEL RAILS.
17 inch Rails. Very strong.
U/8799.—Single ... **3/3**   U/8800.—Double ... **4/11**
U/8698.—Treble ... **9/-**   SILUMIN.

U/9028. SOAP HOLDERS.
6 by 3½ in. Brass, Nickel-plated.
4/- each.
U/9030. With Short Straps.
3/9 each.

U/9109. SHELF BRACKETS.
6 in., 1/4 each. SILUMIN.
U/9110.
PLATE GLASS SHELF TO SUIT.
24 by 6 in., **4/6** each.
Fixing Screws supplied where required.

U/6490.
DOUBLE WARDROBE
HOOKS.
3 in., 5½d. each.

U/8145.
WARDROBE
HOOKS.
2 in. 3d. each.
2½ in. 4d. ,,
2½ in. 4½d. ,,
SILUMIN.

U/8737.
TOILET PAPER HOLDER.
Brass, Nickel-plated.
5 in. Roller, 1/5½ each.

U/7756.
MORTICE FURNITURE.
5/9 per set. SILUMIN.

U/7640.
MORTICE FURNITURE.
4/11 per set.
SILUMIN.

U/8492.
FINGER PLATES.
8 in., 1/5½ 11 in., 1/9 each.
SILUMIN.

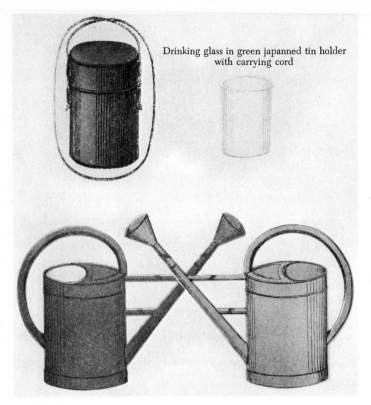

Drinking glass in green japanned tin holder
with carrying cord

changed his concepts. "The sharp American and English atmosphere removed all my prejudices against the products of my own time." In another essay, he said: "The English and the engineers are our Greeks. From them we get our culture, from them it spreads over the globe. They are the ideal men of the 19th century." [28] Loos saw as the products of his own time precisely those that had the long underground tradition of the nineteenth century, the machines and instruments, and the vernacular in everyday use, both of hand tradition and of industry: tools, luggage, clothes, shoes, saddles, glassware, spectacles, cigarette cases—all of an undecorated, simple, functional form, and therefore modern. He reiterated in all his writing that modern was neither new nor artistic, that the best design was produced not by designers but by artisans and manufacturers simply making as good a product as could be made. This put him, of course, in opposition to all of the Art Nouveau and

the Vienna Secession, and what made his position so interesting and important is the fact that he fought as fiercely and as much, or more, against the new and fashionable Art Nouveau as against the dying eclecticism. He was the only one who, recognizing the modern qualities of many objects being produced in his time, logically proclaimed them modern. While every other artist, designer, or architect wanted to reform and renew and thought he was laying the basis for the design of the twentieth century by creating individual works of artistic expression, Loos insisted with complete assurance that modern design already existed, was being produced anonymously by artisans and factories, and that artistic designers could only ruin it. Whereas van de Velde says: "Wherever the artist intervenes, he improves!," Loos says that as soon as artists and architects concern themselves with the design of a given craft with sound traditions, that craft is ruined and its products take on

269. *Items from a catalogue of the hardware firm Nürnberger Metallwaarenfabrik, Gebrüder Bing, Nürnberg, 1893.*

270. *"Bauhaus" lampshades, from a catalogue ca. 1900 of the firm of N. A. Schjorring, Copenhagen, Denmark.*

271. *Pressed-glass bottles, designed by Richard Riemerschmid, ca. 1905, for industrial production. (Courtesy Neue Sammlung, Munich. Photo: S. R. Gnamm)*

the aspects of fashion and will be unbearable in a few years[29] (*Fig. 274*). He, more than anyone else, saw the functional form with the quality of *Sachlichkeit* as the constant and as the continuum that linked the nineteenth with the twentieth century.

Loos pointed out that there *is* a distinction between art and design. The eighteenth century freed science of art—and he cites earlier anatomical textbooks in which engravings showed the gods of Greece with the skin removed from their bellies, to demonstrate anatomy (he might also have cited the scientific instruments discussed earlier in this book that were embellished with the gods and ornaments of Greece). It was the great achievement of the nineteenth century to have brought about the clear separation between art and design. The cultivated products of our time have no connection with art, and modern man considers it a degradation and prostitution of art to mix it with design. To waste art on an article of utility is bar-

baric in modern eyes. Modern man wishes to enjoy art as art and to have utilitarian objects about him that serve him well but are otherwise neutral, indifferent, unassuming. Ornamentation, artistic embellishment of the utilitarian object, belongs to earlier, less sensitive eras. Modern man is incapable of cutting his meat on a plate with a mythological scene of naked gods and goddesses.[30]

There are remarkable parallels in the writings of Loos and Greenough. Both despised ornament and thought it was somehow a weakness of primitive man. The eradication of ornament from modern life was the ruling passion of Loos's life. He believed that mankind progressed from ornament to pure form, that the more primitive man was, the more he used ornament. If man used ornament in the modern era, he betrayed signs of primitivism, either through lack of education and social status or as a stunted or perverted personality, in any case more prone to criminal tendencies than a truly modern man; thus, in his famous essay "Ornament and Crime," he established a connection between the two, and by implication equated ornament with crime. Greenough had also connected ornamentation with primitivism: "I understand . . . by embellishment, THE INSTINCTIVE EFFORT OF INFANT CIVILIZATION TO DISGUISE ITS INCOMPLETENESS." (Capitalization his.) And further, "the savage who envies or admires the special attributes of beasts, maims unconsciously his own perfection, to assume tints, their feathers or their claws; we turn from him with horror and gaze with joy on the naked Apollo." [31] Loos spoke of the English and the engineers as our Greeks, and continued that "Greek vases are beautiful, as beautiful as a machine, as beautiful as a bicycle"; Greenough said, "The men who have reduced locomotion to its simplest elements, in the trotting wagon and the yacht *America*, are nearer to Athens at this moment than they who would bend the Greek temple to every use." [32] Loos reiterated again and again that all things truly modern were without ornament—our machines, instruments, bicycles, carriages, glasses, umbrellas, luggage, our plumbing fixtures and bathtubs—and absence of ornament was not unattractive but acted as a new attraction, enhancing the form; Greenough said, "In nakedness I behold the majesty of the essential, instead of the trappings of pretension. The agendum is not diminished; it is infinitely extended." [33] Loos also echoed the eighteenth-century philosophers who formed part of Greenough's background; in 1898, he wrote, "There is no absolute beauty in a utilitarian object. Its beauty lies solely in its appropriateness to use." David Hume had commented on utilitarian objects: "their beauty is chiefly derived from their utility and from their fitness for that purpose to which they are destin'd." [34]

Loos was remarkable for defining modern design in exactly the sense that the modern style postulated it in the following decades. But beyond that, he was aware that modern did not mean new, that as a quality of fitness it was timeless, possessing both a history and a future, while "new" design, the decorative art of Art Nouveau, was merely a passing fashion. "We have more in common with the truth, though it be hundreds of years old, than with the lie which walks next to us." [35] His most important essays were translated and published in France, first in 1913 and again in 1920 and 1923. [36] He himself moved to Paris and worked there from 1923 to 1928, thus establishing an ideological and personal link with the decade in which many of his ideas came to fruition. Le Corbusier acknowledged his debt to Loos explicitly. [37] Loos's own work shows at an early date a concentration on smooth, cubic forms, frequently without embellishment except in the luxury of materials and proportions. Loos was primarily an architect and not an industrial designer, though he designed some furniture (*Fig. 272*) and also glassware. He was the first to champion the use of Thonet furniture, although he did occasionally also use forms of the past—not to imitate stylistic forms but because he considered them to be perfect functional solutions to the problem at hand, and therefore he considered it pointless and wasteful to design anew. For example, he used Chippendale dining chairs copied by a local craftsman from museum specimens. For his own living room, in 1903, he used Windsor armchairs (*Fig. 273*), because these were to him also timeless valid forms; and he used precisely the same chairs again in one of his last houses, the Villa Khuner, in 1930. But his ideas and writings are of immeasurably greater significance than the relatively small amount of his own work in the design field, though, because his design is consistent with his words, it reinforces and enhances them.

188

The common image of the turn of the century was entirely dominated by the glitter and glamour of Art Nouveau. It was hailed as the turning point, as the first sweeping break with eclecticism and the first valid expression of a modern style (*Fig. 274*). It was all that, but at the same time it excluded the possibility of modern design. Robert Schmutzler calls Art Nouveau the dreamworld of an elite, and recalls the words of Hugo von Hofmannsthal, who said, "if those who think, so lose themselves in dreams, the masses get nothing." [38] Gerhard Bott, writing on design in the new edition of the famed Propyläen Art History series, comes to the conclusion that

this artistic revolt, supported by only a few bourgeois circles, was an erroneous course which ended in the same machine-made *"Kitsch"* against which it had revolted. The only significant works of this epoch are those products which cannot be classified under the usual stylistic concepts of the turn of the century. They are the precursors of a *"Neue Sachlichkeit,"* which triumphed soon after 1900.[39]

As a matter of fact, Art Nouveau had to become outmoded and be discarded before modern design could take the stage. One of the things Loos helps us see is that modern design was not created, was not an achievement of a few individuals of that period, but was there to be brought to light. When Riemerschmid, who, in 1899, had designed a fine exhibition chair of classic modern design (*Fig. 275*), began in 1904 to design furniture to be made by machines, it was hailed by the magazines of decorative art as a great achievement and a significant initial step, though it was not anywhere near as consistent and successful as his earlier individual chair.[40] Nowhere, except in Loos, does one find any reference to Thonet furniture, produced by machines for at least fifty years and in many of its designs more refined and elegant than Riemerschmid's. Peter Behrens's initial designing activity for AEG (*Allgemeine Elektrizitäts-Gesell-*

schaft, the German equivalent of General Electric), in 1907, has been celebrated as the first instance of industrial design. His arc lamps have been published and republished as unique achievements, ever since Pevsner first included them as "pioneer" work.[41] Behrens did redesign the AEG arc lamps because they (and similar ones by Siemens, another large German electrical concern) were of an outrageously eclectic design until he came. However, if one cares to look, one finds that even in 1906 (and earlier), the world was full of arc lamps as modern, as devoid of acanthus leaves, as those designed in 1907 by Peter Behrens; they were, in fact, very similar [42] (*Figs. 276–79*). And if one looks at other electrical products, lamps, fans, heaters, flatirons, and so on, that were produced anonymously in Europe and America for decades in clear functional forms, it becomes increasingly difficult to see the validity of the pioneer role created for Behrens in the field of industrial design, especially if a few of his products other than street lamps are considered—such as tea kettles, fans, and heaters—that are clearly tainted as decorative art by beading, hammering of the surface, and other attempts to make them genteel (*Figs. 280, 281*).

Just as functional modern design had been produced all through the nineteenth century as an ironic commentary on all the pretentious and pious reform efforts, so now, too, it was being produced by industry, not as a result of the efforts of artistic renewal and reform but entirely outside them, simply as a matter of course in the continuum of the functional tradition, in England, America, Germany and elsewhere (*Fig. 282–89*). It gave the impulse and ideological foundation for the modern style as it developed after 1918, but it was not the same as that style itself, in spite of the similarity of terminology. In fact, once the modern style (the Functionalist or International Style) became established, the timeless, styleless functional

273. *Windsor chair, from the living room of Adolf Loos, 1903.*
(Historisches Museum der Stadt Wien)

274. *Chair by Charles Rennie Mackintosh, Glasgow, ca. 1901–2. Back and seat of natural linen with stenciled decoration in mauve and green. A startling esthetic statement in the personal and original idiom of the artist, but a chair only incidentally.*
(University of Glasgow, Mackintosh Collection)

275. *Armchair of mahogany, by Richard Riemerschmid, 1899. The photograph is of a contemporary version, virtually identical with the original, manufactured since 1953 by the Dunbar Furniture Corp. of Indiana, by agreement with the designer, who died in 1957. The original chair was designed by Riemerschmid for his music room in the 1899 art exhibition in Dresden. Not until 1904 did he begin to design furniture specifically to be made by machines, and this was not manufactured until 1905 and 1906.*
(Courtesy Neue Sammlung, Munich)

190

276. *Lantern of copper, France, 1814–30.*
(Musée Carnavalet, Paris. Photo: Roger Viollet)

277. *White metal lantern, made by Post & Co.,*
Cincinnati, Ohio, late nineteenth century.
(Courtesy of The New-York Historical Society,
New York City)

278. *Arc lamps, United States Electric Lighting Co.,*
1883.

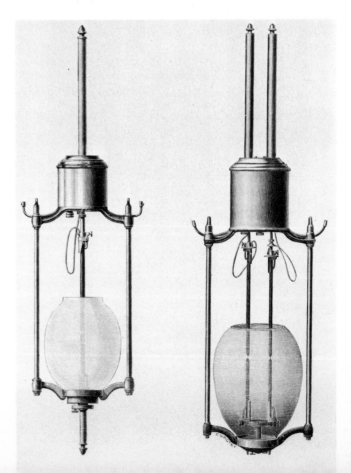

form, though ostensibly constituting the style was, in actual fact, once more submerged and continued its existence largely beneath the surface. The Functionalist style was based on the verbal claim of functional fitness and sought its legitimacy in the practice and pronouncements of the functional tradition of the nineteenth century; but in reality, it was a style of geometric forms subject to the ruling canons of Cubism, later modified by stream-lining, in both cases often unreasoned and un-related to function but adopted for their emotional appeal. Ozenfant wrote in 1928 that "manufac-tured forms are geometric, and we respond to geometry. No doubt that is so, because intuitively geometry communicates to us a feeling that some higher dispensation is being subserved, which thus becomes a pleasure of the mind, and a feeling that we are satisfying the laws that govern our being." Foreseeing changes in technology, he continued, "By the time we have got to disintegrating the

279. *200-volt quartz lamp, manufactured by Quartzlampen Gesellschaft, Pankow, Germany, 1907.* (From Electrical World, 1907)

280. *Fan and motor, American, manufactured by Bernstein Electric Co., 1892.* (From Electrical World, 1892)

281. *Electric heater, designed by Peter Behrens for AEG, 1906.* (Courtesy AEG-Telefunken, Abt. Formgestaltung)

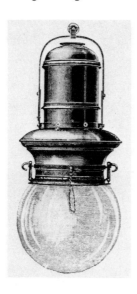

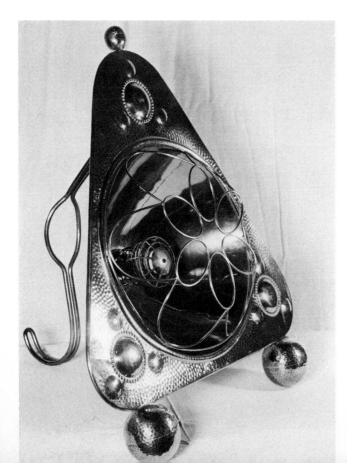

atom, it may be there will be nothing at all worth looking at. Our mechanism is primitive, and that is why it still looks gratifyingly geometric."[43] In the catalogue to an exhibition entitled "The Object Transformed," held at The Museum of Modern Art in 1966, Mildred Constantine and Arthur Drexler wrote:

That the dominant forms of modern industrial design have been largely geometric is usually explained in terms of functional suitability, although, in fact, geometric forms have a strong emotional appeal, associated not only with painting and sculpture but also derived from the values established by what used to be called "moral Philosophy."

When the early nineteenth-century engineers spoke of geometric forms as being the inevitable result of their search for the best functioning form for their machines, their premises were practical, while those of the designers in the first half of the twentieth century were formal.

192

282. *Motion-picture camera and stand, English, made by R. W. Paul, 1896.*
(British Crown Copyright. Science Museum, London)

283. *Ship's Chronometer, German,* ca. 1905.
(Deutsches Museum, Munich)

284. *Sleigh, of wood and iron, made by A. E. Perren of Buffalo, N.Y., 1895.*
(Courtesy of The Henry Ford Museum, Dearborn, Michigan)

285. *Racing sulky, 1900, made by The Faber Sulky Co., Rochester, N.Y.*
(Courtesy of The Henry Ford Museum, Dearborn, Michigan)

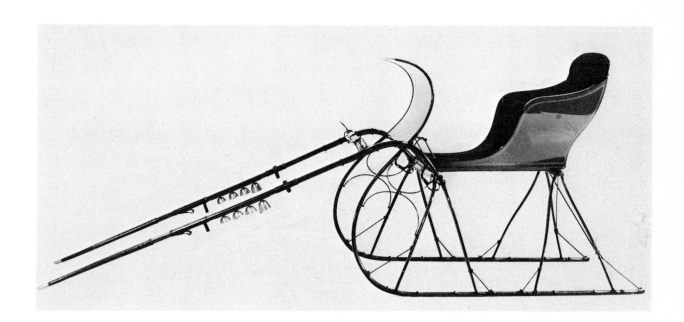

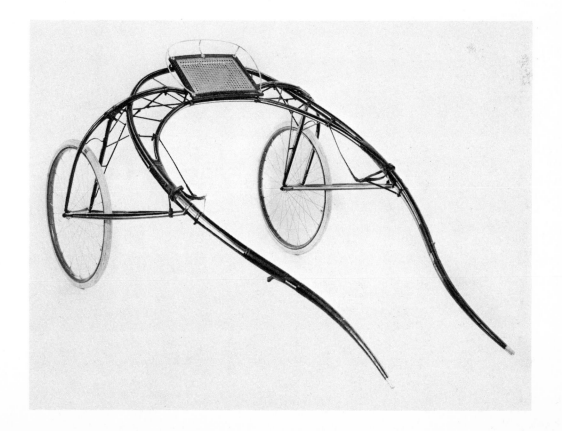

286. *Cunard Liner* Campania, *1893.*
(Courtesy Cunard Line Ltd.)

287. *Locomotive, 1911. Manufactured by the*
locomotive factory of Graffenstaden, Bas-Rhin, Alsace.
(Deutsches Museum, Munich)

288. *Peugeot automobile, 1903.*
(Deutsches Museum, Munich)

289. *Model of the Wright brothers' first double-decker plane, 1908.*
(Deutsches Museum, Munich)

What we think of as modern design in its classic phase, from the late 1920's through the 1940's, was not only a *style*—precisely what its initiators had hoped to avoid—but was also, to a large extent, exhibition and museum design; thus it was brought into the realm of art while simultaneously being alienated from the simple purposes of practical life. The raising of the anonymous industrial product of functional form to the status of an art form began soon after 1900. To be sure, such industrial products had been shown throughout the nineteenth century in the recurring industrial exhibits of the international exhibitions, but something new now occurred: These products began to be shown in art museums as art, and not only were they taken by artists as motifs but the actual substance was elevated to the status of works of art.

In 1906, the exhibition of applied art in the Dresden Museum showed not only the work of artist-craftsmen but also anonymous products of industry of simple utilitarian design. There were stoves, lamps, ship's lanterns, industrially made furniture (including the series designed by Riemerschmid), classroom furniture, workers' model apartments, even railway carriages and ship cabins.[44]

An almost entirely forgotten American museum director pioneered in a similar venture. John Cotton Dana of the Newark Museum showed, in 1912, an exhibition of modern German products assembled by Karl Ernst Osthaus and sent through the German *Werkbund*. Although offered to The Metropolitan Museum in New York as a traveling exhibition, and turned down by them, it did travel subsequently from Newark to other American museums. The exhibition consisted of 1,300 items, including, in addition to the various fields of design proper, work by Ernst Barlach, Käthe Kollwitz, and, in photographic form, the architectural work of Peter Behrens, Walter Gropius, Josef Hoffmann, Hermann Muthesius, and Henry van de Velde. Dana constantly had small one-case exhibitions of what he called "Every Day Art," or "Fifty Cents Exhibits," of inexpensive objects he picked up at Woolworth's or other stores in town, nickel-plated tableware and drinking glasses at 10c apiece, a 25c enamelware cooking spoon. One of his favorite slogans was that "beauty has no relation to price, rarity or age."[45]

With these ventures, Dana anticipated by decades the proliferation of such exhibitions in American and European museums in the 1930's, 1940's, and 1950's. In the interim, a series of prestigious design exhibitions were produced by the German *Werkbund* as part of its campaign to educate design taste and understanding among consumers, manufacturers, the commercial middlemen, and even political entities, such as city administrations. The first significant exhibition took place in 1914, in Cologne;[46] "Form without Ornament" was held in Stuttgart, in 1924.[47] (Loos refers to this exhibition, of special interest to him because of its theme, in the foreword to his volume *Trotzdem*: "I have emerged from a thirty-years' battle as victor: I have liberated mankind from superfluous ornament. 'Ornament' was once an epithet for 'beautiful'; today, thanks to my life's work, it is an epithet for 'inferior.'" He then continues: "To be sure, the echo that returns, believes to be the voice itself. The perfidious book *Form Without Ornament*, published in Stuttgart in 1924, ignores my battle and falsifies it at the same time.") There followed the *Werkbund* exhibition of a model housing-project, complete with all furnishings in the modern style, at Weissenhof, near Stuttgart, in 1927;[48] exhibits in Breslau, in 1929; in Paris, in 1930; and the exhibition "Wohnbedarf" in Stuttgart, in 1932. They are landmarks and represent the fulfillment of the modern style.

The use of vernacular industrial forms for artistic purposes begins with soft irony. In 1911 an

Englishman, Edward Verral Lucas—an editor of *Punch*—in collaboration with George Morrow, illustrated a facetious autobiography, *What a Life!*, with pictures of common objects taken from the catalogue of a household furnishings store, using them as visual puns in a whimsical way.[49] This means that a sensitive person consciously *saw* these common objects and used them, because he knew he would be evoking the knowledge of them out of the subconscious of his readers.

In the same years, the Cubist painters were using similar objects in their compositions. They were among the first to feel and see the worth of vernacular objects—pipes and bottles, glasses and musical instruments. Kahnweiler has pointed out how Cubism "by its very subject matter . . . made us 'see' and love so many simple, unassuming objects which hitherto escaped our eyes . . . It has increased the world of our aesthetic vision by introducing us to new objects." [50]

In the early 1920's, Le Corbusier wrote didactically about the modern style and used for his illustrations the gamut of what constitutes the functional tradition: technical machinery, vehicles, and many items of the industrial vernacular. He complained of "eyes that do not see" these things, and by his publications, in which the illustrations take on some of the magic of images, he, of course, contributed to their being "seen." [51] Ozenfant echoed Le Corbusier a few years later: "Where are the chair-chairs, the table-tables, the lamps that illuminate? Yet they exist, and in quantities, everywhere: but unperceived because of their polite neutrality, decent and worthy though they are of any interior." [52]

Though in an earlier phase of recognition, Loos had been the first noted architect to use Thonet chairs, in a café designed by him,[53] Le Corbusier demonstratively took up the Thonet chair—that model piece of industrial vernacular—in the 1920's and used it in several of his interiors, most notably in 1925 in the Pavillon de l'Esprit Nouveau at the Paris Exposition Internationale des Arts Décoratifs.[54] Le Corbusier himself wrote about his choice of the Thonet chair: "We have introduced the humble Thonet chair of steamed wood, certainly the most common as well as the least costly of chairs. And we believe that this chair, whose millions of representatives are used on the Continent and in the two Americas, possesses nobility." [55]

If Le Corbusier's choice conferred nobility, that of other artists did more: In the same years that the Cubists were painting everyday objects, other artists, the Dadaists, took the objects themselves and, solely by virtue of their choice, the objects were sublimated and given the status of works of art. Marcel Duchamp, who called them "Ready-Mades," set a bicycle wheel on a stool (1913); he also selected a bottle-drying rack (1914)—which Robert Motherwell declared to have "a more beautiful form than almost anything made, in 1914, as sculpture" [56]—a snow shovel (1915), a Thonet bent-wood hat rack (1917), and a urinal (1917). By taking them from the unseen environment, isolating them, exhibiting them, he made them into the anti-environment, into art. The urinal of 1917 disappeared from an exhibition and Duchamp wrote "The Richard Mutt Case" in the Dadaist review *The Blind Man*, in 1917: "Whether Mr. Mutt with his own hands made the fountain or not has no importance. He CHOSE it. He took an ordinary article of life, placed it so that its useful significance disappeared under the new title and point of view—created a new thought for that object." And as for the accusation that it was merely a plain piece of plumbing: "that is absurd. The only works of art America has given are her plumbing and her bridges." [57]

Duchamp's, Le Corbusier's, the Cubists' and Dadaists' objects, in fact, are all of the kind that is straight out of the nineteenth century. Every one of them (except for the airplane) could have been taken from the corpus of material presented in this book: Le Corbusier's pipe, his metal garden chair, his glasses and bottles, his luggage, his metal office furniture, the Thonet chairs, and his ocean liners; the guitars, flutes, bottles, and bowls of the Cubists all have a far longer history than the moment in which they were chosen to be illustrated and to be "seen."

Not by chance, at this same time, in the late 1920's and in the 1930's, the interest in Shaker furniture reawakened and its simple beauty was revealed and appreciated. What was once a functional part of a living environment is resurrected as an art form, was collected, exhibited, and published. Marshall McLuhan has postulated that a functioning environment is invisible and is perceived as an art form only after it has become obsolete and ceased being a viable, practically functioning entity, and been superseded by a new environment. That is an intriguing idea, in view of what seems to have happened in those decades. In a similar vein, Ozenfant wrote much earlier "lovers of machinery by preference collect implements long out of date. Imagining that they worship mechanism, in reality they offer sacrifice to a taste for antiques." [58]

On a more practical level, the Bauhaus, that single most influential institution in the creation and dissemination of the modern style, under the direction of Walter Gropius sought to engender in its students an attitude toward design that was essentially the one of the functional tradition. Of the many famous design solutions that we associate with the Bauhaus, some, particularly from its earlier Weimar phase, are stylistically Cubist and expressionistic, but others, such as the tubular metal chairs by Marcel Breuer, the lamps, and other metalwork and pottery, are sophisticated equivalents of the more naïve and direct solutions of the nineteenth century. In these instances, the functional tradition is maintained and clearly revealed as the core ingredient of the modern style. [59]

In the later 1920's, these ideas, books, exhibitions, and works began to exert a reverse influence on America. The *Little Review*, which had for years championed all forms of modern art, from Joyce's *Ulysses* to the work of the Cubists, the Dadaists, Futurists and Surrealists, in May, 1927, put on an exhibition in New York entitled *Machine-Age Exposition*. It was organized by one of the review's editors, Jane Heap, who had spent some years in Paris as one of that famous band of expatriates of those years, and who came home in 1925 full of Corbusian ideas about design. The exhibition was announced as "an international exposition of modern architecture, painting, sculpture, and constructions, shown in juxtaposition with engineering and the industrial arts. First exposition of its kind anywhere. First showing of modern architecture in America." The catalogue, which appeared as a supplement to the spring, 1927 issue of the *Little Review*, had on its cover a design by Fernand Léger; the exhibition consisted of works by Juan Gris, Jacques Lipchitz, Naum Gabo, Fernand Léger, Charles Demuth, Theo van Doesburg, and others; of an astonishingly complete photographic review of modern European architecture; and, finally, of American industrial design: pumps, valves, gears, time clocks, light bulbs, radios, coffee grinder, meat carver, tractor, plow, airplane engine, propeller, oil burner, thermostat. The exhibits were drawn from such companies as Crane Co., International Harvester Co., I.B.M., General Electric, Curtiss Aeroplane Co., and others. The exhibition was planned to show the interdependence and interrelation of art and design; it was to present and justify the new art and the related new dynamic forms of architecture and design. Almost paraphrasing Le Corbusier, Jane Heap wrote in the catalogue: "When it is admitted that the general public must be educated over and over again to the simplest new thing, is it surprising that, without any education at all, it is unable to see that it is surrounded by a new beauty, and beyond that . . . who could expect it to see beauty in a thing not made for beauty: the machine." The exhibition took place in an office building on West 57th Street, in which a whole floor, unpartitioned, was given over to it; walls of unpainted white-plaster finish, columns, beams and girders, and ordinary tin pails, inverted as reflectors for lighting fixtures, made the setting. The exhibition was also to "act as a fore-runner of a permanent exposition such as the industrial arts museums in many foreign cities." Though extraordinary for its time, this exhibition went almost unnoticed—it was perceptively and appreciatively reviewed only by the architect Herbert Lippman in *The Arts* magazine of November, 1927—and it was soon entirely forgotten. Certainly the Museum of Modern Art in its later similar ventures never referred to it. But it was only a few years before such exhibitions would have much more resonance and influence.

In 1934, The Museum of Modern Art staged its Machine Art Exhibition, in which even the kitchen sink was included, and for which Plato's definition of beauty—"straight lines and circles, and shapes plane or solid, made from them by lathe, ruler and square"—served as motto.[60] In an introductory essay to the Machine Art catalogue, Philip Johnson illustrated one of Whitworth's drill presses and called it a "remarkable exception" in machine design in the mid-nineteenth century and claimed that it had received no more approbation from the designers of the day than the Crystal Palace had from the architects. It would perhaps have diminished his own enthusiasm and joy of discovery

in the 1930's if Philip Johnson had been aware of the extent of machine design like Whitworth's and its keen appreciation by the engineers. Their enthusiasm for the designs they created and Philip Johnson's as a latter-day aesthete mark the difference between the vital creative phase and the later appreciative phase.

This exhibition—ranging from ship's propellers, gasoline pumps and cash registers, chemical ware and dental instruments, compasses and calipers and scales, microscopes and telescopes and dictaphones, toasters, saucepans, glass and ceramic tableware, to spoons at 25c apiece and paper cups at even less—brought modern functional design within the orbit of museum art and gave it equal prestige. Subsequent exhibitions and the building of a collection of design confirmed and accentuated this. With its very special charisma, The Museum of Modern Art succeeded as well as any artist in sublimating an ordinary object by choosing it for exhibition and giving it the cachet of being in its collection. A display stand for oranges in its collection can well stand comparison with Duchamp's bottle rack, but it is perhaps true to say that without Duchamp's bottle rack there would be no orange stand.

Exhibitions of "Useful Objects," "Good Design," and "Everyday Art" flourished for a few decades, along with catalogues and periodicals that document these efforts. During the 1950's, they came almost to a complete end.[61] The exhibitionist phase of the modern style was in a sense an aftermath of its creative phase in the interwar decades. But both creative and established phases have ended, and we are now in a new period or phase whose image or form is not yet clear.

We have entered what might be called the postmodern era in design, when modern design, as understood in the first half of the century, no longer has the convincing prestige of a ruling style; in fact, it has become distinctly démodé. The age of faith is over. Instead of dedication, at least in theory, to pure, rational, functional form on the part of informed opinion, we now have a confusing permissiveness, which not only produces but also accepts the bizarre and decorative as well as the rational and meaningful form. Of course, one can also see it as a liberation, a freeing from tight dogma, and an opening toward new forms, new possibilities and relationships. However, the present also accepts more and more uncritically the revival of all the historical revivals of the nineteenth century, as well as a replay of Art Nouveau (whose appeal at the time lay in its freshness and newness)—and now also Art Deco, the superficial Cubist decorative art of the mid-1920's—with enthusiasm, equanimity, or resignation, depending on the degree of defection from the modern style. As in the nineteenth century, functional design is, once more, often better the further it is removed from the general consumer.

The English historian Reyner Banham has been the most articulate critic and the first to announce a shift in the prevailing aesthetic. "The machine aesthetic is dead," he declared in an article in 1955, and he chided critics for expecting eternal museum values from expendable, disposable objects made by an industry that must produce ceaselessly for consumers who must buy insatiably to keep the economic system going. He emphasizes the legitimacy of the question "Will it sell?" in judging design, and he sanctions all forms of saleable design by declaring it Pop Art, equivalent to our films, television, magazines, comics, and other forms of commercial, reproducible mass-market goods. In his book, *The First Machine Age*, published in 1960, Banham is the first to see "modern" architecture and design objectively, from the outside, as an uninvolved observer, as one of a new generation who can analyze forms and motives of

the modern movement more detachedly than anyone who was part of that movement himself, if only as a consumer or spectator of it. Pevsner, the doyen of historians of the modern style, announced, in a lecture in 1961, his discovery that the modern style was a thing of the past. With some wonderment he declared that, while it lasted, it was thought by all to be the millennium, a final and unchangeable condition.[62]

As for the change itself, it has been attributed variously to the Eameses, the Beatles, Carnaby Street, Pop Art, the economic system, and human nature. A number of articles in more or less amusing form give these various viewpoints, but, most recently, Misha Black, the English designer, has restated a reasoned and humane position for design in a lecture given before the UNESCO Conference at Tbilisi, U.S.S.R., in April, 1968.[63] He said that it was the job of the designer "to ensure that the common things which man uses are as economic and efficient as they can be: that they are properly related to the convenience of the user or operator: that they give minor aesthetic pleasure from their formal mathematical elegance: that they be as few in number as is consonant with the real needs of mankind." As to the confusion engendered by emotion-laden claims on design, he said, "When art apes design or design assumes that it is art, then only mediocrity remains." With that, he is squarely within the functional tradition.

Just as the functional tradition in the nineteenth century provided the grass roots from which the modern style could spring, so today it stands as a point of reference; when the pendulum swings again, it will be there for model and measure, not for specific form, but for quality of form derived from attitude and method. Form changes with technology, but the logic of function that gave this quality of form to the product of the early nineteenth century will give the same quality to that of the future.

1. A letter from the Frenchman M. Blanqui quoted by John Tallis, *History and Description of the Crystal Palace and the Exhibition of the World's Industry in 1851* (London and New York, n.d.), I, 234.

2. Quoted by C. R. Fay, *Palace of Industry, 1851* (Cambridge, England: Cambridge University Press, 1951), p. 57. The journal has not been published and survives only in a transcript made from the original by Princess Beatrice and kept in the Royal Archives (Fay, p. 44, note 1).

3. Lothar Bucher, *Kulturhistorische Skizzen aus der Industrieausstellung aller Völker* (Frankfurt: 1851), pp. 142–45. In his fascinating little book, Robert F. Dalzell, Jr., *American Participation in the Great Exhibition of 1851* (Amherst, Mass.: Amherst College Press, 1960), has gathered a number of such estimates and comparisons, including some self-righteous American ones (pp. 37–57). See also H. J. Habakkuk, *American and British Technology in the Nineteenth Century* (Cambridge, England: Cambridge University Press, 1962), pp. 122–24, who points out some of the technical and sociological reasons for the production of simpler, standardized industrial goods in America.

4. Richard Redgrave, *Report on Design: Prepared as a Supplement to the Report of the Jury of Class XXX, of the Exhibition of 1851,* Reprinted from the Official Edition (London: 1852), pp. 30, 3.

5. Gottfried Semper, *Wissenschaft, Industrie und Kunst* (1851), republished with some of his other writings and edited by Hans M. Wingler in the series *Neue Bauhausbücher* (Mainz: Florian Kupferberg, 1966), p. 33.

6. *The Times* (London), July 1, 1851, p. 5, cols. 4–5. This essay from *The Times* was republished by Tallis, *op. cit.,* III, 61–64.

7. *Journal of Design and Manufactures,* Vol. VI (September, 1851–February, 1852), p. 135.

8. The 1901 essay was reprinted in *Jugendstil,* ed. Helmut Selig (Heidelberg and Munich: Keyersche Verlagsbuchhandlung, 1959), pp. 416–18; the later essay, "Neue Möglichkeiten in der bildenden Kunst," in *Kunstwart,* XVI, part 2 (1903), 22.

9. The debate itself, and numerous comments by other members present, appeared in the minutes of the meeting: Hermann Muthesius, *Die Werkbundarbeit der Zukunft* (Jena: Eugen Diedrichs, 1914). The ten theses and countertheses of Muthesius and van de Velde were republished in *50 Jahre Deutscher Werkbund,* ed. Hans Eckstein (Frankfurt and Berlin: Alfred Metzner Verlag, 1958), pp. 32–33.

10. Henry van de Velde's writings are scattered through many periodicals, but a few collections of essays appeared: *Kunstgewerbliche Laienpredigten* (Leipzig: Hermann Seemann, 1902); *Essays* (Leipzig: InselVerlag, 1910) contains the famous "Amo" as part of the chapter "Vernunftgemässe Schönheit," pp. 114–22; more recently, many of his significant essays were collected and published by Hans Curjel under the title *Zum Neuen Stil* (Munich: R. Piper, 1955). His autobiography appeared under the title *Geschichte meines Lebens* (Munich: R. Piper, 1962). His work was published by Karl Ernst Osthaus, *Van de Velde* (Hagen: Folkwang-Verlag, 1920). A commemorative exhibition took place at the Kunstgewerbemuseum in Zürich, in 1958, for which a catalogue was published under the title *Henry van de Velde, 1863–1957, Persönlichkeit und Werk* (Zürich: 1958); and in 1963 an exhibition of his work took place in his native Belgium, at the Paleis voor Schone Kunsten in Brussels, for which a catalogue was also published, entitled *Henry van de Velde 1863–1957* (Brussels: 1963).

11. Abraham Hammacher, *Die Welt Henry van de Veldes,* trans. from the Dutch by Dr. Karl Jacobs (Cologne: M. Dumont Schauberg, 1967), p. 125.

12. Karl-Heinz Hüter, *Henry van de Velde, Sein Werk bis zum Ende seiner Tätigkeit in Deutschland* (Berlin: Akademie-Verlag, 1967), pp. 8, 50, 72. It was through the kindness of Prof. Hüter that I was able to obtain the photograph of the van de Velde cabinet in Fig. 244.

13. Stephan Tschudi-Madsen, *Sources of Art Nouveau* (New York: George Wittenborn, Inc., 1955).

14. Robert Schmutzler, *Art Nouveau* (New York: Abrams, 1964).

15. Jost Herman, *Jugendstil: Ein Forschungsbericht 1918-1964* (Stuttgart: J. B. Metzlersche Verlagsbuchhandlung, 1965).

16. Hans Eckstein, "Idee und Geschichte des

Deutschen Werkbundes 1907–1957," in *50 Jahre Deutscher Werkbund* (Frankfurt and Berlin: Alfred Metzner Verlag, 1958), pp. 7–16; *"Die Form" Stimme des Deutschen Werkbundes 1925–1934*, eds. Felix Schwarz and Frank Gloor, Bauweltfundamente 24 (Gütersloh: Bertelsmann Fachverlag, 1969); Reyner Banham, *Theory and Design in the First Machine Age* (New York: Praeger, 1960), pp. 68 ff.

17. Lothar Bucher, *op. cit.*, p. 71.

18. F. Reuleaux, *Briefe aus Philadelphia* (Braunschweig: Friedrich Vieweg, & Sohn, 1877), p. 59.

19. Georg Seelhorst, *Die Philadelphia Ausstellung und was sie lehrt* (Nördlingen: C. H. Beck, 1878), pp. 93–96, 122–23.

20. Julius Lessing, *Berichte von der Pariser Weltausstellung 1878* (Berlin: Wasmuth, n.d.), pp. 94–99.

21. *Idem*, "Kunstgewerbe," *Amtlicher Bericht über die Weltausstellung in Chicago, 1893*, II (Berlin: 1894), 766.

22. *Idem*, "Neue Wege," *Kunstgewerbeblatt*, VI (1895), 3–4.

23. Wilhelm Bode, "Moderne Kunst in den Vereinigten Staaten von Amerika, Eindrücke von einem Besuch der Weltausstellung zu Chicago. II. Die Architektur und das Kunstgewerbe," *Kunstgewerbeblatt*, V (1894), 137.

24. Hermann Muthesius, *Das Englische Haus* (Berlin: Ernst Wasmuth, 1904–5), II, 237.

25. *Idem*, "England," in *Die Krisis im Kunstgewerbe*, ed. Richard Graul (Leipzig: S. Hirzel, 1901), pp. 13–14.

26. *Idem*, *Das Englische Haus*, III, 238–39.

27. Loos originally published his writings as essays and commentaries in newspapers and journals and later assembled them in two volumes: *Ins Leere Gesprochen 1897–1900* (Paris: Georges Crès, 1921); and *Trotzdem 1900–1930* (Innsbruck: Brenner-Verlag, 1931). A second edition of *Trotzdem* appeared the same year (Innsbruck: Brenner-Verlag, 1931), and the first volume, *Ins Leere Gesprochen*, was republished by the Brenner-Verlag in 1932. Both volumes have been published once more, under the editorship of Franz Glück, as the first volume of a two-volume edition of all his writings: Adolf Loos, *Sämtliche Schriften* (Vienna: Herold Verlag, 1962). The first important monograph on his work was Heinrich Kulka, *Adolf Loos* (Vienna: A. Schroll, 1931); a second was the small book by Ludwig Münz, *Adolf Loos* (Milan: Il Balcone, 1956), in the series "Architetti del movimento moderno," and, finally, Ludwig Münz and Gustav Künstler, *Der Architekt Adolf Loos* (Vienna and Munich: Anton Schroll, 1964). This has appeared in English as *Adolf Loos, Pioneer of Modern Architecture* (New York: Praeger, 1966), with an introduction by Nikolaus Pevsner. It also contains the translation of three of Loos's most significant essays, including "Ornament and Crime," pp. 219–31.

28. Loos, *Ins Leere Gesprochen* (1898), pp. 13, 58.

29. van de Velde, *Essays*, p. 158; Loos, *Trotzdem*, p. 71.

30. Loos, *Trotzdem*, p. 72.

31. Horatio Greenough, *The Travels, Observations, and Experience of a Yankee Stonecutter* (1852; Gainesville, Fla.: Scholars' Facsimiles & Reprints, 1958), pp. 201, 165.

32. Loos, *Ins Leere Gesprochen*, p. 58; Greenough, *Travels*, p. 33.

33. Loos, *Trotzdem*, p. 203; Greenough, *Travels*, p. 202.

34. Loos, *Ins Leere Gesprochen*, p. 49; David Hume, *A Treatise of Human Nature*, Vol. II, *Of the Passions* (1739; London: Longmans, Green, 1882), p. 151.

35. Loos, *Trotzdem*, p. 23.

36. Herwarth Walden, in his avant-gard magazine *Der Sturm*, published five of Loos's essays in Berlin, in 1912, and thus brought them to the attention of an international audience. "Ornament and Crime," which was not included, appeared in a French translation in *Les Cahiers d'aujourd'hui* in June, 1913, was reprinted in 1920, in *L'Esprit Nouveau*, and again in 1923, in Albert Morancé's *L'Architecture vivante*. Franz Glück, in Loos, *Sämtliche Schriften*, I, 457–58, noted that this most famous of his essays did not appear in German until 1929, after it had appeared in all languages of the civilized world, including Hebrew and Japanese. Thieme-Becker also noted (in 1929)

that it had been translated into all languages but had not appeared in German. *Allgemeines Lexikon der Bildenden Künstler,* XXIII (Leipzig: E. A. Seemann, 1929). Banham's account, *op. cit.,* pp. 89, 90, is not quite accurate on this point.

37. Le Corbusier, *L'Art Décoratif d'aujourd'hui* (Paris: G. Crès, 1925), pp. 85, 137.

38. Schmutzler, *op. cit.,* p. 274. The von Hofmannsthal quote is from "Aufzeichnungen 1890 bis 1895," *Corona,* X, 4 (1941), 443.

39. Gerhard Bott, "Kunstgewerbe," in *Die Kunst des 19. Jahrhunderts,* Vol. II of the new edition of the Propyläen Kunstgeschichte, ed. Rudolf Zeitler (Berlin: Propyläen Verlag, 1966), p. 152.

40. Ernst Zimmermann, "Künstlerische Maschinenmöbel," *Deutsche Kunst und Dekoration,* XVII (October 1905–March, 1906), 247–63. See also Charles Roux, "Le Concours de Mobilier à Bon Marché," *L'Art Décoratif,* XVII (1907), 74–80, a review of an exhibition of French inexpensive manufactured furniture in the Grand Palais.

41. Nikolaus Pevsner, *Pioneers of Modern Design from William Morris to Walter Gropius* (New York: The Museum of Modern Art, 1949), p. 129 and fig. 121. Wend Fischer, *Bau, Raum, Gerät,* in the series *Die Kunst des 20. Jahrhunderts,* ed. Carl Georg Heise (Munich: R. Piper, 1957), pp. 104–5.

42. Going through one year's issues of the *Electrical World* (1906–7), one finds Vol. XLVIII, No. 7 (August 18, 1906), 341, the Marquette Arc Lamp; Vol. XLVIII, No. 11 (September 15, 1906), 532, the General Electric Arc Lamp; Vol. XLIX, No. 25 (June 22, 1907), 1274, a British Arc Lamp, made by The Thomson-Houston Co., of Rugby, England; Vol. L, No. 16 (October 19, 1907), 770, an arc lamp manufactured by the Quartzlampen-Gesellschaft of Pankow, Germany. Earlier volumes of the same magazine, going back to the 1880's, show lamps, fans, clocks, heaters, flatirons, and a multiplicity of other electrical products, none of them in need of Peter Behrens's attention.

43. Ozenfant, *Foundations of Modern Art* (New York: Brewer, Warren & Putnam, 1931), pp. 152–54. The original French edition appeared in 1928.

44. *Die Kunst,* XIV (1906), 393 ff, 433 ff, 481 ff. See also Wend Fischer, *op. cit.,* pp. 100–102.

45. Dean Freiday, "Modern Design at the Newark Museum, A Survey," *The Museum,* IV (Winter-Spring, 1952), 1–19, gives interesting information about this as well as other design exhibitions at the Newark Museum; also *The Museum,* I (September, 1926), 84; II (March, 1929), 41.

46. *Deutsche Form im Kriegsjahr, Die Ausstellung Köln 1914. Jahrbuch des Deutschen Werkbundes 1915* (Munich: F. Bruckmann, 1915). See also note 9 above.

47. *Die Form ohne Ornament, Werkbundausstellung 1924* (Stuttgart: Deutsche Verlags-Anstalt, 1924).

48. The international importance of the Weissenhof project is well known. It is fully documented in two volumes: *Bau und Wohnung* (Stuttgart: Verlag Dr. Fr. Wedekind, 1927); and *Innenräume* (Stuttgart: Verlag Dr. Fr. Wedekind, 1928).

49. E. V. L. (Edward Verrall Lucas), and G. M. (George Morrow), *What a Life!* (London: Methuen, 1911). The illustrations were taken from *Whiteley's General Catalogue. What a Life!* was included in the exhibition *Fantastic Art, Dada, Surrealism,* at The Museum of Modern Art in 1936, catalogue No. 146.

50. Daniel-Henry Kahnweiler, *Juan Gris: His Life and Work* (New York: Valentin, 1947), p. 117. Kahnweiler expressed similar thoughts in another book on Cubism, written earlier, *Der Weg zum Kubismus* (Stuttgart: Gerd Hatje, 1958 [it was originally written in 1914 and 1915 and first appeared in *Weisse Blätter,* Zürich, 1916]). On p. 37, he speaks about "the indirect values of lyrical painting. It taught us to see the beauty of form of the simplest things, which we would otherwise have ignored."

51. Le Corbusier, *L'Art Décoratif d'Aujourd'hui* (Paris: G. Crès, 1925), especially pp. 64–115; *Towards a New Architecture* (originally published in 1923, by G. Crès, under the title *Vers Une Architecture;* New York: Praeger, 1959), pp. 81–138.

52. Ozenfant, *op. cit.,* p. 159.

53. The Café Museum, 1899; see Münz and Künstler, *op. cit.,* fig. 15.

54. Le Corbusier and Pierre Jeanneret, *Oeuvre Complete de 1910–1929* (new ed., Zurich: Girsberger,

1937); House for Ozenfant (1922), pp. 55, 57; House for Jeanneret (1923), p. 67; House in Pessac (1925), p. 80; Pavillon de l'Esprit Nouveau (1925), pp. 101–8; Weissenhof project (1927), p. 153.

In 1929, Loos wrote that he had recognized the Thonet chair as the only modern chair thirty-one years earlier. He adds that Le Corbusier had now also seen this and used the chairs in his buildings. "However," he adds, "unfortunately he used the wrong model!" *Trotzdem*, p. 254.

55. Le Corbusier, *Almanach d'Architecture* (Paris: G. Crès, 1925), p. 145. The English translation used here is taken from Sigfried Giedion, *Mechanization Takes Command* (New York: Oxford University Press, 1948), p. 492.

56. Quoted by William C. Seitz, *The Art of Assemblage* (New York: The Museum of Modern Art, 1961), p. 46.

57. Walter Hopps, Ulf Linde and Arturo Schwarz, *Marcel Duchamp, Ready-Mades, etc. (1913–1964)* (Paris: Le Terrain Vague, 1964). On p. 62, the book reproduces the article by Marcel Duchamp, "The Richard Mutt Case," which appeared in *The Blind Man*, 1917.

58. Marshall McLuhan, "The Emperor's Old Clothes," in *The Man-Made Object,* ed. Gyorgy Kepes (New York: George Braziller, 1966), p. 90, and his introduction to the paperback edition of *Understanding Media: The Extensions of Man* (New York: McGraw-Hill, 1965), especially pp. vii–viii. The Ozenfant quote is from *Foundations of Modern Art*, p. 155.

59. The first authoritative book in English on the Bauhaus was published in conjunction with an exhibition at the Museum of Modern Art: *Bauhaus 1919–1928*, eds. Herbert Bayer, Ise Gropius, and Walter Gropius (New York: Museum of Modern Art, 1938). Though much has since been written about the Bauhaus, the scope of this book was not superseded until very recently, when Hans Maria Wingler's *Bauhaus*

(which had first appeared in German in 1962), was published, in 1969, in an enlarged English edition by the M.I.T. Press.

60. *Machine Art* (New York: Museum of Modern Art, 1934), unpaged.

61. See Bernard Karpel, "The Idea of Design, A Suggestive Bibliography," in *International Design Annual: idea 55* (Stuttgart: Gerd Hatje, 1955), pp. 137–57.

62. Reyner Banham, "Machine Aesthetic," *Architectural Review*, CXVII (1955), 225–28. He elaborated on his ideas in a second article: "Industrial design e arte popolare," *Civiltà delle macchine,* (November, 1955), pp. 12–15. Both articles were republished in *Industrial Design* (March, 1960), pp. 45–47, 61–65. Nikolaus Pevsner delivered his lecture on January 10, 1961, at the Royal Institute of British Architects, and it was reported as "Modern Architecture and the Historian, or the Return of Historicism," in *RIBA Journal*, LXVIII (April, 1961), 230–40. In 1966, Pevsner celebrated the thirtieth anniversary of the first publication of the *Pioneers of Modern Design* by giving a lecture on "The Antipioneers" over the BBC that was published in *The Listener*, LXXVI, No. 1970 (December 29, 1966), 953–55, and LXXVII, No. 1971 (January, 1967), 7–9.

63. Peter Smithson, "Just a Few Chairs and a House: An Essay on the Eames-aesthetic," *Architectural Design*, XXXVI, 9 (1966), 443–45; Corin Hughes-Stanton, "What Comes After Carnaby Street?" *Design*, CCXXX (February, 1968), 42–43; Christopher Cornford, "Cold Rice Pudding and Revisionism," *Design*, CCXXXI (March, 1968), 46–48; Abraham A. Moles, "Die Krise des Funktionalismus," *Form*, XLI (March, 1968), 36; Werner Nehls, "Die Heiligen Kühe des Funktionalismus müssen geopfert werden," *Form*, XLIII (September, 1968), 4. Misha Black's speech appeared in a German translation in *Form*, XLII (June, 1968), 27–29; it has not been published in English as far as I know.

BIBLIOGRAPHY

The following bibliography makes no pretense at being exhaustive on the subjects of technology and aesthetics in the nineteenth century. Lewis Mumford, for one, has done this much more thoroughly in his bibliography for *Technics and Civilization*. I offer the following as a selection of books that have been helpful in guiding my own thinking and searching and that may also be helpful for others so interested. Many more detailed sources have been left as notes at the end of each chapter, where they are more immediately pertinent and accessible to those whose curiosity carries them into footnotes. In the last analysis, the text and thesis of this book are best documented by the objects illustrated, and it is first and foremost to them, and to others like them, that I send the reader for confirmation of what I have had to say.

AHLERS-HESTERMANN, FRIEDRICH. *Stilwende. Aufbruch der Jugend um 1900*. Berlin: Gebr. Mann, 1941.

BANHAM, REYNER. *Theory and Design in the First Machine Age*. New York: Praeger, 1960.

BARR, ALFRED H., JR. *Cubism and Abstract Art*. New York: The Museum of Modern Art, 1936.

BØE, ALF. *From Gothic Revival to Functional Form*. Oslo: Oslo University Press, 1957.

BOTT, GERHARD. "Kunstgewerbe." (In *Die Kunst des 19. Jahrhunderts*, Vol. II of the new edition of the Propyläen Kunstgeschichte.) Berlin: Propyläen Verlag, 1966.

CHECKLAND, S. G. *The Rise of Industrial Society in England 1815–1885*. London: Longmans, Green, 1964.

CLARK, VICTOR S. *History of Manufactures in the United States*. New York: McGraw-Hill, 1929.

DALZELL, ROBERT F., JR. *American Participation in the Great Exhibition of 1851*, Amherst, Amherst College Press, 1960.

DE ZURKO, EDWARD ROBERT. *Origins of Functionalist Theory*. New York: Columbia University Press, 1957.

DEANE, PHYLLIS. *The First Industrial Revolution*. Cambridge, England: Cambridge University Press, 1965.

Deutscher Werkbund. *"Die Form" Stimme des Deutschen Werkbundes 1925–1934*, eds. FELIX SCHWARZ and FRANK GLOOR. (Bauweltfundamente 24.) Gütersloh: Bertelsmann Fachverlag, 1969.

DEXEL, WALTER. *Deutsches Handwerksgut, eine Kultur- und Formgeschichte des Hausgeräts*. Berlin: Propyläen Verlag, 1939.

———. *Das Hausgerät Mitteleuropas*. Braunschweig: Klinkhardt & Biermann, 1962.

ECKSTEIN, HANS (ed.). *50 Jahre Deutscher Werkbund*. Frankfurt and Berlin: Alfred Metzner Verlag, 1958.

GEDDES, NORMAN BEL. *Horizons*. Boston: Little, Brown, 1932.

GIEDION, SIGFRIED. *Mechanization Takes Command: A Contribution to Anonymous History*. New York: Oxford University Press, 1948.

GRAUL, RICHARD (ed.). *Die Krisis im Kunstgewerbe*. Leipzig: S. Hirzel, 1901.

GRAY, CHRISTOPHER. *Cubist Aesthetic Theories*. Baltimore, Md.: Johns Hopkins Press, 1953.

GREENOUGH, HORATIO. *Form and Function*, ed. HAROLD A. SMALL. Berkeley: University of California Press, 1947.

———. *The Travels, Observations, and Experience of a Yankee Stonecutter* (1852). Gainesville, Fla.: Scholars' Facsimiles & Reprints, 1958.

HABAKKUK, H. J. *American and British Technology in the Nineteenth Century*. Cambridge, England: Cambridge University Press, 1962.

HAMMOND, J. L., and HAMMOND, BARBARA. *The Rise of Modern Industry* (8th ed.). London: Methuen, 1951.

HENDERSON, W. O. *Britain and Industrial Europe 1750–1870. Studies in British Influence on the Industrial Revolution in Western Europe* (2d ed.). Leicester: Leicester University Press, 1965.

HERMAN, JOST. *Jugendstil. Ein Forschungsbericht 1918–1964*. Stuttgart: J. B. Metzlersche Verlagsbuchhandlung, 1965.

HERMANN, GEORG. *Das Biedermeier*. Oldenburg: Gerhard Stalling Verlag, 1965.

HOBSBAWM, E. J. *The Age of Revolution 1789–1848*. Cleveland, Ohio: World, 1962.

HOFFMANN, WALTHER. *Stadien und Typen der Industrialisierung*. Jena: Gustav Fischer, 1931.

Journal of Design and Manufactures. London: 1849–52.

KARPEL, BERNARD. "The Idea of Design, A Suggestive Bibliography." In *International Design Annual: idea 55*. Stuttgart: Gerd Hatje, 1955.

KOUWENHOVEN, JOHN A. *Made in America*. Garden City, N.Y.: Doubleday, 1948.

LANDES, DAVID S. "Technological Change and Development in Western Europe, 1750–1914." In *Cambridge Economic History of Europe*, VI, 274–601. Cambridge, England: Cambridge University Press, 1965.

LE CORBUSIER. *L'Art Décoratif d'Aujourd'hui*. Paris: G. Crès, 1925.

———. *Towards a New Architecture*. New York: Praeger, 1959.

LICHTWARK, ALFRED. *Eine Auswahl seiner Schriften*. 2 vols. Berlin: Bruno Cassirer, 1917.

LINDINGER, HERBERT. "Design Geschichte." *Form*, No. 26 (June, 1964) 18–26; No. 27 (September, 1964), 26–32; No. 28 (December, 1964) 37–43; No. 30 (June, 1965) 36–44.

LOOS, ADOLF. *Ins Leere Gesprochen 1897–1900*. Innsbruck: Brenner-Verlag, 1932.

———. *Trotzdem 1900–1930*. Innsbruck: Brenner-Verlag, 1931.

METZGER, CHARLES R. *Emerson and Greenough: Transcendental Pioneers of an American Esthetic*. Berkeley: University of California Press, 1954.

MUMFORD, LEWIS. *Technics and Civilization*. New York: Harcourt, Brace, 1934.

MUTHESIUS, HERMANN. *Das Englische Haus*. 3 vols. Berlin: Wasmuth, 1904–5.

———. *Die Werkbundarbeit der Zukunft*. Jena: Eugen Diedrichs, 1914.

OZENFANT. *Foundations of Modern Art*, New York: Brewer, Warren & Putnam, 1931.

PEVSNER, NIKOLAUS. *Gateway to the Twentieth Century*. New York: McGraw-Hill, 1962.

———. *Pioneers of Modern Design, from William Morris to Walter Gropius*. New York: Museum of Modern Art, 1949.

POSENER, JULIUS. *Anfänge des Funktionalismus*. Berlin: Ullstein, 1964.

REDGRAVE, RICHARD. *Report on Design: Prepared as a Supplement to the Report of the Jury of Class XXX of the Exhibition of 1851*. Reprinted from the Official Edition. London: 1852.

RICHARDS, J. M. *The Functional Tradition in Early Industrial Buildings*. London: The Architectural Press, 1958.

ROE, JOSEPH WICKHAM. *English and American Tool Builders*. New Haven, Conn.: Yale University Press, 1916.

ROLT, L. T. C. *Tools for the Job*. London: B. T. Batsford, 1965.

SCHMUTZLER, ROBERT. *Art Nouveau*. New York: Abrams, 1964.

SEDLMAYR, HANS. *Verlust der Mitte*. Salzburg: Otto Müller, 1948.

SEMPER, GOTTFRIED. *Wissenschaft, Industrie und Kunst* (1851). Republished in the series *Neue Bauhausbücher*, ed. Hans Maria Wingler. Mainz: Florian Kupferberg, 1966.

SINGER, CHARLES (ed.). *A History of Technology*, Vols. IV and V. Oxford: Clarendon Press, 1958.

TSCHUDI-MADSEN, STEPHAN. *Sources of Art Nouveau*. New York: George Wittenborn, 1955.

VEBLEN, THORSTEIN. *The Theory of the Leisure Class*. New York: Macmillan, 1912.

WAENTIG, HEINRICH. *Wirtschaft und Kunst*. Jena: Gustav Fischer, 1909.

SOURCES OF OBJECTS

Nineteenth-century objects of the kind illustrated in this book can be found in a great variety of museums, but by and large not in what are usually called art museums. Certainly, the great museums of art, such as The Metropolitan Museum of Art in New York, the Museum of Fine Arts in Boston, or the Art Institute in Chicago have, in the catholicity of their collections, many things that would make admirable illustrations for this book. Equally, the prestigious museums devoted more specifically to the decorative arts—such as the Victoria & Albert in London, the Musée des Arts Décoratifs in Paris, the Kunstgewerbemuseums in Berlin, Hamburg, and Vienna, the Bavarian National Museum in Munich, the Danske Kunstindustrimuseum in Copenhagen, the Nordiska Museum in Stockholm, and the Henry Francis du Pont Winterthur Museum in this country—all will have objects of interest to this point of view. In most cases, however, one is compelled to feel that they are there *faute de mieux*, because these museums seek objects primarily for their artistic merit and not their functional propriety.

One is more likely to find simple objects of functional form in the museums with a more general cultural and historical approach. Here, they were collected for interest in their performance and their role in society rather than for artistic or stylistic characteristics. Such museums range from our own Smithsonian Institution's Museum of History and Technology in Washington, The Henry Ford Museum in Dearborn, Michigan, and such national museums as that of Finland in Helsinki and that of Switzerland in Zürich, to an endless number of local historical museums, historical societies, and historic houses in almost every city and town in Europe and America. These museums endeavor to show how the average person lived and thereby cannot help but exhibit the simple, useful objects of his everyday life.

There are also museums specifically devoted to small-town and rural life, such as the Shelburne Museum, near Burlington, Vermont, Old Sturbridge Village in Massachusetts, the collection of American farm and folk culture of the New York State Historical Association at Cooperstown, New York, the Norsk Folkemuseum outside of Oslo, the Museum of English Rural Life at the University of Reading, and, of course, the various Shaker collections, most notably that at Hancock Shaker Village, in Pittsfield, Massachusetts.

On quite a different plane are the technical and scientific museums, with their more intellectualized functional forms for their specialized demanding purposes. Of these the Deutsches Museum in Munich undoubtedly represents the peak, and a close second is the Science Museum in London. Similar collections are in the Musée du Conservatoire National des Arts et Métiers in Paris and in the Technisches Museum für Industrie und Gewerbe in Vienna, Austria. In these museums, the functional form is found in its purest most explicit form, in the instruments, tools, and machines that have shaped and at the same time characterized our modern civilization.

There are transportation museums in Lucerne, Switzerland, and in London, the Baltimore & Ohio Transportation Museum in Baltimore, Maryland, and the beginnings of one also in St. Louis, Missouri. Early automobiles are collected in a number of places (aside from such obvious places as the Henry Ford Museum in Dearborn, which also collects so much else), for example, the Antique Auto Museum, Larz Anderson Park, Brookline, Massachusetts, and the Musée de l'Auto, de la Motor et du Cycle, in Geneva, Switzerland. The most polished and beautifully displayed is the Daimler-Benz Museum in Stuttgart, Germany. Carriages are shown in many larger museums, such as the Smithsonian, the Ford Museum, and the Deutsches Museum, but also in such specialized museums as the Suffolk Museum and Carriage House in Stony Brook, Long Island, and, of course, in such princely collections as that at Nymphenburg Castle outside of Munich, and at Schönbrunn outside of Vienna.

Maritime history and all the functional design connected with it, from ships to all their gear and lore and instruments, are found in the maritime museums in Greenwich, near London, in Amsterdam and Rotterdam, the Altonaer Museum in Hamburg, Germany, the Peabody Museum of Salem, the Marine Historical Association Museum in Mystic, Connecticut, and the whaling museums of New Bedford and Nantucket Island.

And one can become ever more selective and specialized: there are glass museums, such as the elegant and scholarly Corning Glass Museum, in Corning, New York, and the more modest one at Zwiesel in the Bavarian Forest, where glass has been blown since the Middle Ages. The Wedgwood Museum in Stoke-on-Trent, in Staffordshire, shows this ware and its history, while the museum in Bennington, Vermont, has much of the pottery produced locally there.

Clocks and watches are found, as might be expected, in horological museums in Switzerland, in Chaux-de-Fonds and in Geneva, but also in a special museum in Vienna, Austria, the Uhren-Museum, and in the James Arthur Collection of Clocks and Watches at New York University in New York City. Cutlery is collected in the German Cutlery Museum in Solingen and flatware for the table in the Bodo Glaub Museum in Cologne, Germany. In New Haven, Connecticut, there is the Winchester Gun Museum and also the Edward Clark Streeter Collection of Weights and Measures. In Rochester, New York, there is the George Eastman House, with its collection of photographs, films, and photographic apparatus. A small but interesting collection of Thonet furniture is shown at the Thonet factory in Frankenberg, Germany, and the local museum in High Wycombe shows the modest chairs produced locally there. In London, the Pinto Collection of Wooden Bygones is devoted to wooden objects of the past, including such things as shooting sticks, some made by Thonet. In Philadelphia, there is even a dairy museum,

belonging to the Pennbrook Milk Company. It has a number of handsome examples of nineteenth- and early twentieth-century utensils, tools, and containers used in the dairy industry.

The Administration Building of the John Deere Company in Moline, Illinois, has perhaps the most interesting and extraordinary American collection of nineteenth-century tools, utensils, and devices, installed in the form of a huge three-dimensional mural, or collage, that was assembled and designed by Alexander Girard in 1962–64. His object was not to collect and display museum pieces, but to re-create the quality of a time as expressed in its simple, everyday artifacts.

None of the above is devoted to the collection of objects for the sake of their functional form per se. The objects in these museums are there because they are part of a larger scheme of things. I know of only two museums that are specifically devoted to functional design: the Formsammlung (Form Collection) in Braunschweig, Germany, and the so-called Neue Sammlung (the New Collection), in Munich. The former was originally the personal collection of Walter Dexel and came to the city of Braunschweig after World War II. It is now housed there in a handsome gallery in the School of Design. The latter has a collection from the period of William Morris on, and in its acquisition and exhibition policy has long been oriented toward functional design.

Index